Y0-BRW-651

Art for Travellers
GREECE

The Essential Guide to Viewing Art in Greece

Poseidon Temple, Rhodes

Art for Travellers

GREECE

The Essential Guide to Viewing Art in Greece

BILL AND LORNA HANNAN

ILLUSTRATIONS BY DEE HANNAN

Central Islip Public Library
33 Hawthorne Avenue
Central Islip, NY 11722-2498

Interlink Books

An imprint of Interlink Publishing Group, Inc.
Northampton, Massachusetts

3 1800 00224 0360

First published in 2006 by

INTERLINK BOOKS
An imprint of Interlink Publishing Group, Inc.
46 Crosby Street, Northampton, Massachusetts 01060
www.interlinkbooks.com

Text copyright © by Bill and Lorna Hannan 2006
Edited and designed by Ed 'n' Art, Newport, Sydney

Cover illustration: *Priestess at an altar*, detail from a sarcophagus from a tomb at Ayia
Triada, Crete, Late Minoan Period, c. 1390 BC (painted plaster on limestone),
Minoan/Archeological Museum of Heraklion, Crete, Greece, www.bridgeman.co.uk

All rights reserved. No part of this publication may be reproduced, stored in a
retrieval system, or transmitted in any form or by any means, electronic, mechanical,
photocopying, recording or otherwise without the prior permission of the publisher.

Library of Congress Cataloging-in-Publication Data
Hannan, Bill.
Greece : the essential guide to viewing art in Greece / by Bill and Lorna
Hannan ; illustrations by Dee Hannan.— 1st American ed.
    p. cm. — (Art for travellers)
Includes bibliographical references and index.
ISBN 1-56656-592-8 (pbk. : permanent paper)
1. Art, Greek—Guidebooks. 2. Art—Greece—Guidebooks.
3. Greece—Guidebooks. I. Hannan, Lorna. II. Title. III. Series.
N6891.H36 2005
709'.38—dc22   2005006207

All paintings are used in this book with the kind permission of Bridgeman Art Library.
Photographs are from the Corel CD *Greece*

All quotes from Pausanias, *Description of Greece*, are reprinted by permission of the
publishers and the Trustees of the Loeb Classical Library from Pausanias: Volume 1,
Loeb Classical Library Volume 93, translated by W.H.S. Jones and H.A. Ormerod,
Cambridge, Mass.: Harvard University Press, 1918. The Loeb Classical Library is a
registered trademark of the President and Fellows of Harvard College.

The epigraph on page 9 is from C.P. Cavafy's *Ionic* (Ikaros Press). The English
rendering is by the authors.

Printed and bound in China

Acknowledgments

Many thanks to Shelagh Hannan, George Xylouris, and Sean Byrne for their hospitality, help, and advice. Thanks also to Dee Hannan, Psarandoni, and Katina for their help and to Carol Floyd for her meticulous editing and advice.

Below: Harbor scene from Oia, Thera

Residential quarter, Lindos, Rhodes

Table of Contents

Just because we smashed their statues
Just because we drove them out of their temples
In no way means that the gods have died.

—C.P. Cavafy

Introduction: Life among the Ruins

The culture of ancient Greece, especially of the Classical period, is a towering presence in Western civilization. The study of Greek and Roman civilization and ancient Greek literature and philosophy was the foundation of European culture for centuries. No other period has had such a far-reaching influence. Today, the preoccupations of ancient Greek art—harmony, significant symbolism, and the human form—remain essential canons in Western art.

The high Classical era is but a moment in a vast artistic history of more than three thousand years, from the Bronze Age through to the Christian revolution that absorbed the Roman Empire. For the early periods, up to about the 1st millennium BCE, archeology gives us a picture of successive civilizations and their arts. From the 8th century BCE, we enter an historical phase where we draw on literary sources and archeology to understand the nature and inspiration of Greek art.

Despite the familiarity that centuries of imitation create, Greek art speaks powerfully to modern viewers. In this guide we try not to insert our artistic judgements between the work and the viewer, but to provide contextual information to enhance understanding of each work.

About the Trails

The Trails take travellers across Greece from prehistoric times to the early Byzantine era. They concentrate on the periods and art styles known as Cycladic, Minoan, Mycenaean, Geometric, Archaic, and Classical. Less attention is given to the later Hellenistic, Roman, and Byzantine periods, generally because much of this art is outside the main centers, for example, in isolated monasteries, or outside Greece in state and private collections.

Many Trails go to places combining an archeological site with an art

INTRODUCTION

museum. It is, therefore, not possible to isolate art from archeology, but we focus on the art. Most "archeological museums" contain astonishing art treasures. Often these treasures are found in Athens or in a central museum, but the Greek government is pursuing a policy of returning art to the original site and it is sometimes possible to see both site and art finds in the same location. In the case of crafts, such as pottery and jewelry, we focus on the finest or the most representative.

The ideal starting point is Athens. Trails 1–3 lead to the Athenian Acropolis, the National Archeological Museum, and noted sites and galleries in central and outer Athens. Subsequent Trails (4–7) move to archeological sites and art collections of mainland Greece: Delphi, Thebes, and Thessaloniki—the second city of Greece—and, in the Peloponnese, Corinth, Mycenae, Epidauros, and Olympia. Trail 8 tours the islands of Crete and Santorini.

The Trails

WHERE	HOW LONG	TRAIL	FEATURES
Central Athens	2-3 days	1	Ancient Athens, the Acropolis, Agora, Keremeikos, Eleusis
Central Athens	2 days	2	The National Archeological Museum
Athens	1-3 days	3	Museum of Cycladic Art, Byzantine Museum, Piraeus, Dafni, private museums
Day trips from Athens	1-2 days	4	Delphi, Hossios Loukas
Peloponnese	4 days	5	Corinth Argos, Nafplio, Mycenae, Epidauros
Peloponnese	2 days	6	Olympia
Northern Greece	3-4 days	7	Thebes & Thessaloniki
The islands	5 days	8	Crete & Santorini

* Car travellers could include Thebes in their trip to Delphi (Trail 4)

Tips for the Art Traveller

Opening hours: Sites and museums open about 8:00 am and close at 4:00 pm. Hours are shorter in winter (and the weather cold). Major sites open every day except Monday when they may be closed.

Churches are best visited in the morning. They close during the early afternoon and have services during the late afternoon. You will be shooed away if you try to see the art in a church during a service. There are no charges, but you can leave donations.

Admission prices: State-run museums follow a pattern. The highest entry price is about 10 euros for big sites such as the Acropolis and Olympia. A small museum is 2 or 3 euros. To allow for inflation, we have given price ranges, as follows:

Low: Euro 1–4
Mid: Euro 4–8
High: Euro 9–12

Admission on Sundays and certain holidays is often free. Also, in state-run establishments, seniors with EU passports and students with identity cards get discounts, usually about half the standard price.

Methods of travel: In central Athens the Metro is the most agreeable and accessible form of travel. Buses are plentiful but stops are sometimes hard to find. Before you get the bus, get a ticket at a *periptero,* which is what the ubiquitous and invaluable street kiosks are called. Cars are hard to park and their fumes damage the art works you've come to admire. The traffic is somewhat anarchic.

Outside Athens on the mainland, there is a wide range of choices. You can go to Thessaloniki by plane, train, bus, or car. Elsewhere, there are plentiful buses and some convenient rail lines. The trains get a bad press in many guidebooks, but they're quite agreeable. You need to keep on the alert to catch buses—they can arrive at unexpected stops and leave abruptly. Between towns and cities, you pay for your ticket on the bus; at the bus terminals in Athens you buy a ticket before you get on the bus.

For long distance trips from Athens, there are two bus terminals and two train terminals, differentiated by whether they are going to places on the mainland or destinations on the Peloponnese. The tourist office has good maps of Athens and the transport system.

Planes and ferries go to Crete and Santorini. The ferries are terrific. The Athens Metro goes to Piraeus where the ferries depart. In Crete, use buses or hire a car.

Snacks, rests, and food: Apart from the obvious bread roll, cheese, salami, fruit, etc., the best local snack is a cheese pie (*tiropitta,* with the stress on the o), bought from bread and cake shops in the morning. Many food shops close between 1 and 4 or 5 pm.

The best way to get a coffee shot is to get the Greek (*elliniko*) coffee (called Turkish coffee in English but don't say that in Greece). If you don't want it too sweet ask for it *metrio.* In summer, a frappé, made with Nescafé, is delicious. Restaurants serve lunch until well into the afternoon and stay open late at night.

Telephones: Telephones work by cards bought at the periptero. Operators use English as well as Greek.

The Art of Ancient Greece: an Overview

The land and islands we call Greece have been home to many remarkable cultures and art movements, which are commonly divided into prehistoric and historical eras. For the art of the prehistoric era, from about 7000 to 1000 BCE, we rely on archeological evidence but have rich, written records from historical times.. Museums and commentaries frequently describe works using these categories: Neolithic, Helladic, Cycladic, Minoan, and Mycenaean are prehistoric; Geometric, Archaic, Classical, Hellenistic, and Byzantine art belong to historical eras.

Where the Greeks came from is a matter for speculation, as are the origins of the peoples who preceded them. Greek speakers are first in evidence during Mycenaean times, between 1550 and 1100 BCE. Earlier cultures ranged widely around the Mediterranean, trading and swapping art styles. Mycenae was, it seems, the first civilization to control most of Greece. The great epic and dramatic literature is set in Mycenaean times.

Prehistoric Art

The prehistory of Greece includes the Neolithic Age, from 7000–3000 BCE and the Bronze Age, from 3000–1100 BCE. Within the Bronze Age are four distinct civilizations.

Cycladic	3000–1100 BCE
Helladic	3000–1100 BCE
Minoan	2200–1100 BCE
Mycenaean	1550–1100 BCE

Neolithic Art: 7000–3000 BCE

Archeological evidence of settlement in Greece goes back 40,000 years with remains of baked clay vessels and figures dating from 6000 BCE. There are also some stone images, and later, some metal work. The transition to the Bronze Age is usually dated at around 3000 BCE, when there is evidence of population movement around the mainland and the islands. The major finds have been on the mainland and Crete where artists showed an early attraction to the human figure. The baked-clay figurines of the Neolithic period are usually thought to represent female gods typical of agricultural societies. In general, figures with big thighs, buttocks, and breasts are taken to represent fertility or a mother figure who guarded over people, animals, crops, and the seasons, These are plausible speculations based on analogies with other creatures but there is no way of establishing their truth. Nevertheless, the images are compelling.

Typical works: Clay pots and human figurines.

Where to see them: Small collections in the National Archeological Museum (Trail 2), and in the majority of other museums.

Cycladic Art: 3000–1550 BCE

The Cycladic islands, dotted between mainland Greece and Crete, were probably settled from the mainland or Asia Minor at the beginning of the Bronze Age (say 3000 BCE). Their art was probably created by groups of artists working within common conventions. The truly distinctive Cycladic style emerges in developments in sculpture between 3000 and 2000 BCE, now termed Early Cycladic, which left us striking marble figures, some life-size, some tiny, all masterpieces of semi-abstract art. Interestingly, their Neolithic predecessors were more realistic in style.

Though they come to us as pure white marble images, they were originally painted and so would have appeared more realistic than they do today. As with Neolithic figurines, the female figures are assumed to represent divinities, but the range of representations is wider and includes musicians. The important centers are the islands of Naxos, Melos, Syros and Paros. From Melos came obsidian, used widely for carving tools. From Naxos and Paros came marble, which would become a favored material in Greek sculpture and architecture. After 2000 BCE, the art of the Cycladic Islands merged with the Minoan culture of Crete and eventually the widespread Mycenaean civilization.

The Bronze Age saw expanded trade and greater interaction with other groups. Pieces found in Crete indicate that there was contact between these two cultures, and Cycladic art found substanial admiration in Crete.

Museums of Cycladic, Helladic, and Minoan art all follow the conventional methods of classifying art and archeology into early, middle, and late phases with numbered sub-divisions within each phase. The divisions, based on a mix of art styles and historical changes, are used to organize museum displays. However, museums in Crete prefer categories based on the development of palace architecture.

INTRODUCTION

Cycladic female figure. 2700–2300 BCE. (National Archeological Museum Athens). Lauros/Giraudon/Bridgeman Art Library

Typical works: Marble statuettes and statues, pottery.
Where to see them: The Goulandris Museum of Cycladic and Ancient Greek Art in Athens, (Trail 3,) the National Archeological Museum (Trail 2), Heraklion Archeological Museum in Heraklion, Crete (Trail 8).

Helladic Art: 3000–1100 BCE

Helladic art is found on mainland Greece during the millennia corresponding to the Cycladic and Minoan periods on the islands. It too is categorized into early, middle, and late phases. Unlike Cycladic art, it lacks evidence of impressive sculpture and is largely represented by clay figurines and pots. Some archeological sites, such as Lerna near Argos, provide evidence of advanced town building with multi-story houses and tiled roofs. The Late Helladic phase merges with Mycenaean art.

About 2000 BCE many settlements both in Greece and elsewhere were destroyed, apparently violently. The end of the next millennium, around 1100 BCE, saw another violent destruction of Helladic, Minoan, and Mycenaean sites. Volcanic eruptions and earthquakes contributed to this destruction but these settlements may also have succumbed to outside invasions, immigration, and economic competition.

Typical works: Clay pots and figurines.
Where to see them: Museums on mainland Greece usually have small collections. The fascinating finds from Lerna are in the Argos Archeological museum (Trail 5).

Minoan Art: 2200–1100 BCE

Crete is the southernmost and largest island of modern Greece, and in prehistoric times was the home of the Aegean's first civilization. What the people called themselves is not known, but modern excavators named the civilization after the legendary king Minos. In 1900, the British archeologist Sir Arthur Evans unearthed ruins of a large palace at Knossos just outside Heraklion. He had the site reconstructed in ways we would not approve of today, and which keep modern visitors on their toes.

Minoan civilizations were generally peaceful and prosperous. Their palaces at Knossos, Phaistos, Malia, and elsewhere were not fortified and were centers to distribute oil, grains, wine, and necessities of the good life. Their first palaces were built after 2200 BCE and destroyed in earthquakes around 1700 BCE. This is the Protopalatial phase. A second lot of palaces grew up in their place—essentially on the same spots. These belong to Neopalatial phase, which lasted nearly 400 years. Knossos was destroyed in 1370 BCE, when Crete seems to have come under Mycenaean control.

It is presumed the Minoans were not Greeks, but when the young English architect and Classical scholar Michael Ventris unravelled the Linear B script in 1952, he demonstrated that towards the end of the millennium, a form of ancient Greek was used, if not by locals, then at least by the new settlers.

Minoan art is immensely vital and exerts a strong influence beyond Crete. It handles both stylized and realistic forms with ease. Both indigenous and exotic plants are used decoratively and perhaps symbolically. Artists recreated animals and people with vigor and perception. Fortunately, samples survive in a range of media. Painting, small-scale sculpture, and pottery are the prize pieces. The palaces, as re-imagined, are impressive. Craft objects such as gold jewelry, seals, and boxes are beautifully made. Wonderful painting comes from Crete and from nearby Santorini, whose ancient city of Akrotiri was buried in an earthquake and massive volcanic eruption that blew half the island away. Although Mycenaeans seem to have taken over Crete around 1400 BCE, Mycenaean art is in most respects a branch of Minoan art.

Typical works: palaces, highly decorated pottery, small sculpture, wall paintings, jewelry.

Where to see them: Heraklion Archeological Museum, Knossos, Agios Nikolaos Archeological Museum, (Museum of Prehistoric Art), Fira on Santorini. All in Trail 8.

Mycenaean Art: 1550–1100 BCE

Linguistically and culturally, Mycenaeans are probably the first Greeks. Whether they came from elsewhere or developed from earlier settlers is not certain, but the great epic stories, from Homer to Euripides, are set in Mycenaean times and establish their preeminence in literature. Although Mycenaean art resembles Minoan art, the massive fortresses surrounding their palaces speak of a very different civilization—a martial culture bedevilled by internal conflict. Gigantic walls and huge stone tombs are on a scale not found either before or after Mycenae's comparatively brief life.

Mycenaean interiors, painting, pottery, and jewelry have much of the richness and dash of Minoan equivalents and were imitated from or made by Minoan artists and craftsmen. However, they often lack the grace and light of Minoan work.

Nineteenth-century archeologists digging at Mycenaean sites were carried away by imagined associations with the characters in Homer and used names like the "Mask of Agamemnon" and the "Tomb of Clytemnestra" that add romance but cannot be taken seriously.

Typical works: paintings on walls and sarcophagi, statuary, pottery, palaces, tombs, jewelry.

Where to find them: National Museum Athens (Trail 2,) Argos Museum, Mycenae and Nafplion Museum (Trail 5).

Historical Art

At the end of the Bronze Age, at around 1100 BCE, there were several centuries of cultural decline across Greece and the islands. Beginning around 900 BCE, historical Greece emerges, its spirit defined by Homer's epic storytelling.

Detail of vase of the geometric period. 750 BCE. (National Archeological Museum Athens)

Geometric	900–700 BCE
Archaic	700–480 BCE
Classical	480–323 BCE
Hellenistic	323–31 BCE
Roman	31 BCE –323 CE
Byzantine	323 CE –now

Geometric Art: 900–700 BCE

From 900 BCE, Greek art develops a geometric style where highly gifted artists use abstracted images rather than naturalistic ones. The Olympic Games started in this period—the first was in 776 BCE. The final century of this period, 700–600 BCE, shows influence from Egyptian and oriental sources. The majority of objects surviving are splendid large vases covered with black images on a rich, brown background. Human and animal figures, highly abstracted, appear in funeral and military scenes and as natural backdrops. In the orientalizing period, plant, animal, bird, and monster images become common motifs. Corinthian pottery emerges at this point.

There is also some impressive small-scale sculpture in terracotta and bronze, often of elongated human figures and closely observed animals. The end of the period sees the emergence of large marble sculptures of human figures. They would become—for us—the most characteristic form of ancient Greek art.

Typical works: vases, bronze, and terracotta statuettes.
Where to find them: National Museum Athens (Trail 2); Goulandris Museum of Cycladic and Ancient Greek Art (Trail 3); Kerameikos museum, Athens (Trail 1); Argos Museum (Trail 5); Olympia Museum (Trail 6).

Archaic Art: 700–480 BCE

During the Archaic period, the art of ancient Greece took shape. Gradually, temples were built of stone rather than wood. Marble statues of athletes or gods and heroes were life-size or larger. Sculpted panels and vases depicted narratives of gods and heroes, normally with black figures painted on a red background. Ancient writers refer to paintings from this time, but none survived. We can, however, see the trend towards naturalism in the vase painting, which scholars assume echoes the themes and techniques of other painters.

The glory of the Archaic period is its sculpture of young men and women. Many fine examples have survived. Their appeal lies in their seeming to belong both to an ideal supernatural world and a perfected natural one. The male statue (a kouros) is naked and stands like an Irish dancer: arms by his side, shoulders back, one foot forward. His hair is carefully shaped into elaborate patterns and he has a peaceful, welcoming smile. The female (a kore) wears a long garment that shows some of the underlying form and a waist-length shawl. She too has a fine hairdo and an agreeable smile. To some viewers, she appears like a young girl; to others, an imposing goddess.

Typical works: Large marble statues of young men and girls, friezes, and pediments on temples.

Where to find them: Archeological museums on the mainland usually have some samples—the best are in the Acropolis Museum (Trail 1); the National Archeological Museum, Athens (Trail 2); the museum at Delphi (Trail 4); and the museum at Olympia (Trail 6).

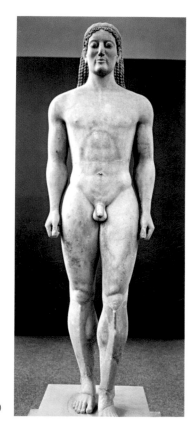

Anavysos kouros. c. 530–520 BCE.
(National Archeological Museum Athens
Lauros/Giraudon/Bridgeman Art Library)

INTRODUCTION

The three orders common in Greek architecture are Doric, Ionic, and Corinthian, each having a distinctive capital. An order comprises column, capital, and entablature. These original designs are simpler than later European versions. The Doric order is considered to be the most ancient. It is sturdy, with a plain capital and decorated entablature. The Ionic order, which came from Asia Minor in the 6th century BCE, has a slimmer column and a voluted capital. The Corinthian developed in the 5th century BCE (see note on Kallimachos, page 30). It is similar to the Ionic order but has leaf motifs in place of volutes.

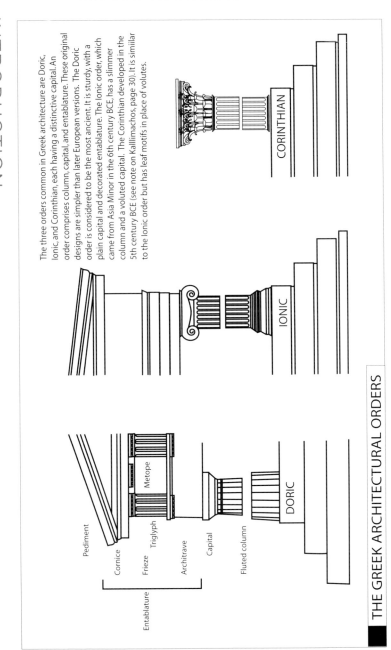

Pediment
Cornice
Frieze
Triglyph
Metope
Architrave
Entablature
Capital
Fluted column

DORIC

IONIC

CORINTHIAN

THE GREEK ARCHITECTURAL ORDERS

Classical Art: 480–323 BCE

The Classical period begins during the 400s BCE. Its center is undoubtedly Athens. The invading Persians who had caused great destruction in Athens, were driven out in 479 BCE. Some 40 years after the Athenian victories, when Athens was at the head of the League of Greek States and the capital had moved from Delos to Athens, Pericles initiated a huge rebuilding program. By this time architecture, sculpture—and, we suppose, painting—had developed to great heights; it was at this time that the Acropolis was built.

In sculpture, the transition from Archaic to Classical styles is to greater realism, particularly in the treatment of the human body. Male figures assume freer poses that show their body weight and musculature. Drapery on female figures becomes agitated and transparent. Narratives are crystallized in essential and dramatic moments, made the more effective because their subjects were familiar to viewers. In a development that is rare in pottery, vase painting became almost entirely narrative, as apparently did painting.

The themes of these narratives in stone and terracotta are taken from mythology, epics, and daily life. Gods defeat giants and centaurs. Herakles, the demigod, performs superhuman feats. Theseus defeats the Minotaur. Incidents from the *Iliad* are replayed. Scenes from daily life include funerals, athletics, religious ceremonies, and warriors departing for battle.

The Classical era is the first to feature large numbers of architects, sculptors, painters, and potters by name and hence to identify styles with individuals. In sculpture, for example, Phidias and Polykleitos are greats of the early Classical period, between 450 and 400 BCE, whilst Praxiteles and Lysippos characterize the late period, from about 350 to 320 BCE. Phidias is the master of long-lost statues of gods in wood, gold, ivory and precious stones, and overseer of the Athenian Acropolis. A century later, Praxiteles makes sensuous, humanized marbles of gods, and famously introduces female nudity to Western art.

For Western art the depth of the legacy from the Classical period is incalculable. Most obviously, it enshrined idealized human figures as central subjects in painting and sculpture and gave architecture a virtually complete language. Its greatest gift, however, and one that goes beyond styles, is a concern for proportion, rhythm, and harmony in art. Whether these principles have been imitated, developed, or rebelled against, they have remained our essential point of reference.

Typical works: Statuary, temples, and vases.
Where to find them: Ancient Athens (Trail 1) and the National Archeological Museum, Athens (Trail 2).

Hellenistic Art: 323–31 BCE

The Hellenistic period covers the time when Greek art styles spread through the Roman Empire and beyond, as far as Afghanistan. Consequently, some of the most spectacular works are outside Greece. It is the art of Greeks rather than the art of Greece, usually dated from Alexander's death in 323 BCE to the Battle of Actium in 31 BCE, when a rival Roman army defeated Anthony and Cleopatra.

Hellenistic art—what survives most is marble sculpture—pushes the tendencies in Classical art towards realism and drama. It can be striking, moving, or charming, but also empty—perhaps because it loses its religious seriousness. However, the profusely ornamented gold jewelry and artifacts from royal tombs are dazzling.

> **Typical works:** Statuary, temples, jewelry, mosaics, some painting, and red figure vases.
>
> **Where to find them:** Vergina, Thessaloniki Archeological Musuem (Trail 7), and the final rooms of most archeological museums, especially Athens (Trails 1 and 2).

Roman Art: 31 BCE–323 CE

The Roman occupation of Greece sees changes of style to suit official and private Roman tastes. Greek art and artists were much sought after by Romans. Their taste for marble copies of earlier Greek works adds to our knowledge of classical Greek sculpture, but the quality is variable and the accuracy unreliable. Ancient sites in Athens, Corinth, or Olympia include Roman buildings and the remains of statuary.

Roman art is outside the scope of this guide, though we will occasionally comment on it.

> **Typical works:** Statuary, mosaics, and architecture.
>
> **Where to find them:** Major archeological sites and the tail end rooms of museums.

Byzantine Art: 323 CE

When Constantine became sole ruler of the Roman Empire in 323 CE, he made Christianity its official religion. Byzantine art developed from early Christian art, especially painting, into a mystical, jewel-like art that persists into modern times in eastern and orthodox churches.

Byzantine art takes its name from Byzantium. Renamed Constantinople (the city of Constantine) and now Istanbul, it was capital of the Byzantine

Empire until it fell to the Turks in 1453 CE.

Byzantine art is mesmerizing. "...The music of its name alone," writes John Julius Norwich, in *Byzantium*, conjures up "visions of gold and malachite and porphyry, of stately and solemn ceremonial, of brocades heavy with rubies and emeralds, of sumptuous mosaics dimly glowing through halls cloudy with incense."

Byzantine art was governed by rules intended to ensure that depictions of human forms were not realistic, but intimations of the sacred: its ensembles of frescoes and mosaics are laid out to communicate predictable stories and church teachings. Some think this formalism rigid but its use of human figures to represent the supernatural world and its taste for working over a fixed set of narratives reflect ancient intellectual preoccupations, even if the style has changed. Ultimately, Byzantine art would be the launching pad for late medieval and Renaissance art in the West, as well as a continuing framework for art in the east.

Apart from the excellent museums of Byzantine art and civilization in Thessaloniki and Athens, much Byzantine art in Greece is in churches and monasteries outside these Trails—Mt. Athos, which excludes women, is an obvious example. As the art of a vast empire based outside Greece, its supreme masterpieces are beyond the reach of a guide based on Greece. Our commentaries on Byzantine works within the Trails are therefore relatively brief.

Typical works: frescoes, mosaics, painted icons, churches.

Where to find them: Athens (museum and churches (Trail 3); outside Athens at the monasteries of Dafni (Trail 3); Hossios Loukas (Trail 4); Thessaloniki museum and churches, (Trail 7); and Kritsa Crete (Trail 8).

Vases in Greek Art

The vessels and vases we often regard as specifically Greek began to be produced in the Geometric era and adorned the Mediterranean world until the late Classical era—in all, from around the 900s to the 300s BCE. They are, on the whole, excellent examples of craftsmanship, but what makes them of particular interest to art historians is the growth and flowering of narrative drawing and painting based on Greek mythology and aspects of contemporary life.

To both archeologists and art historians vases have a special fascination. One reason is that many survive. They are made of a material that breaks but does not deteriorate much, and they were much used in funeral rites, so that many have been found unbroken in graves. They are also widespread. The Greeks were persistent travellers, colonists, and traders. Vases are found in quantity in mainland Greece, the islands, Asia Minor, central and southern Italy, and Sicily. Corinth and Athens were the two great centers of production and trade in Greece, but most Greek settlements had their own potteries and those of Italy became very large indeed.

A further interest is the insight they give into Greek painting. Painting was widely practiced in ancient Greece but apart from some of the wonderful Minoan remains from Knossos and Santorini, next to nothing survives. Ancient texts tell us that certain painters were the most celebrated of artists in their day, and the art traveller Pausanias gives long descriptions of works that have vanished without leaving a flake. Even the decorative painting of statues and temples has almost completely faded, and figurative mural painting is essentially gone. Whether vases reflect this great painting tradition is not known, but it is fair to assume that something of the content and treatment of themes was common to both media, just as some vase painting presages themes and approaches in sculpture.

Before the introduction of figures and narratives, pottery in Greece used motifs common to much pottery in the Mediterranean and the Middle East: flowers, plants, birds, animals, or abstract patterns. The Minoans in particular developed these conventions to a sophisticated level. With the Geometric period, however, the preoccupation of Greeks (and through them, Western art) with the human figure in art appears. By the Archaic period, narrative painting on vases is well developed.

Vases of the Geometric Period

Little art remains from the period between the decline of the Myceneans in about 1100 BCE and the emergence of Geometric art sometime after 1000 BCE. (The best examples of vases are from the 700s). Building was of timber and the surviving sculpture is mainly bronze and ceramic miniatures. The magnificent large vases are therefore of particular importance as a clue to the interests of the period. One of the greatest, the vase by the Dipylon Painter, is displayed on the ground floor of the National Archeological Museum, in Room 7 (see Trail 1). It points both to the splendor of grave monuments of the time and to the importance of Athens as a center of ceramics. The vases are of a fawn-colored clay, decorated all over their surface with horizontal black bands of many geometric patterns. One or two of the bands also feature human and animal shapes. The human figures are engaged in scenes of contemporary life such as funerals and battles.

Towards the end of the period—around 700–650 BCE—artists entered what is called an orientalizing phase, in which they used monsters, flowers, and animals similar to those used in the Middle East at the time. These motifs—sphinxes, griffins, birds, wild animals, and flowers—were developed with great dash by the Corinthian potters, who painted with several colors on a whitish clay ground.

Attic Black-figure Vases

Athens and its province of Attica became the leading center of pottery when, from the early 500s BCE, it developed the narrative painting that we most associate with Greek vases. Funeral scenes continued to appear and other scenes of contemporary life were introduced: banqueting, athletics, religious rituals, and sitting around talking. But the greatest innovation was the profusion of scenes from mythology and literature. The gods of Olympus, in human form and with their popular symbols, were shown meeting and talking. Dionysos, the god of wine, womanizing, and ecstasy, often appears with satyrs on one side of a vase; and then drinking, dancing, and harassing women on the other. Herakles was a particular favorite, both in minor adventures and in his twelve labors. Homer's epics and the tragedies of Aeschylus, Sophocles,

The Dipylon Amphora. c. 750 BCE. (National Archeological Museum Athens)

and Euripides provide many of the narratives. Popular scenes were the judgement of Paris; the combat between Achilles the Greek and Hector the Trojan; the death of Priam, King of Troy; and the stories of Orestes and Electra. The earlier of these prized Attic pieces are drawn as black figures on the red background of the pot.

Attic Red-figure Vases

Black-figure vases were soon complemented by vases with red figures outlined against black backgrounds—a reverse process in which the red of the pot shows the figure and the background and lines on the figures are painted in black.

White Funeral Vases

As well as red and black vases, there was a type of vase with a white background on which red and black figures were painted. These are called *lekythoi* (white). They are small and were much used for funerals.

Greek Artists and Writers

For most of the periods of Greek art in this guide, there are no certain records of the names, or lives of artists. However, once we reach the 5th century BCE there begins to be an abundance of names and in some cases, biographical details. The amount of detail does not necessarily reflect the importance or prestige of the artist at the time. The entries below are brief accounts of major figures whose work is featured in this guide; more minor figures are included in the appendix Other Notable Figures in Greek Art. The list does not include any painters because their work has vanished.

ALKAMENES (5TH CENTURY BCE)

Alkamenes is the most highly regarded pupil of and successor to Phidias. He may have continued Phidias's work as supervisor of the buildings on the Athenian Acropolis. Ancient writers, both Greek and Roman, accord high praise to his marble statue of Aphrodite, which was said to be in a temple set in gardens outside the walls of Athens. Pausanias (see below) thought this statue one of the best sights in Athens. The same writer also mentions a statue in ivory and gold of Dionysos in the god's sanctuary next to the Theater of Dionysos, huge marble statues of Athene and Herakles in Thebes, and a statue of Hermes at the entrance to the Athenian Acropolis. None of these statues have survived, but copies do make mention of the original sculptor.

DAIDALOS (A LEGENDARY FIGURE FROM EARLY IN THE 1ST MILLENNIUM BCE)

An artist and inventor, Daidalos is said in legends to be the founder of the Archaic style in sculpture. An early form of Archaic sculpture is still called Daidalic. Diodoros, an historian from the 1st century BCE, says that statues by Daidalos were so realistic that people believed that they were actually alive, and it was said that the statues had to be chained up so that they would not run away. Daidalos was exiled to Crete where, the legend says, he designed a labyrinth for the Minotaur. When Theseus defeated the Minotaur, the king of Crete jailed Daidalos and his son Icarus. Daidalos used wax to fit wings to himself and the boy so that they could fly away. He escaped, but Icarus flew too close to the sun, the wax melted, and he fell and drowned in the sea.

HOMER (BETWEEN 900–700 BCE)

Homer is the name given to the ancient Greek poet (or perhaps poets) to whom the *Iliad* (the story of the Siege of Troy), the *Odyssey* (tales of ten years of wandering by Odysseus on his way home after the war against Troy) and the Homeric hymns are attributed. We know little of Homer's life, but traditions say he was born either on the island of Chios or in Ionia (western Turkey) and that he was blind. His works have been studied for millennia and widely translated, including some vigorous contemporary translations in English. Along with Hesiod's long poem *The Theogony*, which tells the myths of the Greek gods, Homer is a key source for the stories told in Greek art from the Archaic period onwards. See *The Iliad and The Odyssey,* translated by Robert Fagles, Penguin Books, and the *Homeric Hymns,* translated by Jules Cashford, Penguin Classics.

IKTINOS (5TH CENTURY BCE)

Plutarch's *Life of Pericles* identifies Iktinos and Kallikrates as the architects of the Parthenon on the Athenian Acropolis. Pausanias also mentions Iktinos as the Parthenon architect in the course of praising his temple to Apollo at Bassai in the Peloponnese. The Roman writer Vitruvius records that Iktinos was responsible for a vast roof over the sanctuary of Demeter at Eleusis, which he built in the Doric order and without external columns in order to create more space outside.

KALLIKRATES (5TH CENTURY BCE)

Kallikrates worked with Iktinos on the design and building of the Parthenon. A contemporary inscription refers to him as the designer of doors for the temple of Athene Nike on the Athenian Acropolis. Plutarch says that Kallikrates supervised the building of the "long wall" proposed by Pericles. This project involved building two parallel walls joining Athens and Piraeus, but progress was apparently so slow that the process was the butt of satirists' derision.

KALLIMACHOS (5TH CENTURY BCE)

Traditionally—and according to Vitruvius—Kallimachos designed the Corinthian column. The story is that he took the idea of the acanthus leaves on the capital from the grave of a young girl in Corinth. Vitruvius approvingly noted that the column itself imitated the slenderness of a maiden, but Pliny says that Kallimachos was overly fastidious and attentive to detail, and that his work therefore lacked charm. Pausanias considered him an inferior sculptor but an inventive technician, and records that he made a gold lamp for the image of Athene in the Erechthion on the Athenian Acropolis. Corinthian columns became a favorite adornment of Roman and, in the 19th century, Victorian architecture.

PAUSANIAS (2ND CENTURY BCE)

Pausanias is the author of *Description of Greece*. He travelled around the Greek world in the 2nd century CE and wrote comprehensive descriptions of the sites and works he saw. In many cases, his is the only description of vanished works. He is a lively writer whose work is full of fascinating detail about both the art and the stories surrounding it. *Description of Greece* is reproduced, in Greek and English, on www.perseus.tufts.edu. Another version, entitled *A Guide to Greece* Vol 1, translated by Peter Levi, is published by Penguin Books.

PERICLES (C. 495–429 BCE)

Pericles, an Athenian of privileged birth, became leader of Athens in the 450s. He strengthened Athens as a democracy not only by memorably articulating its vision but also by practical measures, such as employing citizens for carrying out various public duties. In 447 he started on the ambitious building program that resulted in the Acropolis. He did this partly to stimulate the economy with public works that created employment, and partly to lift Athenians from the despair that followed the destruction of the old Acropolis by the Persians in 480 BCE. After that loss, the Athenians had vowed never to rebuild, but Pericles offered them such a vision of the greatness of Athens that they accepted the proposal for a glorious monument that would mark out Athens from the rest of the world. The decades before the Peloponnesian Wars (431–404 BCE) were the Golden Age of Athens, the age of its best Classical art and drama.

PHIDIAS (5TH CENTURY BCE)

No artist of the Classical period draws greater praise than Phidias. He was both architect and sculptor, supervisor of Pericles's famous building program in Athens, and a principal sculptor of the temple of Zeus at Olympia. Phidias's preeminence stems from his skillful portrayal of the gods. He made what are arguably the most famous statues of antiquity: the chryselephantine (gold and ivory) statues of Athene Parthenis in Athens and of Zeus at Olympia, all now vanished. Today, the quality of his work can be seen in the friezes of the Parthenon. Perhaps out of envy, his enemies charged him variously with procuring women for Pericles, with stealing gold and ivory from the material for his most famous statues, and with including portraits of himself and Pericles on the shield of Athene Parthenos. He was tried on this last charge and sent to prison, where he died, according to Plutarch, either of disease or from deliberate poisoning designed to discredit Pericles.

PRAXITELES (4TH CENTURY BCE)

Praxiteles, a celebrated sculptor of late Classical times, was best known in antiquity for his statue of Aphrodite of Cnidos, which, unlike earlier statues of females, was naked. The model is said to have been his mistress Phryne, who was reported in ancient texts to have indulged in naked bathing before a large crowd. Pliny reports at least one attempt by a man to make love to the Aphrodite of Cnidos. The original statue has vanished but there are some copies of the Aphrodite and many other works in various collections, including at the Louvre. Praxiteles worked in both marble and bronze, but was most admired for the soft realism of his marble work.

Harbor view from Phira, Thera

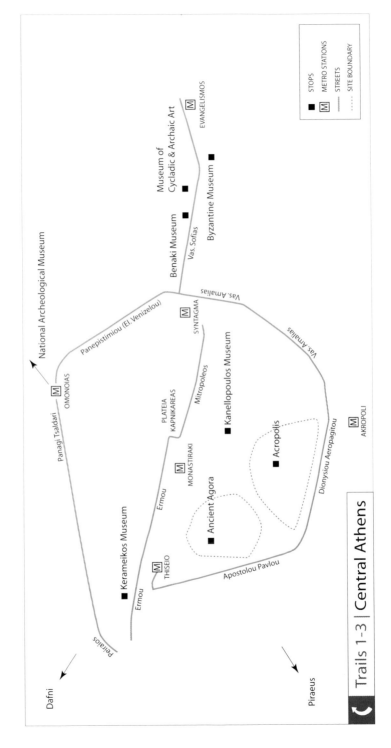

Trails 1-3 | Central Athens

STOPS
M METRO STATIONS
STREETS
.... SITE BOUNDARY

National Archeological Museum

Museum of Cycladic & Archaic Art

M EVANGELISMOS

Benaki Museum

Byzantine Museum

Vas. Sofias

Panepistimiou (El. Venizelou)

Vas. Amalias

M SYNTAGMA

Kanellopoulos Museum

Mitropoleos

PLATEIA KAPNIKAREAS

Vas. Amalias

Acropolis

M MONASTIRAKI

Dionysiou Aeropagitou

M OMONOIAS

Panagi Tsaldari

Ermou

Kerameikos Museum

Ancient Agora

M THISEIO

Ermou

M AKROPOLI

Apostolou Pavlou

Peiraios

Dafni

Piraeus

TRAIL 1:
Ancient Athens

The preeminence of Athens in Greece's Classical age makes this foremost among the Trails. It takes you along the Panathenaic Way, a processional route that linked the Acropolis, the ancient Greek Agora and the Kerameikos cemetery.

A vast walkway of Cycladic marble and stone now links most of the ancient Athenian sites. The circuit, begun in 2000 in the street outside the new Acropolis museum and opposite the gate of Hadrian and Temple of Olympian Zeus, takes in the entrances to the Acropolis metro and joins Dionysiou Areopagitou to pass the theater of Dionysos and the Odeon of Herodus Atticus—at which point a path leads up to the Acropolis. From there the walkway proceeds to the ancient Agora and ends at the Kerameikos. Eventually the project is to follow the Sacred Way from Kerameikos to the site of ancient Eleusis, 22 kilometers (13.7 mi) out of town.

The periods represented on this Trail are the Archaic and the Classical, but you will also see some Geometric pottery. The Trail starts on Pericles's illustrious Acropolis. We first visit the archeological site and then its museum. From there the Trail backtracks along the Panathenaic way to the ancient Agora and the ancient cemetery of Kerameaikos. Allow a long half-day to see the Acropolis and its museum and a day for the Agora and Kerameikos.

The Acropolis towers above the metro of the same name and its museum is next to one of the metro exits. The ancient Agora is a short walk downhill from the Acropolis. Continue through the Agora to visit Kerameikos, or take the metro to Thiseio station.

A ticket for 12 euros gives admission to the Acropolis, Agora and Kerameikos, the Theater of Dionysos, the Olympeion and the Roman Agora, or you can pay a separate entrance fee at each site. The Olympeion comprises some Corinthian columns and is not covered in the Trail.

The Acropolis

Location: When you exit Dionysiou Areopagitou, go left to the Acropolis entrance next to the Odeon of Herodus Atticus.

Contact details: Tel. +30 210 321 4172, 323 6665, 923 8724; www.culture.gr

Opening hours: Site and museum open daily at 8:00 am. From the beginning of April to the end of October, closing time is 7:00 pm; for the rest of the year, 2:30 pm.

Admission: The entrance fee, covering both site and museum, is in the highest range for national museums (Euro 9–12). Consider a second visit on a Sunday when entrance is free. Alternatively, a ticket for Euro 12 provides admission to the Acropolis, Agora and Kerameikos, the Theater of Dionysos, the Olympeion, and the Roman Agora.

Other information: Food is forbidden and kiosk drinks are priced for tourists. Take a drink with you. On a cold, windy day, it is extra cold up among the gods, and paths can be slippery when wet.

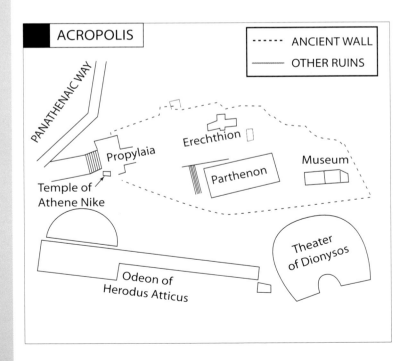

The Site

The Acropolis has been inhabited since Neolithic times. The remains of huge ramparts date from the Mycenaean period. During and after the Archaic period, the site was reserved principally for the goddess Athene. Today's ruins are mostly those of a huge building program begun by Pericles in 450 BCE. The site is remarkable for its views to the sea and its rocky terrain, which here and there one can see were incorporated into the base of buildings. The diagram shows the layout of the site. The Olympeion, of which only some columns remain, and the Roman Agora are not commented on in this guide.

An acropolis means the high point of the city. Any city-state of substance built an acropolis to symbolize its power and house its patron god, but Athens built one to beat them all. The Persians had destroyed a previous acropolis, with its temple to the goddess Athene, 30 years before, in 480 BCE. Once the Greek David had finally broken the Persian Goliath, Pericles proposed an ambitious building program to stimulate the Athenian economy and display the grandeur of Athens. In his *Life of Pericles*, the 1st-century CE writer Plutarch says that he appointed the great Phidias as "his general manager and general overseer."

Phidias engaged a team of architects, sculptors, and craftsmen. Iktinos and Kallikrates designed the Parthenon, Kallikrates the temple of Athene Nike and Mnesikles the Propylaia. "It was Phidias himself," wrote Plutarch, "who produced the great golden image of the goddess, and he is duly inscribed on the tablet as the workman who made it" (*The Rise and Fall of Athens*, translated by Scott Kilvert, Penguin Books). No work ascribed directly to Phidias survives, but Plutarch points out, "everything, almost was under his charge, and all the artists and artisans, as I have said, were under his superintendence." On this evidence we can assume that much of the sculpture of the Parthenon was from his workshop or commissioned and approved by him.

Phidias's role (which he owed, says Plutarch, "to his friendship with Pericles") saw him caught up in "envy" and "contumely" was directed at him and his patron. Rumor around Athens had it "that Phidias made assignations for Pericles with free-born women who would come ostensibly to see the works of art."

The works on the Acropolis were executed quickly. Plutarch relates that "all of them were built in the heyday of a single administration." This in no way diminished their craftsmanship or beauty. "The workmen strove to surpass themselves in the beauty of their handicraft" claims Plutarch. Although the works "were created in a short time," they were created "for all time. Each one of them, in its beauty, was even then and at once antique; but in the freshness of its vigor, it is, even to the present day, recent and newly wrought … as though the unfaltering breath of an ageless spirit had been infused into [it[." If anything, the stature of the works has grown in the two millennia since Plutarch expressed his wonder.

When new, Phidias's gold and ivory statue of Athene the Warrior could be seen well out to sea, glinting in the sun. Inside was another gigantic 40-foot (12-meter) high statue of Athene Parthenos (the virgin) made of gold and ivory.

Only three substantial buildings remain on the site from the time of its greatest glory: the Propylaia, or grand entrance, which includes a small Ionic temple to Athene Nike; the unmistakable Parthenon that dominates Athens and the Erechthion.

The entrance gate, just beyond the ticket office, is the Beulé Gate, named after the French archeologist who excavated it in the mid-19th century from underneath later Turkish buildings. The gate with its two towers is Roman, as are the steps beyond, which replaced part of the original Greek building. At the top of the steps and ahead, is the platform of Mnesikles's Propylaia. Above the steps to the right is a small temple of Athene Nike. In the original design, the entrance was past the Temple of Athene Nike rather than up the steps that remain from Roman times.

As you stand in the entrance gate, on your left is another Roman addition, the pedestal for a statue of the famous general Agrippa. Look back from the top of the steps, past the site of Agrippa's monument (about 45 degrees to your right) along the Panathenaic Way. This processional road started at the Kerameikos, (see the map) passed through the Agora, wound up the hill below the Temple of Athene Nike (past where you are now), through the Propylaia, and entered the Acropolis to finish at the Temple of Athene Polias (of the city) with its olive-wood statue, the oldest known statue of the goddess.

The Panathenaic Way was used for the grand Panathenaic festival held, like the Olympic Games, every four years, and said to have been founded by Erechtheus. It included athletics, theater, and music and ended with a gigantic procession from the Kerameikos to the Erechthion, the apparent subject of a long frieze around the interior of Parthenon.

If you can tune out the sounds of the city and passing tourists, you might catch lingering echoes of the horns and music of the procession, the hoof beats of riders, the drums of musicians and performers, and the cries and songs of dancers and athletes, and imagine the color and excitement of a day when these buildings were new.

From the entrance there are two buildings before you. The Temple of Athene Nike, on your right, uses the ornate Ionic order; the Propylaia straight ahead and above uses the plain Doric order.

THE PROPYLAIA

The Propylaia was created by Mnesikles between 438–430 BCE as an imposing entrance. The architect's task was to combine beauty with a feeling of overwhelming grandeur. He used masonry of white Pentelic marble from Mount Penteli, to the east of Athens. The columns of the central part tower over the visitor, especially because they are first seen from well down the slope, but the wings that fan out asymmetrically to each side embrace the ascending visitors. In its pre-Roman form, before access was made even more visible by a grand staircase, it would have struck the visitor more forcibly. The effect is intentionally theatrical.

Building on the Propylaia began just after the Parthenon was finished in 438 BCE and fairly quickly completed. "The Propylaia of the Acropolis," wrote Plutarch, "were brought to completion in the space of five years." In fact it was never quite finished; part of the wall facing to the left of the entrance remains incomplete.

The two wings are of unequal size. The one on the right (south) is constrained by the Temple of Nike and consists of a simple stoa (a colonnaded, covered way). The wing on the left or northwest is much larger and includes a space known as the "pinakotheke"—an art gallery, which displayed paintings, possibly hanging on the walls, and which was probably a reception area with couches for visitors. There is evidence on the east wall that work was interrupted before it was finished. A number of knobs (or "bosses") used during the construction are still exposed. The precise Athenian craftsmen masons would not have left the wall like this unless they had to.

The main order used on the Acropolis is the Doric, but the Ionic order is used in some interior columns within the Parthenon. This mixing of the two orders carries a political message. Use of the Doric order symbolized Athens's solidarity with the other people of mainland Greece, where the Doric order originated (the Athenians were originally Ionians). The Ionic order originated among the Greeks who colonized islands and parts of present-day Turkey. Its delicate lines and somewhat voluptuous decoration lacked the strength of the Doric order, which was associated with mainland Greece. Athens, however, was in alliance with island Greeks against the Persians, so the introduction of Ionic architecture under Pericles indicates solidarity with Athens's military allies.

The Propylaia is purely an entrance and has no sculptural decoration.

You cannot go into the small Temple of the Athene Nike. Before going through the Propylaia, though, look back. It sits up on a raised platform like a military observation post above the ancient ramparts. According to the 2nd century traveller Pausanias, it offered a fine view of the sea. From here, Aegis, father of Theseus, saw his son's ship returning with its black sails hoisted, which they had agreed before the journey would denote Theseus's death. Believing his son dead, Aegis threw himself into the sea that carries his name. In fact, Theseus had simply forgotten to hoist the white sails.

TEMPLE OF ATHENE NIKE

The present Classical temple is on a sacred site. The Persians destroyed the earlier tiny building and altar, along with most other buildings on the Acropolis. Pericles did not rebuild it. The building we now see was eventually built by Kallikrates, one of the Parthenon architects, between 421–415 BCE during a short peace in the Peloponnesian War between Athens and Sparta. This might explain why the Athenians preferred to use the order associated with their Ionian origins. Originally the Temple of the Wingless Nike, goddess of victory, it became known as Athene Nike.

Ionic buildings generally don't have friezes, but the Athenians, as seen in the Parthenon, incorporated friezes. Most items here are copies of originals in the British Museum, except for the ones on the entrance side. As befits the military character of the sanctuary, the frieze depicts battles, and, on the front, gods. In modern times, the temple was demolished by the Turks in 1687, rebuilt in 1834, and the rather inadequate result then restored in 1935. The greatest threat to it today is the Athenian haze.

From the Propylaia you emerge into an open rocky space with the Parthenon ahead and the Erechthion to your left. Evidence of other buildings can be seen in lines of stone on the ground. Here, in a space enclosed by ramparts and crowded with buildings and *ex voto* (votive) sculptures and objects, which largely obscured the Parthenon itself from passers-by, the clashing Panathenaic procession would have wound past Phidias's famous bronze statue of Athene Promachos, carrying the ceremonial *peplos* to the oldest statue of Athene, Athene Polias (the goddess of the city). The Panathenaic Way ended at the altar of Athene, in the space between the Parthenon and the Erechthion. Phidias's Athene Promachus (meaning the champion, the one who fights for you) was taken away to Constantinople in 426 CE and destroyed in the 13th century.

The old forecourt of the Parthenon lies to the right of the spot where the Athene Promachos statue stood.

TEMPLE OF ATHENE PARTHENOS (THE PARTHENON)

In 2,500 years, the Parthenon has had many uses. Built by Iktinos and Kallikrates in 447–438, it was originally the home of Athens's patron god, Athene. Between the 5th and 15th centuries, it was a Christian church. The Turks then made it a mosque, but during the Venetian siege of 1687 it was an arsenal. The Venetians bombarded it from the sea and the roof and some columns were demolished.

In the 19th century, the English ambassador Lord Elgin bought and sold a lot of the Parthenon frieze to the British Museum. His booty is known collectively as the Elgin Marbles, and the Greek government is making efforts to restore the treasures to Greece.

Doric triumph: the Parthenon, on the Athenian Acropolis. Kallikrates and Iktinos. 447–432 BCE.

ANCIENT ATHENS

Despite these efforts, you must still go to London to see most of them. Much of the past century has been spent on restoration of the frieze and dispute about the authenticity of various efforts. By now, the fumes of modern Athens are silently working to complete the destruction.

The image of today's Parthenon, a white ruin in Pentelic marble against a blue sky, is so engraved on our consciousness that it is hard to imagine the multicolored building that it originally was. Try imagining it new and whole with sculptures and architectural ornaments painted in something like Minoan blue, red, and gold.

As with all buildings, we have to reconcile the created object to its natural space. Today we admire architecture that harmonizes relatively simple human geometry with complex natural settings. In earlier ages, architecture aimed to make visible a divine order inherent in the world—geometry was a pre-eminent branch of knowledge replete with mystical meanings. A good building would contain the underlying order and harmonies of the universe.

The purpose of the Parthenon was to house Athene and the Athenian treasure. The goddess herself existed as Phidias's gold and ivory statue inside a room within the temple. The interior also contained a couple of rooms for attendants and for Athene's treasury.

The Parthenon, obviously the main building on the Acropolis, is, accordingly, on its highest point—the same site as a series of earlier temples dedicated to Athene. Its immediate predecessor was a very large temple, begun after the Athenian victory over the Persians in the Battle of Marathon in 490 BCE but destroyed about a decade later by the Persians. The ruins had been left as evidence of the perfidy of the enemy. The Periclean Parthenon, not as long but wider, used some of its foundations.

The exterior, most of what we now see, consists of columns on a stepped platform. The austerity of the ruin focuses the eye on the proportions. Its eight columns across and seventeen along (twice eight plus one) satisfy a proportion of 9:4. The foundations of the preceding temple in part dictated this, but Iktinos repeated the proportion in the ratio of the height of the columns to the distance between them, and in the side elevation of the building. On the façades, from the base line to the tip of the pediment, the proportion used is often referred to as the golden section, or golden mean—an ideal ratio widely used in art and architecture down the centuries. It is approximately a ratio of 1:1.6. Greek mathematicians saw this proportion repeated in the human body and Greek sculptors referred to it when they developed canons of proportions for the human figure.

The Parthenon is a prime example of a Doric temple, but Doric temples could be quite different from one another. The Parthenon has one row of columns whereas some other temples had two. Earlier Doric temples—e.g. the Temple of Zeus at Olympia, built between 470–450 BCE—had six columns on the shorter side; the Parthenon has eight.

We do not know why the Greeks supported their temples with exterior columns when the functional building inside was walled. The tapering of columns and the fluting, as well as the decoration that connects the column to its architrave, seem to derive their inspiration from trees. The same ideas apparently inspired columns in Egypt that were crowned by leaf shapes. The true symbolism may not be known, but the columns certainly make a big rectangular box seem light and varied in its effects of light and shade.

A much-discussed aspect of the Parthenon's geometry is the adjusting of shapes to accommodate the functioning of the human eye. Some commentators say there is scarcely a straight line in the entire building. Horizontal lines bow slightly upward, as you readily see if you look along the steps at the side. The vertical lines of the columns are adjusted: each swells in the middle and leans inward. These refinements would have made life very difficult for the stonemasons who had to fit every piece together without right angles and without mortar, but it was important to the architects. One reason was to compensate for the tricks that straight lines play on our eyes. From a distance, strictly straight lines appear to bend. A tall column looks to be nipped in the middle. A long horizontal seems to sag. The bulges in the columns make them look straight from designated viewpoints. From other viewpoints the architects' distortions are plain to see.

The Roman architectural writer Vitruvius quotes Iktinos's claim that the adjustments were indeed made to compensate for the distortions created by the human eye. There may be other reasons. The architects were probably more concerned with overall symmetry rather than the appearance of specific lines. They may have been striving, as painters often do, with exaggerated perspective, to make the temple look bigger than it is. The Classical scholar J.J. Polites suggests that they were exploiting the tensions between the object and our perception of it—that they were, in other words, exploring, as did much Greek art and thought, the interplay between ideal and real worlds.

Inside the Parthenon are two rooms. The smaller backroom, where you will observe Ionic columns, held Athene's treasury of gifts and money. The larger front room is the cella and contained the statue of Athene Parthénos. Parthénos means virgin. Athene defended her virginity vigorously and in this persona, she symbolizes independence, determination and purity. A double-story row of double columns, no longer extant, adorned the cella walls surrounding the gigantic statue by Phidias. You will get a very rough idea of its features from the small marble copy in the National Museum. Phidias's statue was made of wood, ivory, and gold (known as *chryselephantine*; *chrys* means gold) and stood with its crown almost touching the ceiling. She bore symbols of her role and power: a nike (a figure personifying victory), a spear, a shield, and a helmet. The combination of wisdom, power, and invincibility expresses the city's image as a center of power and enlightenment at its peak in the time of Pericles. Nothing remains of these hugely showy and gigantic assemblages of gold, ivory, and wood, but their reputations live on. Phidias's statue of Zeus, made in this manner for the Temple at Olympia, became one of the Seven Wonders of the Ancient World.

Now look at the metopes—the panels with relief carving.

Unknown sculptors supervised by Phidias
Sculpture on the Parthenon Metopes, 447–442 BCE

The metopes on the exterior of the Parthenon carry sculptured figures, most of which have been removed or destroyed. They were created between 447–442 BCE under the direction of Phidias. They show Athenians dealing with their enemies and whatever monsters and opposing forces might be pitted against them. On these metopes, neither foreigners nor mythical forces can overpower the Greeks. The struggle between the gods and the giants was depicted on the eastern side; on the northern, the conquest of Troy by the Archaean Greeks; on the western, the victories of Athenians over the Amazons; and on the southern, battles between the Lapiths and the half-horse, half-man centaurs.

Phidias and others
Pediments of the Parthenon, 448–442 BCE

The last set of exterior sculptures was on the pediments, the triangular sections at the top of the east and west ends. However, both sets of sculptures, probably crowded with figures, were almost completely destroyed in the 1687 bombardment by the Venetians. The overall design is usually attributed to Phidias. The second-century traveller Pausanias recorded that the west pediment dealt with the contest between Poseidon and Athene for the right to be the city's patron. Athene won. The east pediment recounted the myth of Athene's birth. Together, the pediments identified the power of Athene, born of the gods and more powerful than the god of the sea. What remains of the original pieces are in the museum.

Phidias and others
Parthenon frieze, c. 440 BCE

On the inside surface above the colonnade Phidias and a considerable team of sculptors created an enormous frieze spanning about 525 feet (162 meters), but it was bombarded by the Venetians in 1687 CE and depleted by Lord Elgin in 1815. What remained on the west showed the beginning of the Panathenaic games, with athletes mounting their horses. Several pieces are in the Acropolis Museum. The original frieze was painted in bright colors and parts of it, such as weapons and horse equipment, were of metal. It is widely believed that the whole showed the Panathenaic procession, but some archeologists doubt this. One suggests that it depicts the sacrifice of a daughter of Erechtheus. Whatever the subject, the vivid action and the flowing style of the carving (not in very high relief—a maximum of two inches or five centimeters)—indicate that Phidias exerted strong stylistic control over the sculptors he employed.

The frieze shows a great cavalcade of horses and riders accompanied by musicians, men carrying sheep and cattle (presumably to be sacrificed) and elders carrying olive branches. It also shows a peplos being presented to temple dignitaries under the interested gaze of a number of gods and heroes.

Some of this frieze is now in the Acropolis Museum.

ANCIENT ATHENS

Pausanias on the Acropolis

Pausanias was a Greek writer who travelled around Greece in the 2nd century CE collecting material for his Description of Greece. *On the Acropolis he saw Phidias's statue of Athene, and in the manner of ancient observers, he enjoys relating art works to their associated legends:*

> The statue itself is made of ivory and gold. On the middle of her helmet is placed a likeness of the Sphinx ... and on either side of the helmet are griffins in relief. These griffins, Aristeas of Proconnesussays in his poem, fight for the gold with the Arimaspi beyond the Issedones. The gold which the griffins guard, he says, comes out of the earth; the Arimaspi are men all born with one eye; griffins are beasts like lions, but with the beak and wings of an eagle. I will say no more about the griffins. The statue of Athene is upright, with a tunic reaching to the feet, and on her breast the head of Medusa is worked in ivory. She holds a statue of Victory about four cubits high, and in the other hand a spear; at her feet lies a shield and near the spear is a serpent. This serpent would be Erichthonius. On the pedestal is the birth of Pandorain relief. Hesiod and others have sung how this Pandora was the first woman; before Pandora was born there was as yet no womankind.

                                    Pausanias, Description of Greece

For art travellers, the Parthenon is two buildings: one the white ruin we see before us, the other the original—sculpted, colored, and housing a rather wild, gigantic statue in ivory and gold. The ruin has become a stark symbol of a glorious past and may even appeal more to the contemporary imagination, shaped by 19th-century Romanticism, than would a recreated original.

One of the intriguing questions of Western architecture is why the ruins of this building have so much warmth, while many of the neo-Classical buildings inspired by it seem so cold. It is of course almost impossible to imitate its distortions: Greek architects started with measured proportions but ultimately did things by eye and were acutely conscious that they were making a divine building. Modern imitations, likely to be banks, churches, or schools, cannot seem to capture its beauty. When we speak of the genius of ancient Greece, the Parthenon is one of the images in our mind's eye.

The Erechthion is nearby.

THE ERECHTHION

Architect/artist unknown
The Erechthion, 430s–406 BCE

The Erechthion is the temple of the ancient god, Erechtheus. Some accounts state that Erechtheus reigned over Athens but became merged in legend with Poseidon; others state that Erechtheus had killed Poseidon's son in a war and was killed on this site by Poseidon's thunderbolt (or a trident). The Erechthion's connections with the history of Athens and with a number of gods made it a venerable building on the Acropolis and much wealth and care was lavished on it.

Ionic capitals have volutes and egg-and-dart decoration. The Erechthion columns feature even more ornamentation: there is a floral motif beneath the capital running around the column, which would have been gaily painted. The accompanying egg-and-dart molding is supplemented by other decorations.

The building is complicated and contained several shrines— to Athene, Erechtheus/Poseidon, and Hephaestes. The main portico facing north with its six columns is monumental in scale, whereas at the opposite end of the building, an intimate porch has its roof supported by six caryatids. The caryatids stand symmetrically—three to the right with the right leg forward, three to the left with the left leg forward. Four here are copies whose originals are in protective custody in the on-site museum. The second from the left is a copy of the original in the British Museum. The last on the right was lost and is an imitation rather than a copy.

There are two parts to the building. The eastern and higher part was dedicated to Athene Polias. Unlike the Athene of the other parts of the Acropolis, Athene Polias was an amiable goddess of the countryside. This section contained a cult statue of olivewood said to have fallen from the sky. The lower part was dedicated to Poseidon and Erechtheus, combining sea and countryside.

Fragments of a marble frieze that once adorned parts of the building are in the museum. Its single roof and the friezes held the diverse elements of the building together. An olive tree on the west side of the building—i.e., facing the Propylaia—commemorates the olive tree that Athene gave to her people.

Since Classical times, the Acropolis has been used as a citadel by a series of conquerors from the Romans to the Franks to the Turks. Collectors have plundered the area, and there have been good and bad restorations. Its greatest enemy now is damage from the chemicals in the Athenian smog. In spite of all the damage, all the disrespect and all the exploitation of its image, it remains one of the world's benchmarks of dignity and beauty.

The Acropolis Museum

Location: The museum is on the Acropolis site behind the Parthenon. A separate entry ticket is not needed. A new museum is being built outside one of the exits of the Acropolis metro and on the pedestrian walkway. The metro itself has an excellent display of material found during its excavation.

Contact details: Tel. +30 210 310 185; www.culture.gr

Opening hours: Both site and museum open daily at 8:00 am. From the beginning of April to the end of October, closing time is 7:00 pm. For the rest of the year, both close at 2:30 pm.

Admission: A ticket for Euro 12, valid for four days, provides admission to the Acropolis, Agora and Kerameikos, the Theater of Dionysos, the Olympeion, and the Roman Agora. You could make a second visit on a Sunday when entrance is free.

The Acropolis Museum has an absorbing collection of Archaic and Classical sculpture and is particularly rich in the sculpture of the Archaic period, especially the 6th century BCE. When the Persians sacked the Acropolis in 480 BCE, they smashed a great deal of the Archaic sculpture that crowded the place. The Athenians regained the Acropolis not long after and found these works lying about. They buried them respectfully near the Erechthion, treating them as though they were people rather than trying to re-erect them. The buried statues, mostly korai, lay there until they were found during excavations in 1886 CE.

Although works of the Classical period have been extensively destroyed or plundered, there are still significant pieces from Phidias's times in the collection.

In the entrance foyer

Attributed to Alkamenes
Statue of Prokne, *Exhibit 1358, 440 BCE*

The sculptor Alkamenes was a pupil of Phidias. His figure of a woman with a child clinging to her leg strikes one immediately as an image of great sadness. The legend that inspired the statue is one of tragedy and barbarism. Prokne was a mythical figure, princess of Athens, sister of Erechtheus, and wife of Tireis, King of Thrace. Tireis raped Prokne's sister Philomela and cut out her tongue. However, Philomela told Prokne of the outrage through her weaving. In revenge, Prokne murdered her own son Itys, whose trusting image we see at his mother's side, and served him to Tireis for dinner. The sculptor shows the child drawing close to his mother as though seeking reassurance, unaware of the dreadful fate that awaits him at her hand. She seems absorbed in her own inner conflict and unaware of the child. The barbarity of the story is at odds with the touching beauty of the statue, but it is the genius of Greek art and drama to bring these extremes together. Prokne will use this trusting child to avenge her sister (and by extension Athens) and bring gruesome shame on the house that betrayed her. The realism of the figures and the depiction of deeply felt human emotions are qualities that are profoundly present in the tragedies of Aeschylus, Sophocles, and Euripides.

Room I

Unknown Athenian sculptor
Lioness Savaging a Calf, Exhibit 4, 570 BCE

Lioness Savaging a Calf is probably from the pediment of an early temple of the Athene Polias, about 120 years before the Parthenon we know. The strength and posture of the lioness and its victim are realistic, but in keeping with work of that period, much of the hair and some of the features are treated as decorative geometry. Traces of color can be seen, especially on the eyes of both animals. The subject fits the flattened triangular end of the pediment with ingenuity and naturalness. The flowing line of the lion's back communicates strength. A reconstruction shows the space filled symmetrically with this lioness matched head to head with another lioness and calf.

When you step away and look back, the scene seems more animated and the image itself more three-dimensional.

Unknown Athenian sculptor
Serpent, Exhibit 41, 575–550 BCE

The intimidating line of the reptile ready to strike is a great subject for the Archaic sculptor, because a serpent is both lively and adorned with geometric markings. There are many traces of color on this serpent, which would have made it more realistic, but it has more the appearance of a snake-monster than of an actual snake. For the ancients, the serpent was associated with life and healing. Gods (including Zeus) and the first humans (including Erechtheus, who was part god and part human) were sometimes depicted as snakes.

Room II

Unknown sculptor
Pediment showing Herakles and the Triton, Exhibit 35, c. 550 BCE

This pediment features one of strongman Herakles's many encounters in pursuit of his labors and loves. On the left, the hero wrestles with Poseidon's Triton, who is half-man, half-fish. Herakles crouches over Triton to strangle him. Triton's serpentine tail conveniently but plausibly fills the acute angle of the pediment. Considering that the work is millennia old, traces of color are surprisingly well preserved. The human form of the naked Herakles is sculpted to show powerful thighs and prominent calf muscles.

On the opposite side are three male torsos with wings, entwined serpents' tails, and Archaic beards and smiles. Together they make up the demon Nereas, a benign-looking shape-changer. They are sculpted in full relief, looking in different directions and taking an interest in different things. The one to the rear holds water, represented by wavy lines; the middle one carries fire, represented by straight lines; and the one to the front has a bird. If the bird represents air, the missing element is the earth, where Herakles is in control.

Go past and look back to see how the animation and the movement of Herakles's body follows through into Triton's body. This is a more dynamic view than the frontal one, which focuses the eye on the pattern and the balancing of elements to fit the pediment. The rhythm of the piece is pronounced from this angle and the flow of bodies and the demons' smiling faces more prominent.

Unknown sculptor

Moschophoros: Man carrying a calf, Exhibit 624, 570 BCE

This is an *ex voto* or votive offering of a youth carrying a calf for a sacrifice to Athene. It was dedicated by Romvos, whose name is inscribed on the base. The common name given to the statue, Moschophoros, refers to his carrying the calf. The youth is naked except for a garment (himation) hanging from his shoulders. The garment hanging down the back is relatively simple in detail yet suggestive of the body beneath, as drapery carved in marble often is. He has the appealing body of an active countryman. The face is soft, the smile innocent and tender. The large eyes have been hollowed out for insets. The calf is arranged around his neck and clasped like a friend—a pose that will be taken up, centuries later, in statues of Jesus as the good shepherd. The animal is naturally observed and carved with fewer conventions than the human figure. The rapport between the man and the animal suggests that sacrifice to the gods is not brutal but a proper fate for young things. The more melancholy expression on the face of the calf may suggest a regret that the youth does not share.

Votive statues from the 6th century BCE were frequently of marble from Mt. Hymettos, near Athens, or from the island of Paros, used since Cycladic times and destined to become even more popular with Greek sculptors. Votives of this sort must have once crowded the Acropolis.

Unknown sculptor

Kore (girl), Exhibit 593, 580–570 BCE

This is an early Attic kore (plural korai); such sculptures of women were very popular as votive statues in this period. In this era, the sculpted female was clothed—the reverse of later Western practice in which the female is more often naked than the male. There are traces of paint and the hair shows the same symmetry as that of the typical male kouros with three curled lengths of hair to each side. Such statues were probably not modeled on particular people. They followed quite strict conventions in posture and clothing, but were not uniform and have individual expressions and subtle differences in size, stance, and costume. Overall, they communicate great calm, but the smile and posture also combine to communicate warmth.

Room III

Unknown sculptor
Dying Bull, Exhibit 3, 559 BCE

This savage scene was in the center of the pediment of the earliest Parthenon and probably flanked by the Herakles, Triton, and three-headed serpents of the earlier exhibit. All that remains of the two lions killing this bull are the cruel claws digging into its flesh. The figure of the bull is intact but has lost its coloring. Even as a fragment, this is a most compelling image of the death agony. The powerful creature holds nothing back, but the reconstruction suggests also that the ensemble was made to be balanced in the manner of a coat-of-arms.

Room IV

Unknown sculptor
Dog, Exhibit 143, 520 BCE

This dog knows its job: it is lean, with prominent ribs, its rear haunches lowered, its shoulders raised, its gaze intense, its nose pointing, slinking forward, ready to leap. Wonderfully observed, it demonstrates that realistic sculpture is well within the capacity of Archaic artists and that their stylized treatment of the human is deliberate. The *Dog* is said to have stood guard at a now-vanished sanctuary of Artemis, attribute to her role as the unmarried goddess who cared for pregnant women and wandered free as a huntress.

Unknown sculptor
The Rampin Horseman, Exhibit 590, 560 BCE

The statue takes its name from the French collector who took possession of the head, now in the Louvre. This head is a plaster copy but illustrates the Archaic use of hair and beard for abstract patterning. The hair looks rather like the wigs the Egyptians wore, and the beard is a pattern of dots. The remaining torso captures the consummate ease and command of a truly accomplished rider.

The whole was originally a votive piece of two riders, believed to represent the brothers Hipparchos and Hippias, who, with their father, ruled Athens in the 6th century BCE. During that time, the Athenian economy and arts scene flourished, and the sons arranged to rebuild the old temple to Athene. Both came to sticky political ends. Hipparchos was assassinated in 514 BCE and Hippias exiled in 510 BCE. The date of the piece suggests their father made the votive offering.

Unknown sculptor
The Peplos Kore, Exhibit 679, 530 BCE

This noted kore in Parian marble is wearing a Doric garment known as a *peplos*, from which she gets her name. This figure is thought by some to be the work of the same sculptor as the *Dog* (Exhibit 143). Like other Archaic korai, she has curls hanging on each side. She must have been brightly colored—there are traces of color on her eyes and hair and patterns on her clothing. Her smile is slight and she looks plump and good-tempered if a little haughty. (by comparison the nearby *Lyons Kore,* Exhibit 269, looks somewhat apprehensive). There is a hint of movement on her left, following the direction of the now missing arm that would have held a gift. From different angles, you see more curls and ears pierced for rings, which would have been on the original statue.

Unknown sculptor
Torso of a naked youth wrestling, Exhibit 145, 520 BCE

This is one of the few Archaic male figures in the museum. The more representative collection in the National Museum will allow you to become familiar with the overall style. It contrasts with the very still poses of nearby korai, made during the same period, and has some features that show a change towards the Classical. For example, in comparison with the Archaic style, the sculpting of the abdomen continues to be formalized but the musculature is more pronounced. The body is shown in motion, the arms outthrust. The hand on the shoulder is evidence of a wrestling contest in progress. The figure, with its enviable physique, is often thought to represent the Athenian hero Theseus.

Endoios and unknown sculptors
Athene and various korai, Exhibits (from the left) 682, 684, 615, 674, 670, 625, 633, 685, 505,680, 671, 520–490 BCE

During the 19th century, archeologists unearthed many marble statues and fragments buried on the site in 480 BCE after the Persian victory. These were among them. Some were votive

ANCIENT ATHENS

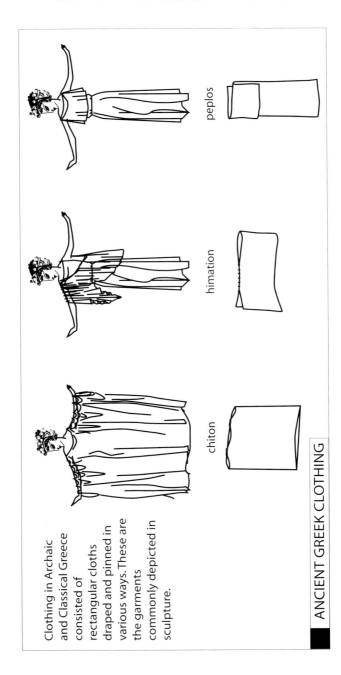

Clothing in Archaic and Classical Greece consisted of rectangular cloths draped and pinned in various ways. These are the garments commonly depicted in sculpture.

peplos

himation

chiton

ANCIENT GREEK CLOTHING

offerings, others made in memory of the dead. Exhibit 625 (seated in the center) is the dilapidated remains of a lively statue of Athene, signed by the sculptor Endoios. As the korai approach the 5th century, they become more solemn.

The figures demonstrate the individual sculptural differences existing within an apparently tight convention. For example, look at the faces, starting with Exhibits 682, 684, and 674. Exhibit 682, from 520 BCE, is a grande dame of appropriately greater size. The work is said to have been influenced by the art of the island of Chios. She greets the viewer with the famous Archaic smile and a look of good humor. Exhibit 674, from 500 BCE, the noted sphinx-eyed kore, is the Mona Lisa of korai—a slight smile at the corner of the mouth, dark eyes, and an air of introspection that accompanies her startling beauty. The smile is a striking indicator of change. Exhibit 684, from the following decade (490 BCE) is solemn if not somber, with the barest hint of a smile.

Art historians discern the change in style towards the coldness or detachment evident in the last piece. The difference may have been provoked by external affairs. Philosophy, science, and poetry flourished in the 6th century BCE, which also saw the beginnings of Greek drama. However, in the opening years of the 5th century BCE, Athens was at war with Persia and despite her victory at the Battle of Marathon in 490 BCE, endured the destruction of the Archaic Acropolis. The proud city-state waited nearly half a century before Pericles's rebuilding scheme brought it back to glory. The years up until 450 BCE are the years of transition to the Classical era, in which the realistic style of that period begins to emerge in sculpture.

Consider the different treatments of clothing. The drapery is an essential feature in the sculpture of female figures, as indeed it will be for centuries to come. The ingenious garments worn—the peplos, the chiton, and the himation—were a gold mine for sculptors, who gloried not only in the bodies they might reveal, but also in the patterns observed or invented in the fall of the cloth. The grande dame, Exhibit 682, stands in the wind. Under her skirt, her knee is tightened. Others gather their drapery in various ways that show the body beneath, and the depth of the carving varies. Look at the back of the figures to see differences in the elaborate hairdos and the fall of their garments.

Alcove off Room V

Attributed to Agorakritos
Frieze from the Temple of Athene Nike, Exhibits 424–427, c. 415 BCE

The Temple of Athene Nike was the small temple perched high up on the right as you entered through the Propylaia. Considering their location, these works are not in bad shape. The central one shows a procession of the gods. Both sides show various scenes of battle—perhaps real, perhaps mythological, but certainly with Athenians winning. Though much worn, the battle scenes show the artist's skill at depicting violent action within the limitations of working in relief. Within the assembly of gods (identified on the explanatory label) the sculptor has contrived to place the figures in postures and positions that suit their reputations.

Room V

Unknown sculptor
Marble kore, Exhibit 683, 510 BCE

This is a short stocky kore, a rustic figure in a rough heavy garment that hangs straight. Paint can still be seen on many parts of the figure, including the hair, eyes, garment, and slippers and suggests how color might have made stylized figures look like the people they depicted. The heavy facial features are strongly and honestly modeled, suggesting maturity and confidence.

Attributed to Antenoros
Large kore, Exhibit 681, 520 BCE

This very large kore might belong to the base next to it, in which case it is a work of the noted sculptor Antenoros and was a gift of the potter Nearchos. It is a massive figure, well over life-size. The drapery has had a great deal of attention.

Unknown sculptor
Fragment of a pediment of the Gigantomachy, Exhibit 631, 525 BCE

A former Temple of Athene dedicated by the sons of Peisistratos had, on its pediment, scenes representing the mythological battle of the gods with the primordial giants. Fittingly, Athene had a central role. The fierce sons of mother earth had attacked the gods because she was disgusted by the way they had treated her earlier sons, the Titans. In the course of the war, Athene was born from the head of Zeus, fully armed and ready for the fight. She promptly assumed a leading role in the battle, which only concluded when the mortal Herakles joined in on the side of the gods. Here, she strides towards the enemy with a shield of snakes held out before her. Her power is mighty. Her first foe is already down (time has left us only his foot). The next in line is already in his death throes. The giants are gathering their strength to launch into battle. As is usual, the female figure is clothed and the males nude.

The sculpting of Athene combines power and aggression, in the posture and the threatening snake, with beauty and grace, shown in the delineation of the legs and the calm face. Despite the fragmentary nature of this piece, we see the artist's ability to grasp the dramatic moment.

Room VI

Attributed to Kritios
The Kritios Boy, Exhibit 698, 480 BCE

This figure of a youthful long-legged athlete is named after the sculptor Kritios, who was the teacher of Myron, another noted sculptor. It is sometimes thought that a contemporary, Nesiotes, may have been the sculptor or have worked with Kritios as he did on other sculptures. Made of Parian marble, it is the first complete example in this museum of the kouros, the male equivalent of a kore. Historians see it as an example of the transition from Archaic to Classical by means of a style that they call the Severe Style. The Archaic characteristics are that it is nude and shown frontally, with one leg advanced. However, the Archaic style had the male posed fairly rigidly, with complicated coiffures comparable to those on the female statues. *The Kritios Boy* has his hair rolled in a comparatively simple way and the anatomical detail is more realistic. The belly appears to be rising with breath and the weight is firmly on the one leg, leaving the other free to move. The face is unsmiling, soft, and innocent, and different than the Archaic style. Viewed from behind, the buttocks emphasize a heaviness that is not immediately obvious from in front.

Unknown sculptor
The Blond Boy, Exhibit 689, 480 BCE

This figure has a plaited head band with his curly locks brushed over the front into a pretty fringe, a seductive tilt of the head, full lips, and a straight nose—altogether a good-looking lad. He is called blond because there are traces of yellow on his head from the time when the figure was painted. His pelvis is exhibited nearby.

Unknown sculptor
The Euthydikos Kore, Exhibit 686, and *base with legs,* Exhibit 609, 490 BCE

This piece takes its name from the dedication to Euthydikos inscribed on its base. Art commentators see this figure as a prime example of the severity in vogue at the end of the Archaic period. Both her clothing and coiffure are more severe than the works of the preceding decades, and the facial expression is so supercilious and sour as to be arresting. Traces of color show red lips that would have highlighted her pout. Below the knee, the dress material is carved so as to appear to be almost transparent.

Room VII

The groups of exhibits in this room are fragments from the Parthenon itself.

Phidias and others
Metope of centaur trying to capture a Lapith, Exhibit 705, 447–442 BCE

A fragment from the *metopes* on the Parthenon's south side (now mostly in the British museum) features the war between the Lapiths of northern Greece and the centaurs. The king of the Lapiths was, according to myth, the first mortal to murder a relative, namely his father-in-law. Purified by Zeus, he then attempted to bed the goddess Hera—Zeus's wife and sister. Zeus put the monster Centaurus in Hera's place. Later, at a Lapith wedding, centaurs tried to carry off the women, including the bride. Guests, including the mighty Theseus from Athens, came to the aid of the Lapiths and the centaurs were defeated. Although the overall message is man's triumph (as is happening in the one piece in place on the Parthenon in the southwest corner), in this fragment, a centaur is making off with one of the women whose body is twisted in its grip. The sculptor's storytelling power is at a peak. The vulnerability of the clothed figure is highlighted against the solid shape of the centaur's horse legs and human trunk.

Phidias and others
Fragment of a horse's head, from the Parthenon frieze, Exhibits 882 and 884, 440 BCE

From several pieces, art historians have concluded that work from the frieze that was inside the Parthenon behind the metopes was more tightly controlled by Phidias than work on the metopes. The remains of a horse's head suggest that the sculptor caught the whole figure at the moment where, much like an eager racehorse, it was tugging, neighing, prancing and tossing its head as it was led out to be mounted. The horse is a piece designed to evoke the excitement, clamor, and action at the beginning of a mighty processional ride. There is tension in the contrast: the man leading the horse is playing cool.

Phidias and others
Fragments of pediments from the Parthenon, from the west pediment: Exhibits 887, 14935, and 885; from the east pediment: Exhibit 881. All from 435 BCE

The models on the walls indicate where these fragments belonged. The male figure (887), which came from the extreme end of the west pediment, next to the now-headless figures of Kekrops and his daughter (14935), represents the Athenian River, the Illisos. Kekrops was the legendary founder and first king of Athens, and taught the people of his city the basics of marriage, literacy, and proper burial. Athene entrusted his daughters with the care of the infant Erechtheus. Thus the pediment is telling the story of Athens. The sculptural style of this pair and of Poseidon (885) has clearly moved away from the conventions of the Archaic period. Figures are in a wide range of postures, which make different demands on representation of flesh, muscle, and balance. Kekrops and his daughter are seated, leaning affectionately towards one another. The river figure is on his side and propped on one hand as though reclining on a riverbank. The emphasis in Poseidon is on dynamic musculature.

From the east pediment (Exhibit 881) the moon goddess Selene is seen with her horses.

Room VIII

Phidias and others

Fragments from the Parthenon frieze, presumed to picture the Panathenaic procession, c. 440 BCE

The frieze runs around both sides of the room. Exhibit numbers are exemplary, not exhaustive. Beginning on the left hand side of the entrance to the room, they are:

Oxen, Exhibit 857
Rams, Exhibit 860
Pitcher bearers, Exhibit 864
Men in discussion, Exhibit 865
Chariots, Exhibit 859, 872, 863
Riders, Cases on the right hand side wall
Gods watching the parade, Exhibit 856

Animals being led to sacrifice, women carrying pitchers on their shoulders, old men chatting, horses and chariots jostling in procession, gods in their Olympian glory—this daring narrative is commonly presumed to be of the Panathenaic procession. Rather than showing one moment of the procession at its solemn climax, the work is alive with innumerable stories. Animals play; riders are fractious; participants and the watching gods chat and relate to one another. In monumental sculpture, the Parthenon frieze is the opposite of pompous, in no way the sort of art we have come to expect in representations of public occasions. Instead, it invites the viewer to engage with the participants as they casually play their role in the scene. It is all the more remarkable because the complexity of the groupings is achieved in very low-relief carving—at its deepest, only about 2.5 inches (6 centimeters) deep.

Half of the original frieze was taken up with riders, then elders, musicians, water carriers, boys leading sheep and cattle, and, on the eastern wall or the front of the temple, women, heroes, and gods. The ultimate focus of the scene was the presentation of the peplos to the priestesses of Athene.

Note the sculpting of old men in Exhibit 865. Rather than presenting them in a solemn processional line, the frieze shows them in a discussion, where some have turned in different directions or are behind others. The arrangement creates an illusion of depth belied only by the way the feet line up at the bottom of the panel, revealing the shallow space the sculptor was working in.

The frieze includes a long sequence of riders and chariots, exemplifying the astonishing variety in the total work. The figures themselves are variously dressed and caught in very different postures. The horses rear and are ready to break into gallop; the riders look around and behind. Look at Exhibits 859, 872, and 863. In the first, 859, the rider leaps onto a chariot as a marshal, keeping others back. In 872, another marshal holds a horse. In 863, a horseman looks back at the marshal who waves others on. The shallow relief work still manages to get several horses side by side.

On the right side of the room's entrance, in Exhibit 856, the gods indulge in their usual habit of watching the human show from their private boxes. On the left, Triton, with his finger upraised, makes a point to an interested Apollo, who has turned back to him, as people will, to make eye contact during a conversation. The arrangement of the figures, as well as the way in which legs overlap seats, gives a surprising depth to low relief sculpture. Alongside, Apollo's sister Artemis turns aside and hitches up a garment that has slipped revealingly from her shoulder. From the waist up, this modeling of the figure shows a goddess of chastity edging towards the female nude. Her perfect profile has something of a sneer, possibly because the occasion is in honor of her sometime rival Athene.

Overall, the gods are doing ordinary human things, chatting like onlookers with all the time in the world to enjoy each other's company.

The nike figures mentioned below may not always be on display.

Unknown sculptors
Two nike figures from the Nike Tower, Exhibits 972, 973, c. 415 BCE

The Nike Tower carried plaques of the goddess Athene and the nike (personifications of victory). Here are two elegant figures created to evoke the admiration associated with the idea of victory. The carving takes advantage of the folds created by garments. The figure in Exhibit 972 is in motion. See the oxen she was leading. Under the folds of her garment, her strong left leg is taking her forward, the right is gracefully posed. Her cloak flows from her left arm, suggesting that her advance sets up a flow of wind. The figure in Exhibit 973 sits to adjust a sandal, her eye on some other event. Under the folds of the generous garment, her stunning body is on view.

In the final room

Unknown sculptor
Four caryatid columns from the Erechthion, 440 BCE

Four of the original caryatids that supported the porch of the Erechthion are here. One remains in the British collection.

To modern eyes the idea of using figures as columns seems a bit Las Vegas, but the ancients trod a very different line between elegance and vulgarity. After all, the entire Acropolis is a piece of grandiose triumphalism.

The very idea of women as columns gives the building a distinctive character but the genius of the execution went well beyond that. They could have seemed condemned to carry a burden for all time. Instead, they stand so easily and gracefully that the weight of the roof seems barely oppressive; it seems as if the roof would stay in place if they stepped down. With those on the right showing their right legs and those on the left showing their left legs, all strong and yet relaxed, they are as eye-catching as any group of models. The fall of their garments seems deeply marked when viewed at eye level but *in situ* the garments accentuate the grace of the figures. One remains in the British Museum.

When you return to the Propylaia, and exit from the Acropolis, you could go to the ancient Agora through the gate beside the prominent rock outcrop known as the Areopagus (the rock of Ares, god of war), or begin anew the next morning at this fascinating spot.

The Ancient Agora

Location: There are entrances from the Acropolis side or from near the Kerameikos. The closest metro station is Thiseio.

Contact details: Tel. +30 210 321 0185; www.culture.gr

Opening hours: 8:30 am–3:00 pm Tues. to Sun.

Admission: Low range (Euro 1–4). The ticket covers site and museum. Alternatively, a ticket for Euro 12, valid for four days, provides admission to the Acropolis, Agora and Kerameikos, the Theater of Dionysos, the Olympeion, and the Roman Agora.

Other information: The agora was the center of Athens's official and commercial life. It is below the Acropolis, on the north side, and joined to both the Acropolis and the Kerameikos by the Panathenaic Way.

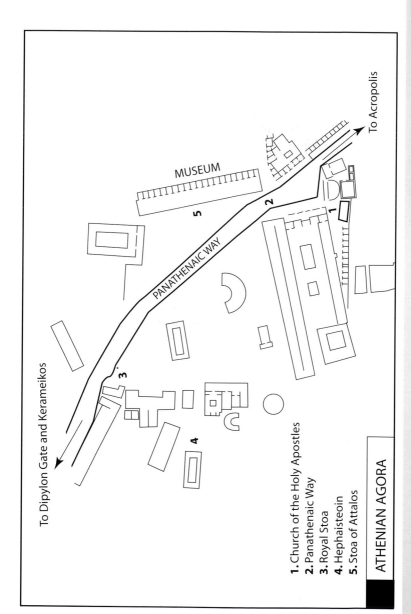

To Acropolis

MUSEUM

5

2

PANATHENAIC WAY

1

To Dipylon Gate and Kerameikos

3

4

1. Church of the Holy Apostles
2. Panathenaic Way
3. Royal Stoa
4. Hephaisteion
5. Stoa of Attalos

ATHENIAN AGORA

The Site

The remains of human habitation on this site span 5,000 years at least. Not much is left of the ancient Greek Agora. Successive phases of building slowly obscured the relatively open public square of the Greeks. Subsequently, the ruins vanished under housing until archeologists reclaimed the area in the 19th and 20th centuries. American archeologists have been the most active in excavating the Agora and housing its finds in a reconstructed stoa.

Entering from the Acropolis end you come first to the Church of the Holy Apostles (Stop 1), a charming Byzantine structure. Walk along the Panathenaic Way (Stop 2) to the Royal Stoa (Stop 3), come back past the Thesion (Temple of Hephaistos) (Stop 4), and finish at the Stoa of Attalos (Stop 5), which contains finds from the site. The ruins you pass along the way come from many different eras and are well labeled.

Stop 1

Unknown architects
Church of the Holy Apostles, c. 1000 CE

The church may be closed, but if so, you can still view the typically fine exterior work on the exterior. The cross shape towards the altar end allows for a small octagonal dome that lets in heavenly light through its slim double windows. Arches are rounded but elongated to add height and slenderness. The brickwork is polychromatic and very detailed, requiring no further decoration. The tiling has the feel of an organic rather than a geometric material.

Stop 2

Panathenaic Way

This broad thoroughfare is the supposed location of the activity in the Parthenon frieze, as riders and others prepared for the procession. The Panathenaic Way began at the Dipylon, the main entrance gate to ancient Athens. Outside this gate was the cemetery of the Kerameikos. The Way then crossed the Agora diagonally and, past the Agora, climbed the hill up to the Propylaia of the Acropolis. It is, needless to say, much worn and rutted by use over centuries. In Greek times the square was fairly open. Roman buildings eventually filled it.

Stop 3

Royal Stoa

The so-called Royal Stoa was a small building at the Kerameikos end of the Panathenaic Way. It was destroyed several times even in antiquity and little trace is left now. Its importance was as the seat of one of the main magistrates of Athens (known as the Royal Archon) and as the place where the Laws of Solon were on display. Socrates was brought before the magistrate here to be examined on a charge of "corrupting the young." He was tried and executed in 399 BCE.

Stop 4

Unknown artists
The Hephaisteion, temple of Hephaistos and Athene. Also called *The Thesion*, 450–440 BCE.

Hephaistos, the son of Zeus and Hera, is the god of fire, and used flame as a weapon in the Trojan War. In peacetime he developed the art of forging metal. Renowned as a brilliant inventor and in demand for equipping heroes for battle, he taught his crafts to workers around the world. Although lame, he was immensely attractive to beautiful women. Apparently he shared this temple with Athene in her role as patron of arts and crafts. In one tradition he also lusted after the goddess.

Workshops of potters and bronze and metal workers were nearby. Archeologists have found evidence that at one stage during its use, the temple was surrounded by a formal garden. It is similar to the Parthenon and though smaller—six columns by thirteen—is of similar proportion. When seen from below, a second row of columns at both back and front add to the depth of the building and give greater prominence to the outside columns. Time and warfare have been fairly kind to this temple, which has remained relatively complete.

The sculptures remaining on the outside illustrate incidents in the lives of Herakles and Theseus (the hero closely identified with Athens) but it is difficult to identify or appreciate them in their present state.

Stop 5

Stoa of Attalos

As well as ruins, the Agora contains a reconstructed building known as the Stoa of Attalos. Attalos II was the ruler of Pergamon, a noted Hellenistic city. He donated the stoa to Athens in recognition of the education he gained there.

Attalos's original stoa was put up in the 2nd century BCE when the Agora was half enclosed by huge colonnades. The ancient shopping center was rebuilt in the 1950s—with Rockefeller money—to house archeological records and serve as a museum for pieces found around the Agora. It is a faithful reproduction of the original. About twenty shops would have opened on to the colonnaded areas at each level—a good vantage point from which to watch the goings on in the ancient Agora.

Agora Museum

From the Acropolis end of the Stoa, you will see a row of marbles running the full length of the colonnade. To your right as you enter the colonnade, against the south wall, is a huge marble statue of Apollo.

Attributed to Euphranor, an Athenian sculptor
Statue of Apollo Patroos, c. 350 BCE

This Apollo is missing its head and arms as well as a musical instrument once held against his left side, signifying his role as god of music. He is in peplos and himation. (There is a miniature copy of the original on Shelf 47 inside.) Ancient writers attributed this statue to the artist Euphranor, a noted Athenian sculptor and painter from around 350 BCE. By this time, sculpture had entered a baroque phase that would continue into Roman times. The treatment of drapery is flamboyant and figures appear as though in vigorous motion or caught in a high wind.

Immediately to the left of the Apollo on a marble pedestal is the autograph of the most famous Athenian sculptor of the 4th century BCE, Praxiteles. Further still to the left against the main wall of the Stoa is an illustration of how the nearby Ionic capital would have been colored.

The museum entrance is some distance along the stoa. It is a single, long, narrow room lined on both sides with cases arranged in bays in chronological order. There are also some free-standing central cases and on the left side explanations of the periods represented in the bays. The cases are not numbered.

The first bay contains prehistoric work. The cases of the second and third bays, especially on the right hand side, are fine examples of pottery from the Geometric period. Bay 4 initiates the Archaic period. In the center is the much-loved *Kneeling Boy*.

Unknown sculptor
Kneeling Boy, 540–530 BCE

This terracotta piece is from the Archaic period at its best. It represents an athlete tying a ribbon around his head as a sign of victory. The figure is apparently hollow and likely to have contained oil, which athletes would have carried to rub themselves down with. Greek athletes—all male—competed nude. The large eyes, half-smiling mouth, patterned hair, and slim, smooth-skinned body are all typical of the extraordinary high-quality sculpture of the period. The formality of the treatment does not diminish the erotic appeal. Something of the young man's pleasure in his own prowess is captured and heightens the erotic element, which enhances its attractiveness. The position of the ribbon is justified by comparison with vase paintings.

Go to the sixth bay on the right side where there are groups of cups in cases.

ANCIENT ATHENS

Vase symbolizing an athlete's victory. Kneeling Boy, ceramic, 530 BCE.
(Agora Museum, Athens).

Attributed to the Chairias painter
Group of cups, Case 30, 525–475 BCE

On the bottom shelf of a case is a group of three cups attributed to the Chairias painter. These are examples of red-figure work and can be compared to examples of black figure at the other end of the same case. From left to right, there is a woman at an altar, a maenad, and a lyre player. Each figure is fitted into a clearly defined circle at the base of a double-handled cup. There is great economy of line in the drawing. The woman at the altar is nude, though women were still commonly clothed in most other works, while men were shown virtually naked.

On the top shelf of the same case is:

The Gorgos painter
Cup, Case 32, c. 500 BCE

This is a red-figure cup painted on both sides. The easy-to-see side has a youth carrying a hare, perhaps as a gift of some sort. The other side has to be seen in the mirror and depicts popular subjects for cups and vases—a Dionysian feast and the duel between Achilles and Memnon. Achilles (son of the goddess Thetis) and Memnon (son of Eos the dawn) fought each other during the Trojan War. The tears that Eos shed for her son reappear again and again as morning dew.

Next to these are:

Epiktetos
A pair of cups, c. 520–510 BCE

The first cup shows a satyr on a donkey. The satyr, as usual, has an erection, and his donkey follows suit to emphasize the nature of satyrs. The red-figure cup alongside it is another by Epiktetos. A girl is carrying her shoes presumably after bathing, which allows her to be shown naked.

Marking the end of the sixth bay is a large fragmentary piece.

Exekias
Calyx krater with black-figure work, c. 530 BCE

Black-figure preceded red-figure works and Exekias was the top black-figure vase painter of the mid 6th century BCE. Apparently, this is the first known object of the shape known as a *calyx krater*, used for mixing.

Some of the scenes come from the height of Greek myth. One side shows a battle over the body of Patroklos (Patroklos died in the Battle of Troy and his friend Achilles fought with legendary fury to avenge his death), and, on the other side, Herakles is being made a god. The story is that as Herakles prepared to die there was a thunderclap, and he was taken to Olympus to live among the gods, where he married the goddess Hebe.

The names of many of the characters are written on the surface of the vase. From left to right, easily decipherable ones are the gods and goddesses: APOLON, ARTEMIS, POSEIDON, HERMES (the one with the hat); and reading the letters from right to left: DIOMEDES and MENTOR and probably PATROKLOS (Diomedes and Mentor were friends of Odysseus who fought at Troy, for Patroklos).

On the lower part of the vessel, lions attack a bull as in the sculptures on the pediments on the old Parthenon. A grapevine decoration shades a maiden who is not yet aware of the satyr stalking her from beneath.

Now go past some domestic objects to the eighth bay, where a nike floats high in a case.

Unknown sculptor
Nike, 3rd century BCE

Here is a small victory figure, a charming and gracious piece that uses the flamboyance of the Hellenistic period to striking effect. There is great power and vigor in the diminutive image, the sweep of the gown accentuating its strength and speed of movement. The figure with its one exposed breast may have lost its head and wings but not the headlong rush of energy associated with winning.

In the end cases opposite are samples of the realism that characterized the Roman phase of art in Greece.

Outside in the colonnade, the second exhibit on the left of the museum exit is a relief work.

Unknown sculptor

Fragment of a monument of victory in an equestrian contest,
c. 360 BCE

According to the inscription, the tribe Leontis won the games pictured here. Horsemanship was greatly admired in the period around 360 BCE. You can see the enormous pleasure taken by the sculptor in showing high-spirited horses and handsome youths being directed by an older officer. In the original, the horsemen would have carried bronze spears. Xenophon wrote an essay on horsemanship, remarking that "...men who manage horses gracefully have a magnificent appearance"(*On Horsemanship*, X1, 8).

On the end wall, to the right of the museum exit, is a nike.

Unknown sculptor

Nike or *Winged Victory,* c. 400 BCE

This marble nike, which probably stood on a roof, is now missing its arms or wings and part of its head. Sculpted some 50 years after the Parthenon, the figure, though incomplete, undoubtedly demonstrates how rapidly Athenian artists developed a flamboyant baroque style, with enormous skill in depicting figures in dramatic poses and using drapery to reveal the body beneath and to accentuate dramatic movement.

From the Stoa you can take the path that exits on Ermou Street, turn left and follow the walkway to the Kerameikos site and museum or to the Thiseio metro station, just before the Kerameikos.

Kerameikos

Location: Ermou Street near Metro Thiseio
Contact details: Tel. +30 210 346 3552; www.culture.gr
Opening hours: 8:30 am–3:00 pm Tues.–Sun.
Admission: Low range (Euro 1–4). Alternatively, a ticket for Euro 12, valid for four days, provides admission to the Acropolis, Agora and Kerameikos, the Theater of Dionysos, the Olympeion, and the Roman Agora.
Other information: The area is being done up as part of a grand plan for remodeling the monumental part of central Athens. If you are in the Agora, you could take the exit beyond the Temple of Hephaistos (the Thesion) and be a short walk from the Metro station and the Kerameikos.

The Site

Kerameikos is an area that included the ancient cemetery of Athens just beyond the Agora. Honored Athenians were buried here. Around the site are copies of some funeral sculpture. The site has been worked upon and studied by the German Archeological Society and has a small museum known as the *Oberlander* with good finds from the 12th to the 7th centuries BCE and some later red and black figure and white vases (see the Introduction for more information about Greek vases). Most of the site is on a lower level, and around it are several brass-plate maps orienting viewers to significant points on the site.

Pausanias ascribes the name of the site to Keramos, an Attic hero said to have invented the art of pottery—hence the word "ceramic." Originally marshland along the course of the Eridanos River, part of Kerameikos had been used as a burial place since 1200 BCE. It was also an area housing Athens's potters, which gives a prosaic and plausible origin to its name.

Kerameikos contained two of the greatest gates of Athens: the Dipylon Gate and the Sacred Gate. They were close to one another in the middle of the site. The Panathenaic Procession departed from the Dipylon, which is at the Agora end of Kerameikos. The Sacred Gate marked a Sacred Way that went in the opposite direction through Kerameikos and on to the distant sacred site of Eleusis.

The museum is just inside the entrance. Outside the museum a concrete path descends to the lowest level of the site and joins the Sacred Way where there are copies of some noted works, the originals of which are in museums. The orientation map, headed by the Street of Tombs, indicates where the works originally stood. The best known is probably the Stele of Hegeso. A copy is set on high ground on the right of the Street of Tombs.

Unknown sculptor(s)
Copy of the Stele of Hegeso, late 5th century BCE

The original stele is in the National Archeological Museum. There are two figures: the deceased Hegeso and a servant girl holding a jewelry box. Hegeso is seated, wearing a chiton buttoned down her arm, which invites the eye to follow the lines of her body beneath, thus seeming to emphasize the life that has gone out of her. She holds a jewel—it was originally painted—but is gazing somewhere into the distance beyond it, lost in thought.

The Museum

The museum rooms are arranged around a courtyard. When you enter, you are in a room with a display of sculpture. The succeeding three spaces round the courtyard are lined with cases arranged in chronological order.

In the entrance room and to the right is another noted grave stele:

Unknown sculptor(s)
Stele of Demetria and Pamphile, late 4th century BCE

This stele originally stood on the rise above the path joining the Sacred Way to the museum. It shows Demetria and her sister Pamphile together. The dead Pamphile is seated, gazing reflectively out at the world that she has left. Under the folds in their clothes, the sculptor shows us the strength and poise of the sisters as living people. The image records the close bond that existed between the sisters as one that is not destroyed by death. A second stele in the National Archeological Museum shows the two sisters again. This time it is Demetria who has died, but they are together and holding hands.

To the left of the entrance is a fascinating group of sculptures unearthed on the site in 2002. The centerpiece is a kouros.

Unknown sculptors
Kouros, lions, and sphinxes on columns, c. 600 BCE

There is an account on the wall of the unusual circumstances that allowed these pieces to survive and be recovered. The centerpiece, the kouros, is notably slender in the body and long in the face. His eyes are large and his hairdo very studied, so that the soul he represents will stride into the next world prepared and at his peak. The sculptor, like many of his contemporaries, achieves a remarkable effect of inwardness in the face. The conventions for portraying animals and mythical beasts in Archaic times parallel those for human figures. Animals too are shown at the peak of their strength and nobility, but, in contrast, they look on the outer world, over which they presided, with confidence and hauteur.

The display of (mostly) small objects found over millennia in the cemetery is laid out chronologically in a series of cases.

Unknown potter(s) and painter(s)
Geometric urns, Cases 1 and 2, 12th, and 11th centuries BCE

These urns demonstrate many of the motifs of geometric work—concentric circles, zig-zag, meanders, triangles, hatching, and dots. We may suppose, given the nature of the age and the attention given to symbols, that each device has a meaning, but we do not know what the meanings might be. A figurative element occurs on the urn between cases 2 and 3 where handles are shaped as goats' heads—a device seen on other geometric vases.

Unknown potter(s) and painter(s)
Pottery, 9th century BCE, Cases 4, 5, and 6

These cases present a number of attractive pieces. On the bottom shelves, urns have lids depicting both horses and birds. Others have one or the other. Pieces on the upper shelves are especially rich in decoration. The painters seem to have been impelled to fill up the space so that the areas between the birds are filled in with ovals and dots. However, what now look like abstract decoration may in fact have represented aspects of the natural world such as the water holes where birds gather.

Unknown sculptor
Sphinx, Case 6, Exhibit 8, c. 650 BCE

This piece was designed as an incense burner. The sphinx is a very linear creature, here as elegant as a supermodel. She has long slim legs, her head and shoulders are upright and her wings do an upsweep to join the incense bowl as a sort of support. There is an irony here since a sphinx has wings but cannot fly. She once was painted, perhaps making her even more glamorous.

The first display inside the last room is of objects from a presumed mass burial. The story is told inside the case. The grave objects in the remaining cases include touching miniatures from children's graves, which were perhaps left as toys for the dead. The practice lasted for many centuries and is touching still today. A number of small pieces show the ritual expression of grief performed by women.

The final cases of the collection display red-figure, black-figure, and white vases usually adorned with tales from mythology and scenes of revelry.

Unknown potter(s) and painter(s)
Amymone and the Satyrs, Case 13, Exhibit 21, 5th century BCE

A prominent vase portraying satyrs illustrates the reliance on line in this kind of vase painting. The figures are outlined and blocked in. The details are then incised on the figures in a form that is best described as drawing. Given the medium and the popular demand across the Greek world for vases, the subjects are often freely treated and open to bawdiness. Note however that these satyrs do not have erections as they often do on vases. The story represented is that of Amymone, one of the Danaus who was sleeping when a satyr tried to rape her. She called on Poseidon for help. He dispatched the satyr and then made love to her himself.

Further Trips in Ancient Athens

Below the Acropolis, on Dionysiou Areopagitou, are two theaters: the theater of Dionysos and The Odeon of Herodus Atticus.

Theater of Dionysos

Location: On the side of the hill of the Acropolis, off the walkway of Dionysiou Areopagitou.
Contact details: Tel. +30 210 322 4625; www.culture.gr
Opening hours: 8:30 am–2:30 pm daily.
Admission: Low range (Euro 1–4). Alternatively, a ticket for Euro 12, valid for four days, provides admission to the Acropolis, Agora and Kerameikos, the Theater of Dionysos, the Olympeion, and the Roman Agora.

The theater dates from at least the 500s BCE, and is set in an area where festivals for the gods were held. Following on from the mime, choruses, and dancing of the festivals, theater is a logical, though not inevitable, development. Beginning with a stage, theater facilities were progressively added (for more detail, see the section on Epidauros in Trail 6). The present condition of the theater results from 19th-century restorations, chiefly of the Roman version of the buildings. It was here that many of the great tragedies of Aeschylus, Sophocles, and Euripides, and the comedies of Aristophanes, were first played.

The Odeon of Herodus Atticus, closer to the Acropolis entrance, was built for musical performance and is still used for this purpose. It was originally roofed, and was completed in 161 BCE for a generous patron of the arts, Herodus Atticus.

Ancient Eleusis

In the industrial suburb of Elefsina is the site of ancient Eleusis. It is the destination of the Sacred Way that started at Kerameikos.

Demeter, the goddess who looked after crops, was especially honored at Eleusis, where there were secret ceremonies in her name. She spent much time there grieving for her daughter Persephone, who had been captured by Hades. Only the initiated could attend these secret ceremonies or "mysteries" (from *myo*, to keep your mouth closed), which were preceded by a 15-mile (23-kilometer) pilgrimage on foot from Athens. The mysteries and their elaborate rituals remained remarkably secret.

Location: Elefsina (Ancient Eleusis) is 14 miles (22 kilometers) out of Athens. The A16 bus goes from the Plateia Eleftheriou (also known as Koymoundouro) near Kerameikos.

Contact details: Tel. +30 201 554 6019; www.culture.gr

Opening hours: 8:30 am–3:00 pm Tues. to Sun. Closed Mondays and public holidays.

Admission: Low range (Euro 1–4).

Eleusis now is chiefly an archeological site. Its layout and appearance in Roman times can be gauged from model reconstructions in the museum. Among the statuary in the small collection is an excellent kouros from the 500s BCE.

TRAIL 2:
The National
Archeological Museum

The National Archeological Museum has one of the world's great art collections. The artists of ancient Greece—like their philosophers—went very close to covering all the big questions of art. A single visit does not do the collection justice. If you can, make two trips, one to view prehistoric art and a second to cover art from historical periods. Although this museum is highly recommended, there are alternatives if you don't feel up to tackling such a large museum. You can get a comfortable overview of Greek art at the Benaki Museum in Athens; you will find directions and brief information for this smaller museum at the end of Trail 3, page 132.

Location: No 44 of the street named 28 Oktovriou (Patission), halfway between two Metro stations. From Metro Omonia, you go north along 3 Septemvriou; from Metro Victoria, you go south along 3 Septemvriou, and in both cases 28 Oktovrfiou (Patisson) is one block to the east.

Contact details: Tel. +30 210 821 7717, 821 7724; www.culture.gr

Opening hours: From March to November 8:00 am–7:00 pm Tues.-Fri.; 8.30 am–3:00 pm weekends; closed Mondays; from November to March 8:30 am–5:00 pm, Mon. 10:30 am–3:00 pm.

Admission: Mid-range (Euro 5–8).

Other information: A leaflet given out from the counter where you buy the entrance ticket shows the ground plan of the museum with room numbers. The rooms are numbered on the wall above each opening. The upper floor of the museum has been closed for some years.

THE NATIONAL ARCHEOLOGICAL MUSEUM

Gold death mask from Mycenae c. 1550 BCE. (National Archeological Museum Athens).

Prehistoric Art: First Visit

The first visit includes the collections of Neolithic, Cycladic, and Mycenaean art. This collection is particularly crucial for those interested in Mycenaean art, as very little of this art is shown at Mycenean archeological sites.

The Cycladic, Neolithic and Mycenaean collections are in Rooms 4, 5, and 6. These are entered directly from the entrance hall. Straight ahead from the vestibule is Room 4, full of Mycenaean exhibits. Off that room to the right, Room 6 contains Cycladic exhibits and, on the left, Room 5 contains Neolithic works.

The Neolithic material is from the Greek mainland and from Troy from the 5th to the 2nd millennium BCE. Cycladic art from the 3rd and 2nd millennia BCE is from islands scattered from the mainland to Crete. The Mycenaean material (Mycenae was in the Peloponnese in central Greece) dates from the 15th to the 11th centuries BCE. It is contemporaneous with and often resembles the Minoan art of Crete. In fact some of the work is certainly by Minoan artists. (Minoan art is represented chiefly by frescoes from the island of Santorini—ancient Thera—and pottery, which is normally exhibited on the upper floor of the museum.)

Room 6

The major pieces in the museum's collection are large female figures and musicians from the most striking period of Cycladic sculpture. They are generally of marble, particularly from the islands of Paros and Naxos, and shaped with bone or copper tools and emery.

In a case beside the entry to Room 6 is a sculpture of a head.

Unknown sculptor
Cycladic Head, Exhibit 3909, c. 2400–2200 BCE

This 28-centimeter (11-inch) head, found on Amorgos, is of the white marble that is plentiful on Paros and was for many centuries the prized material for Greek sculptors—a taste that was picked up in the Renaissance. Marble is a hard stone but Neolithic sculptors made tools of harder stones such as emery and obsidian, which they used to chip, incise, and abrase the surfaces of their work. This head shows the long, straight nose typical of many Greek periods, a typical sculpted mouth, and very small ear sockets. There are traces of paint on the eyes. Now eyeless, the face is soft around the upper lip, below the cheeks and in the line of the chin. If you focus on the lower half of the face or imagine large eyes, you begin to see the face of a very handsome woman enhanced by a long Modigliani neck. It is interesting to speculate whether this is the beauty of an imagined goddess figure representing the spirit of a dead person or the beauty of a real person. The former is more likely.

On your right as you enter Room 6 are cases and a wall chart giving details of the provenance and styles of the works.

THE NATIONAL ARCHEOLOGICAL MUSEUM

Unknown sculptor

Large female statue, Exhibit 3978, c. 2200–2000 BCE

This female statue is life-size—152 centimeters (5 feet and 2.5 inches). Most folded-arm Cycladic figures are female. Now very abstracted in appearance, they would have had more painted detail. Sculptures like this one, with their prominent breasts, are thought to be images of a mother goddess but this is an extrapolation based on general views about primitive art and is far from certain. This figure was found on the island of Amorgos; small versions seem to have circulated widely around the Cycladic Islands, Crete, and the mainland. The proportions are based on a canon of four—head to shoulder, shoulder to waist, waist to knee and knee to toe. This lends weight to the view that the sculptors of the 3rd millennia BCE, like most thereafter, worked to rules of proportion. The flat back and stretching out of the feet, which leads to a slight raising of the knees, suggest it was made to lie rather than stand, or had its back to a wall. If this is indeed a goddess and not, for example, a piece of funeral sculpture, then the Greek habit of making their gods in human images dates well back.

Unknown sculptor

Harpist, Exhibit 3908, c. 2400–2200 BCE

The statuette of the *Harpist* is an immensely attractive piece about 9 inches (21 centimeters) in height, of Parian marble and found on Keros. Move to see it in the round, but concentrate on the view from the harpist's left to see how three-dimensional the conception is. The figure, though seated, fits the proportions of a body divided into four. The tilt of the head not only shows the musician absorbed in his performance, but also creates a simple sweeping line with the arm of the harp. The various hollowed shapes of the harp and the seat echo one another and give a play of light and shade on the composition.

Working such a complex shape with the material and tools available surely required enormous patience and judgement. The shafts of light that fall into the hollows of the piece heighten the inner light that is often characteristic of marble. The *Harpist* was found in the same tomb as the neighboring flute player. We cannot know if the pieces were made especially for the burial in the hope of a musical after-life or if, perhaps, the deceased was a musician or a patron and they were possessions prized in life and taken to the grave.

Unknown sculptor
Flute player, Exhibit 3910, c. 2500–2200 BCE

The *Flute Player* has been caught in the somewhat comic, constipated posture that the effort of blowing into a woodwind instrument can bring about—knees bent, belly out, head back to get the best fill and flow of air from the lungs. The figure is relatively squat, seemingly based on a proportion of three, with a long neck and short legs below the knee. It is made as a standing figure and conceived in three dimensions. Its unusual proportions in no way detract from its elegant lines and the assured balance of the piece.

In spite of an immediate impression of simple uniformity of conception, each Cycladic figure gradually acquires some individuality of feature and posture.

Unknown potter and painter
Painting of fishermen on the stand of a vase, Exhibit 5782, with a modern impression of the original displayed nearby, c. 1500 BCE

This painting is on the stand of a vase from Melos. The postures are frontal in the Egyptian manner; the eyes of men and fish are extraordinarily large, even Picassoesque. The eyes and the elongated bodies and legs give the scene an air of exuberance. The coloring as well as the postures are typical in works across the Aegean.

Browse around the rest of Room 6 noting designs of geometric, floral, and spiral decoration on pots and the élan of the design of jugs. Markings like abdominal muscles on violin figures strengthen the view that the violin figures are intended to be human figures. (In the Neolithic room, Room 5, you will see a violin figure, Exhibit 8970, with a head.)

Room 5

Opposite Room 6, Room 5 contains Neolithic Art from the 5th and the 4th millennia BCE. Immediately outside the room, left of the entrance, are two key works.

Unknown artist
Seated male god, end of the 4th millennium, from Thessaly

The focus of this seated statue is clearly the phallus, though the fragmentation of the scupture leaves it unclear what he was doing with his hand. The piece has been made to view from the front; the back is flat. The head has indications of eyes, mouth, nose, and ears. The arms are very oddly shaped and bent, the left arm quite uncomfortably twisted and the right arm, as it reaches up towards the ear, much shorter looking.

Next to this figure is a large vase. Its shape is a striking combination of beauty and utility. Inside the room, two cases of figurines (towards the middle of the left-hand wall) are interesting.

Unknown artists
Female figurines, Neolithic period

Figurines of this period are the fat females thought to be mother goddesses that were major objects of worship throughout the Aegean in pre-Hellenic times. There is probably a greater attention to sculpting from natural forms in these early millennia than in later Cycladic work, where artists seem more interested in their own canons of proportion and style.

Unknown artist
Mother and Child (called a *kourotrophos*), 4th millennium BCE

About 6 inches (15 centimeters) high, this is a big-hipped, seated figure bent slightly forward as one does to rock a baby. The arms and the baby are boldly formed with smooth curves, the baby snuggling in to the mother's shoulder. The painted lines perhaps suggest clothing and further emphasize the roundness and directions of the two bodies.

From here go back into the large, central Room 4.

Mycenaean Art

Room 4

Mycenae flourished from about 1550–1100 BCE and eventually either controlled or influenced most of Greece, including the islands. It was apparently an authoritarian and militaristic culture, with massive fortifications around its sites. Not surprisingly, a fair proportion of weaponry and depictions of soldiers are among the

Mycenean vase. 1500–1400 BCE. Unknown potters (National Archeological Museum Athens. Lauros/ Giraudon/Bridgeman Art Library)

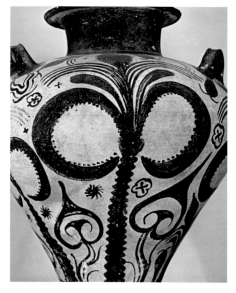

remains that have been found. The deciphering of the famous Linear B script revealed that the Mycenaeans spoke an archaic form of Greek.

To later generations, this is the era from which the Homeric epics are drawn. These epics provided 19th-century archeology with many clues as to the location of ancient sites. The main sites known today are at Mycenae and Tiryns near Argos in the eastern Peleponnese and Pylos in the southwest (see Trail 5). In general, the pieces come from graves, many taken to be the graves of royalty. The Mycenaean room has a lot of gold, both jewelry and useful objects.

The cases in Room 4 are arranged as circular bays with the prime exhibits in central cases. Cases are not numbered. In the first bay as you enter, the central case contains gold masks and other goldwork.

Three gold death masks

Exhibits 253, 259, 264 are in the front of the case. (There are two more, 623, 624 in the rear of the case), c. 1580–1550 BCE

In 1876 the single-minded dilettante Heinrich Schliemann discovered the three gold death masks displayed here in a Mycenaean palace tomb. They are presumed to be of royal personages and the differences between them show that they portrayed individual people.

THE NATIONAL ARCHEOLOGICAL MUSEUM

The gold itself, with its ability to reflect light, and the image it conjures up of sunlight, contrasts starkly with the subject, a person for whom the light—at least of this world—has gone. "A void beneath the mask," as the poet George Seferis put it.

The masks were originally laid on the faces of the dead, obviously to honor and perpetuate them. Today, however, the preciousness of the material mocks the capacity of the subjects to own it, which gives a touch of irony to an otherwise rather gruesome subject. The faces only partially emerge from the flattened surfaces and, in Exhibit 259, the partially spherical form resides inside a larger sun-shape. The precious object owes its shape to observations of a person recently dead.

Heinrich Schliemann (1822–1890)

With the belief that the Homeric stories had an historical basis, the German-born wealthy businessman Heinrich Schliemann retired from business at the age of 41 to pursue his lifelong ambition to find Homer's Troy. On the site of Troy he discovered not one but nine cities, one on top of the other, and established a reputation for himself as an archeologist. He dug up graves at Mycenae and claimed that they supported the historical basis of Greek literature. He predicted the finds at Knossos in Crete, but was not prepared to pay the price asked by the owners of the land and so did not dig or make finds there. The Knossos finds were later made by Arthur Evans, who began his work there at the time of the British Protectorate and continued for some 30 years to dig and recreate the "Minoan world." Schliemann's mansion in Panepistimiou now houses the Numismatic Museum.

Unknown goldsmiths
Gold rings, especially Exhibit 240, *ring with a hunting scene* and Exhibit 241, *ring with a fight*, c. 1550 BCE

Found like the masks and *Cup of Nestor* in Tomb 4, many of these rings, presumed to be seals, are wonderfully designed works of miniature art. They are typically about an inch and a quarter (3.3 centimeters) across. The impressions and drawings displayed are a great help in appreciating them. Was it because such items were widely used and needed to be individually identified that their creators got so much from simple shapes, designs, and representations? Like small modern objects, such as coins and stamps, such limitation attracts artistic skill and invention. Exhibits 240 and 241 compress complex scenes of action into a minute area. In Exhibit 240, a hunt scene shows two men in a chariot shooting arrows at deer. Exhibit 241 contains a battle scene where a warrior, armed with a dagger, fights three opponents and, though outnumbered, is winning.

In the reverse side of the case, you will see:

Unknown sculptor
Gold Mask, known after Schliemann as the *Mask of Agamemnon*, Exhibit 624, c. 1550 BCE

Exhibit 624, in the reverse side of the case, is the mask Schliemann dubbed, over-enthusiastically, the *Mask of Agamemnon*. It comes from Tomb 5 and dates from some 300 years before Agamemnon's appearance as a leader of Greek forces in the *Iliad*. However, this discrepancy has not robbed it of the name. The indented lines used to build up eyebrows and moustache are rather heavy but they give shape to the face, as does the beard surrounding the shaven cheeks and chin. The lips, though thin, give the face an ease of expression that suggests the peace beyond the grave.

In another case in the center of the first bay is a celebrated piece of goldwork.

Unknown goldsmith
Cup of Nestor, Exhibit 412, c. 1550 BCE

The *Cup of Nestor* comes from the same tomb as several of the masks. The *Iliad*'s Nestor was the king of Pylos. He and Agamemnon of Mycenae called on the Greek heroes and kings to make war against Troy. The tomb where the 6-inch (15-centimeter) cup was found was one of six grouped in a circle (Grave Circle A) with two to five people buried in each, and a glittering treasury of gold jewelry, weapons, and ceremonial vessels. Schliemann, who had a habit of interpreting his good luck as astute foresight, called it the *Cup of Nestor*, because he thought it resembled a description in the *Iliad* (in Book 11).

With the cup in front of you, the description from the *Iliad* seems inconclusive: It describes the cup as being studded with golden nails and having four handles, each featuring two golden doves bending over to drink. When full, its weight made it very hard even to lift. (Based on *The Iliad*, translated by Robert Fagles. Penguin Books.)

No matter whose cup it was, the somewhat battered piece is attractive and the drinking doves are a truly elegant touch.

In a case on the right hand wall beside the masks:

Unknown artist
Gold lion head, rhyton, or libation cup, Exhibit 273, c. 1550 BCE

Used for ritual drinking or libations poured to honor the gods or spirits of the dead, such vessels were often of precious materials. Minoans and Greeks of the Classical period also used this style. This lion head was in the same grave as the *Cup of Nestor* and the three gold death masks. It gains in charm if you look from below and take in the modeling of the mouth and beard. The detailing shows a keen appreciation of the ways in which sheet metal can be used to represent the animal's features. The supremacy of a lion in battle is a frequent subject of art and a lion's head as a libation cup may have been thought to add potency to the fluid.

Unknown Minoan artist from Crete
Bull's head rhyton, Exhibit 384, c. 1550 BCE

The form of this 13-inch (31-centimeter) rhyton is the head of a bull, the powerful animal much favored in Cretan art. It, too, is from Tomb 4, which was undoubtedly the richest and contained five skeletons. The curving horns and nostrils of this piece are of gold. There is a gold rosette on the middle of the animal's forehead and a large, round, silver eye. The animal looks benign, partly because of the flower on its head and partly because the horns seem to be curved more for grace than for any threat they may represent.

Now go to the second bay, first to the central case.

Unknown artist
Plaster female head, Exhibit 4575, c. 1200 BCE

Although there is more detail, thanks to the paint and molding below the cheek line, this painted lady, excavated in a house on the Mycenaean acropolis, is similar to the Cycladic figures of a thousand years earlier. The plaster has preserved her careful paint and beauty spots. The eyelining and arranged curls no doubt reflect the cosmetic fashions of her time, but she has a harsh mouth and chin; if this is a portrait, it is of a rather formidable character. Her powerful features stay in the mind's eye.

In the reverse side of the central case is the magnificent *Warrior Vase*.

Unknown potter and painter
Warrior Vase, Exhibit 1426, c. 1200–1100 BCE

Schliemann found the *Warrior Vase* in 1876 in an excavated building, not a tomb. For a *krater* (a bowl from which wine could be served) it is relatively large.

A long-nosed woman bids farewell to warriors who march off in full armor, with horned helmets, waistcoats, and short, fringed tunics, leggings, shields, and spears. Each has a food bag or water bottle attached to his spear. The nose guards on the helmets are barely adequate for the faces depicted. Inside each handle of the vase are a goat and birds.

Walk around the piece to get the full effect. The drawing is slightly comical—especially the succession of prominent noses— but the moment shows the warriors at their hopeful best. Parades of troops through the streets on their way to any war share this innocent spring in the step and this sense of adventure. In a wall case to your left as you face the *Warrior Vase* there is:

Unknown goldsmith,
Large gold ring, Exhibit 6208, c. 1500 BCE

Found in the Treasury of Tiryns, not far from ancient Mycenae, (see Trail 5), this comparatively large gold ring is over 2 inches (5.6 centimeters) wide. It shows four virtually identical bird-like figures, each with a lion's head, in procession towards a seated goddess. They carry libation vases. The goddess, eagle behind her, holds a large vase ready to receive the libations. On the top of the ring are a sun, moon, and ears of wheat; on the bottom, a frieze. The complex image is packed into a miniature space.

To the left and the right of the entrance to the second bay are a number of fresco fragments. Start on the left:

THE NATIONAL ARCHEOLOGICAL MUSEUM

Unknown painter

Large fragment of a fresco of a Mycenaean lady, Exhibit 11670, late 1200s BCE ·

This fresco, found in a house on the Mycenaean acropolis in 1970, is a noted work of which the upper section is well preserved. The woman is painted from the front with her head in profile. Note however that her head is not turned: her neck is entirely relaxed. She is of generous build. The painter has made much of the patterning and coloring of her garments, which fall in a regular way and yet suggest the shape of the breasts just beneath the fabric. Following Minoan and Mycenaean convention, her flesh is white. She seems to be a lady of leisure and some wealth; she is wearing jewels and admiring or selecting more in her right hand. Her hair is curled on the forehead—as on the plaster head nearby—then drawn into a tress and tied. A very long plait falls down to her neck and trails across her shoulder. The long fingers—especially of her left hand—are carefully outlined with the nails short and not painted. The small double chin might have been thought an attractive feature at the time.

Although much of the painting depends on line, the hair, bust, and arms show an adept sense of mass. The observable similarities between Minoan and Mycenaean art reinforce the view that Minoan artists had a status in Mycenaean civilization comparable to that of Greek artists in Roman times.

Underneath this painting is:

Unknown painter

Fragment of fresco picturing evil spirits, Exhibit 2665, Case 21, c. 1300 BCE

These evil spirits, on a fragment also found at Mycenae, either have goats' heads or are wearing them, suggesting that frescoes dealt with popular subjects—as does a neighboring piece showing women framed in a window. The drawing—redolent of modern comic illustrations—captures the grotesqueness of popular superstitious figures with very few and freely drawn lines.

To the right of the entrance to the bay, you will see:

Unknown painter

Installation of fragments of a fresco of a wild pig hunt, with modern extrapolations, Exhibit 5878, c. 1300–1200 BCE

Painting on this fresco, also found at Tiryns (see Trail 5), pictures a hunt at its peak. The boar is fully extended in flight, the dogs are fastening on to him, and a spear is about to penetrate his forehead. It is just the scene for the dining-room wall. The animals appear to be literally in full flight among trees against a blue sky, caught at a moment when their feet have left the ground. What we see is a tribute to the ingenuity of the restorers and the lively imagination of the artist.

Unknown painter

Reconstruction of a fresco of a chariot from fragments, with modern extrapolations, Exhibit 5882, c. 1300–1200 BCE

This much re-imagined piece shows how fragments provide clues to the whole. With the aid of scholarly imagination, we are able to revisit the work of three millennia ago. From the original, we have first a horse's hoof and a section of the frieze below; next, its dressed tail and a piece of the shaft that draws the chariot, then an outline of the front of the chariot and the reins. On the left are parts of the wheel rim, spokes, and the back of the chariot. A white elbow above indicates that one of the figures was female, while the blue and the buff indicate that there were two figures. Finally, fragments show that the chariot is moving among formalized trees, which suggests a country event, perhaps a hunt.

Unknown painter

Installation of fragments of a fresco of a female head, with modern extrapolations, Exhibit 5883, c. 1300 BCE

Though found in a palace at the Mycenaean site of Tiryns, this woman is dressed in Minoan fashion with a decorated red gown or blouse open at the front to expose her astonishingly prominent breasts. They add a new dimension to the Homeric term "deep-breasted." Going on good authority, the restorers have provided a decorated nipple. Most of the exhibit is extrapolated from a relatively limited fragment, the nose, eye, and curls having been preserved in the original. Some commentators argue that she is in a religious procession carrying offerings to a god. Whatever the subject, what remains of the original of the frieze, and especially her hair, indicate that the artists were painstaking in their attention to decorative detail.

Unknown painter
Installation of fragments of a fresco of bull leaping, with modern extrapolations, Exhibit 1597, c. 1300 BCE

This final piece is of a subject dear to the Minoan artists of Crete. Bulls had high, probably sacred, status in Minoan culture and images of both young men and women leaping over charging bulls occur in painting, sculpture, and ceramics. No doubt it was more than a sporting activity or even a demonstration of courage and daring, but its exact significance is not known. We can see, however, that it produced wonderfully graceful images.

Go to the end bay. Proudly displayed in the central case are two gold cups.

Unknown goldsmiths
Two gold cups with bulls, Exhibits 1758 and 1759, 15th century BCE

The pick of the gold work, apart from the masks and rings, are these two Minoan gold cups, found in a tomb at Vaphio, south of Sparta. One is of hunted bulls and is quite violent; the other is of tamed bulls. On the hunting cup, a bull caught in a net is tied to trees while two other bulls run off terrified, one to the right and one to the left. One bull has knocked a hunter to the ground and tossed another in the air.

On the second cup, the bulls are tame. A cowherd holds one by a rope. On the other side, a cow and bull watch an embracing pair of lovers. The ground and trees are placed with much skill. The design takes advantage of the curved surfaces and the work is detailed enough to show a considerable range of expression on the faces of people and animals.

Minoan Art

To see more Minoan art, go through Rooms 34 and 35 to the stairs at the back of the building and up to the next floor to Room 48. Here you will find the most significant Minoan holdings in the museum's collection: the astonishing frescoes and pottery unearthed in the 1960s on the island of Thera (modern Santorini), which was known in ancient times for its great beauty. The frescoes and ceramic pieces have emerged with a great deal of visible color. Since Plato's time, the volcanic eruption of about 1500 BCE that buried these objects under meters of ash and destroyed a great part of the island has been linked to tales of the legendary island of Atlantis. For more discussion about Minoan art, see Trail 8.

The rooms containing these paintings were slightly damaged in an earthquake and have not been on display for several years. In accordance with Greek policy, most of the paintings will return to Santorini to a new museum of prehistoric art on the island (See Trail 8). A few, however, still remain in the National Museum.

Room 48

Unknown Minoan painter(s)
The Spring Fresco, fresco of a landscape around three sides of a room,
c. 1550–1500 BCE

This work was discovered almost intact in a room where there was a bed, shelving at about dado height, and a wall recess full of terracotta vases. The decoration shows a landscape with rocks, flowering lilies and mating birds, justifying its name. The stylized rocks and lilies and the vertical banding of the colors give it a highly decorative tone, akin to modern wallpaper, but the swallows caught kissing in flight are fetchingly realistic. Clearly this painter chose to mix realism with decoration. This work indicates that Minoan painting was of exceptionally high quality.

Unknown Minoan painter(s)
Fresco of two boxers and antelopes, c. 1550–1500 BCE

Modern artists have reconstructed sections of the fresco of these boxing children, as well as the neighboring, fluent line drawings of antelopes. There is enough of the original in both figures to suggest that the child on the left, with earrings and necklace, is a girl, and the other a boy. Each is wearing a glove on the right hand, which suggests that boxing was a popular and fairly vigorous pastime. The girl does not have the white skin typically used in Minoan paintings of females, perhaps because all young children spent time outside playing and were suntanned, while older women worked more indoors. The painting captures the grace of the children and the equality between them. Their eyes stare out from the wall, straight at the viewer, but unlike other figures in the room, they are engaged in vigorous action and shown mainly in profile, making them much more lifelike. A result is that they appear more rounded as figures.

THE NATIONAL ARCHEOLOGICAL MUSEUM

Dolphins in Ancient Greece

The qualities in dolphins that so appeal to people today—their grace, speed, sociability, readiness to help human beings, their effortless mastery of the oceans—attracted the ancient Greeks in even greater measure. Dolphins adorn Greek art from the paintings of the Minoans to the sculptures of Classical times, often with men riding them. It is more than likely that they would have figured in the prolific ancient painting that has now vanished.

Often, dolphins appear to be sacred creatures or beings especially favored by the gods. The Homeric Hymn to Pythian Apollo *relates that in part of his journey from Crete to Delphi, Apollo transformed himself into a dolphin. Apollo's tripod in Delphi was accompanied by images of dolphins. The very name Delphi is close to the Greek word for dolphin. Symbolically, dolphins represented the powers of water and the sea and the capacity of creatures to change shape and to regenerate. In this last capacity, dolphins are associated in mythology with the journey to the next world.*

Unknown Minoan potters and painters
Tables, vases, pitchers, and jugs, c. 1550–1500 BCE

The tables and some of the vases have the graceful dolphin decorations much favored in Minoan decoration. Their lithe figures appear either among other marine plants and animals or bordered by curved geometric shapes. The geometric shapes may well have been inspired by waves and then used in borders above and below to complement the arching bodies of the dolphins.

Other vases carry vegetal motifs, namely lilies and ears of corn. A pitcher decorated with birds has free-flowing lines redolent of those of the dolphin work. Most curious are the pitchers with long necks and bird-like beaks, eyes, necklaces and nipples, the nipples colored and decorated, as apparently was common among women. Nipple decoration suggests a culture in which breasts were not necessarily concealed and perhaps less the focus of erotic thought.

Historical Art: Second Visit

The periods represented in the rooms on this second visit include the Geometric, Archaic, Classical, and Hellenistic.

Geometric Vases and Archaic Sculpture

From the entrance vestibule go to the left and enter Room 7, which contains a huge vase that acted as a tomb marker and is a masterpiece of the Geometric period. Rooms 7–13 feature a fine collection of sculpture from the Archaic period (700–500 BCE), often regarded as the most attractive of all Greek periods. The principal pieces are naked standing male nudes called kouros, (plural kouroi) and standing females called kore (plural kourai).

Room 7

The Dipylon Painter
Attic Geometric vase, Exhibit 804, 760 BCE

The Mycenaean period ended abruptly around 1100 BCE. Little has been found from the following two centuries, but work gradually emerged in the splendid style now called Geometric. This huge (nearly 5-foot/155-centimeter) amphora was a tomb marker in the Kerameikos Cemetery of Athens, the site of the Dipylon gate at the beginning of the Panathenaic Way, hence the name given to the unknown artist. Artists of the Geometric period often covered the whole surface of vases with decoration, mixing geometric with abstracted figurative motifs. This amphora, however, has the restraint of great art. It gains in grandeur from being covered mostly with variations on a meander pattern, thus bringing the relatively spare figurative motifs into prominence. The scene between the handles is one of lamentation for the dead woman (seen in the center). The immense pathos of the procession of figures is achieved with staggeringly simple means—a few silhouettes abandoning themselves to ritual grief. The upper part of the neck is encircled by grazing deer represented as silhouettes in the most typical of postures. The surface—an all-over rich brown decorated in black—has a wonderful patina and depth. There are more Geometric vases in the vase collection upstairs in this museum and in other museums, but this one may be the benchmark.

The various timeworn statues around the room show the beginnings of the Archaic style, which is well represented in the rooms beyond. Legend attributes the invention of the style to Daidalos. The sculpture dates from about 100 years later than the vase itself and shows connections with Egyptian styles.

Room 8

Unknown sculptor
Sounion Kouros, Exhibit 2720, 580 BCE

Walk around the huge (10-foot/3-meter) *Sounion Kouros* and take it in from several angles. Kouroi were found in sanctuaries and cemeteries. Sometimes they represent gods, but are often offerings to gods or markers of graves. Like this one from Sounion, most stand with one foot ahead of the other, their arms held firmly at their sides, their hands lightly clenched. The essential bulk—calves, thighs, buttocks, arms, chest—is sculpted, but the figure relies a fair bit on line, especially at the knee but also at the groin, abdomen, and on the face.

Many kouroi are famous for their slight smile, but this one from Sounion is fairly solemn. The curled hair ringing the head and falling to the back is typical of Archaic kouroi. Its size suggests it was intended to represent a god. The nudity, though common enough in male sport, would emphasize that the body is common to men and gods.

Room 11

Aristion of Paros
Phrasikleia, Exhibit 4889, 540 BCE

The sculptor of this kore is identified on the base as Aristion of Paros. Various symbolic details indicate that Phrasikleia died when she was still a young woman. In her left hand, an unopened lotus flower indicates that she died a virgin. Some color still shows on her himation, belt, and peplos.

Her long garment falls in gentle curves, the lines of which are carved down her back—while they heighten her sense of easy grace, they also make her seem vulnerable. Her right hand holds the folds of her garment, bunched. Her dress is carved with low relief chrysanthemum, stars, and meanders—symbolic of day and night, journey, birth and death. The detail of the sandals is an extra touch of elegance, and she wears a crown. If the male kouroi representing the dead are poised perhaps to walk smiling into the other world, Phrasikleia, too, seems ready, waiting to greet whatever gods or ancestors she will meet in her next life.

Unknown sculptor
The Kouros of Melos, Exhibit 1558, 550 BCE

This kouros, a little later than the Sounion figure, is from a sepulcher on Melos and shows an adolescent balancing rather than walking. His arms hang at his sides. He is slim with flat hips and made even more glamorous from behind with a high, tight bottom and slim thighs. This is a tender work; perhaps the sympathy shown for the subject's youth indicates that the figure stood on the tomb of the figure of a youth, or commemorated one who died young and would live on in an idealized image.

Unknown sculptor
Volomandra Kouros, Exhibit 1906, 550 BCE

This figure has one of the nicest examples of the Archaic smile. Perhaps the kouros is greeting his future companions in the next world. Like many others, this kouros expresses the cult of male adolescence. He is lithe, with muscled arms and legs. His is the body of an athlete who has spent much time in the gymnasium. His face is indeed lit up by the smile—and rendered handsome by the hairdo.

Unknown sculptor
Winged Victory, the Nike of Delos, Exhibit 21, 550 BCE

The running motion of some Archaic statuary is reminiscent of some Asian statuary. This piece was possibly an offering to a temple. Little remains of her wings. The raised right knee dictates the fall of the garment, and she wears a crown. The holes would have been filled with bronze ornaments, and she would have worn bronze earrings and been painted to some extent. Her figure is clearly shaped beneath the clothing. On the whole, the island sculptor has managed to make a very cheerful-looking figure.

THE NATIONAL ARCHEOLOGICAL MUSEUM

Room 12

Unknown sculptor
Standing female figure, Exhibit 11974, 550–500 BCE

The very elongated, high-breasted figure from Cyprus is well outside the Archaic conventions and, with the exception of the head, closer to those of much earlier periods.

Room 13

Unknown sculptor
Anavysos Kouros, Exhibit 3851, 530–520 BCE

This is a funeral statue to a dead warrior identified in the inscription as the Kroisos taken by "furious Ares ... as he fought in the front ranks" and found at Anavysos in Attica. His arms have a very slight bend at the elbow. The image has signs of change to freer Classical sculpture, but, in general, he has the Archaic characteristics of the heavily built adult rather than the adolescent—thick thighs, defined abdomen, heavily shaped calves, Archaic curls, and an ever-so-slight smile.

As he steps into the next life, he is represented by a fully perfected body that fits his move to the world of the gods. His face seems to express the confidence of those who know that their souls will live when the lamentations are over. Note how he contrasts with Aristodikos, nearby.

Unknown sculptor
Aristodikos, Exhibit 3938, 530–520 BCE

Sculpted only about 20 years after the *Anavyssos Kouros*, this funerary monument to Aristodikos unmistakably marks the change from the Archaic to the Classical. The arms are freer, the body more relaxed, the curls gone in favor of short hair (note faint traces of red color). The positioning of the legs makes this image one of the last of the Archaic rather than the first of the Classical images, but clearly the old view of the world has gone; the world that the Renaissance would later want to revive is in the wings, waiting to make its entrance.

Unknown sculptor
The Apollo of Ptoion, Exhibit 124 2005, 520 BCE

In three ways, this figure shows how kouroi of this time were changing from the Archaic to the Classical style. His arms are more mobile—though the elbows are still thrust back so that the shoulders are very squared. The face has arguably become softer and more expressive, and the hairdo is highly ornamental with curls that surround the face and allow it greater prominence.

Unknown sculptor
Relief of a running Hoplite, Exhibit 1959, 510 BCE

Hoplites were the infantry of Greek armies. They fought in armor, so the nakedness of this warrior is a sign that we are looking at his funeral monument. He looks back, perhaps at pursuers, perhaps casting his head down as he tears at his chest to get some breath. His fingers are sunk into his chest. The detail of leg muscle is beautifully sculpted. Both the posture and tension indicate that a violent death is close.

At the end of Room 13 on the left is:

Aristocles
Stele of Aristion, Exhibit 29, 510 BCE

The names of both the warrior and the sculptor are engraved on the base of this tall (over 7-foot/240-centimeter) funerary marble. It is a striking example of the kind of detail beloved of Archaic sculptors. The hair, beard, undergarment, and selected pieces of armor provide material for decorative patterns using fine lines. There are traces of color, but it is impossible to say how the paint appeared with such fine incisions.

Classical Sculpture (480–330 BCE)

Despite its standing as a great museum, the National Museum has relatively few works from the best-known period of ancient Greece. This is the penalty of fame. Commerce and plunder were already depleting Greek art in Roman times and the archeological activity of the 19th and 20th centuries dispersed Greek art around the empires

THE NATIONAL ARCHEOLOGICAL MUSEUM

of the times: Britain, France, Germany, Russia, and the USA. On the other hand, the same empires have done much to excavate and preserve ancient sites with their accompanying museums.

Except where specified as bronze, sculptures are in marble.

Room 15

Unknown Attic sculptor
Votive relief from Eleusis, Exhibit 126, 440 BCE

This is usually referred to as the *Great Eleusian Relief*, presumably because of its size, but perhaps also because of its fame and quality. It was extremely popular in antiquity and much copied. A cast of it adorns the vestibule of the site museum at Eleusis.

Its subject is the moment when Demeter, goddess of agriculture, on the left, bids farewell to Triptolemos, king of Eleusis, who is preparing to teach mankind how to cultivate the soil and grow wheat. The female on the right is Demeter's daughter, Persephone. The story is told at length in the Homeric *Hymn to Demeter*. Demeter's daughter Persephone was out with the daughters of Okeanos gathering flowers when Hades—lord of the underworld— seized her and rode off with her in his golden chariot. Demeter searched for her daughter, grieving. She neglected her duties, and as a result, crops failed. At last, she came as an old woman to the well in Eleusis, and was cared for by the king and his daughters. In the underworld, Persephone also grieved and longed to return home, refusing to eat anything in the underworld.

Ultimately, to save the human race, Hermes persuaded Hades to give up Persephone. Demeter immediately rejoiced. She made the crops grow again and the fields to yield an abundance of trees, fruit and flowers. Persephone, in her relief, was finally convinced by Hades to eat—a few pomegranate seeds. Hades knew, but did not tell her, that eating the food of the underworld binds one to the world of the dead forever; by convincing her to eat he thought that he could still keep her with him. The gods were angered by his trickery, and yet could not entirely undo the power of the food of the dead. They struck a compromise; Persephone would stay in the underworld for only one third of the year. In this way, winter was born: when her daughter left her, Demeter would grieve, making the earth cold and barren.

In return for their kindliness, Demeter revealed to Triptolemos, King of Eleusis, and to other rulers who had supported her in her search for justice, the secrets of her rites and her visions. These became the basis for the Eleusian rites, which were guarded by the deepest secrecy among their initiates. According to the Homeric Hymn, initiates into the rites were blessed by the gods, provided they held to their secrecy, but the initiated were doomed to darkness when they died. The divine figures are much bigger than the human king and carry their customary symbols.

Ancient Greek descriptions of female beauty make much of blonde hair, generous bosoms and neat ankles. Demeter, whose esteemed ankles are not visible in the relief, has a scepter and is giving the king ears of wheat. Persephone, with the much-praised breasts, holds a long torch. She is crowning the king. The missing crown and the ears of wheat were of gold or bronze. The women are wearing graciously draped chitons—Demeter a relatively plain Doric one and Persephone a more pleated, Ionic one under a himation. Triptolemos is a golden youth, naked despite his cloak, and deeply impressed by the gift of the god.

Bronze statue of Poseidon of Artemision, 460 BCE. (National Archeological Museum Athens)

THE NATIONAL ARCHEOLOGICAL MUSEUM

Possibly Kalamis
Poseidon of Artemision, Exhibit 15161, bronze, 460 BCE

This superb bronze was found, fittingly, under the sea at Artemision. Clearly, it aims to glorify the Poseidon of the Homeric hymn: "He who moves the earth and the desolate sea," "shaker of the earth," "Tamer of horses," "Helper of those who sail upon the sea in ships."

The dates suggest homage to the divine ally of the Athenians at the decisive sea battle of Salamis. The god has the stance of a spear thrower, but his javelin, like his eyes, is now missing and his bronze has been greened by the sea. The body is gracefully relaxed and superbly balanced. The muscles of the torso bespeak easy effort. Much is made of his hair. The beard is studiously curled. The hair of the head is plaited and wound around the head to display a youthful fringe.

The attribution to the Athenian Kalamis is speculative.

Trail 2 Classical section

Room 16

Possibly Agorakritos
Gravestone stele, Exhibit 715, 420 BCE

Among several grave steles, this one is left of the exit from the room. The experts see signs of the workshop of Phidias in this sculpting and speculate that it may be by one of his pupils, Agorakritos. The dead person is a youth at the peak of his beauty. A noble head in profile sits on a graceful body, facing frontally so that the greatest depth can be had from the low relief carving. His garment falls elegantly. In his left hand he holds a bird. His raised right hand combines a gesture of farewell with the handling of what might be a cage. He is perhaps about to free a pet. The sad little boy beneath the cat might be a servant. The cat, presumably another pet, adds a tender note to the moment of departure for the next world.

Unknown sculptor
Gravestone from Piraeus, Exhibit 716, 410 BCE

This stele, though broken, has some of the common and touching

Central Islip Public Library
33 Hawthorne Avenue
Central Islip, NY 11722-2498

Athene of Varvakeion. Roman copy in marble of Phidias's original on the Athenian acropolis. First century CE. (National Archeological Museum Athens, Bridgeman Art Library/Alinari.)

conventions of Greek gravestones. The dead person is the seated woman on the left. She is perhaps the daughter of the couple bidding her farewell. The couple are posed as still, calm, loving figures making very restrained gestures of grief and farewell. The fine folding of their robes underlines the stillness of the scene.

Room 19 (entered from Room 17)

Unknown Roman copyist
Athene of Varvakeion, Exhibit 129, Marble copy of Phidias's
Chryselephantine Athene of 438 BCE

This is more of historical than artistic interest. Apart from being a dwarfed and stodgy version of Phidias's legendary gold and ivory wonder, it is not entirely accurate when compared with Pausanias's description of the original, which had Pegasus rather than griffins on the helmet, a shield instead of a spear in the hand and other ornaments on the shield and the base.

Room 18

Unknown Attic sculptors
Two grave steles from Kerameikos (back to back); Exhibit 3624,
Stele of Hegeso and Exhibit 717, *A Farewell*, 400 BCE

A reproduction of the *Stele of Hegeso* (Exhibit 3624) is in situ in the Kerameikos cemetery. Here, in the original work, we see the dead woman, seated. Identified in the inscription on the horizontal of the pediment over her head, she is already finely dressed and adding a piece of jewelry from the box proffered by her young servant. Both are melancholy as they go through this last imagined ritual before Hegeso's journey to the next world.

Directly behind in Exhibit 717 a middle-aged woman, also seated, is bid farewell by a younger woman whom we take to be her daughter. Not surprisingly, it is the mother who is consoling the daughter. The father, too, focuses on the bereaved daughter.

Hellenistic Sculpture

Hellenistic sculpture mirrors the gradual merging of the Greek and Roman worlds between the 4th and the 1st centuries BCE. The tendency to realism, already strong in the art of Classical Greece, develops apace and is put to the service of secular and political subjects. Works of this period have been popular with international collectors and patrons since ancient times and therefore not much remains in Greece. Exhibits are often copies by Greek or Roman craftsmen of the popular originals from earlier centuries.

Room 21

Unknown sculptor

Jockey of Artemision, Exhibit 15117, bronze, 2nd century BCE

This exceptionally charming and skillful piece was also found in a shipwreck off Cape Artemision. It was probably being shipped east. It is an extraordinarily animated and finely observed study of both rider and beast. The diminutive bareback rider is all energy and eagerness, cleaving to the horse but with an eye to other riders racing beside him. The horse thrusts forward at full tilt, its neck and head muscles straining and its nostrils dilating. Both material and subject have been mastered. Realism of this sort and secular subject matter are features of Hellenistic sculpture.

Copy of Polykleitos

Diadumenos, Exhibit 1826, marble copy from the 1st century BCE of a bronze original, 420 BCE

Polykleitos was a master from Argos, ranked in his day with the greats such as Phidias. This copy probably does not do justice to his original bronze but it does reproduce the relaxed, idealized beauty of male sculptures of the Classical period. In the Hellenistic copying it has almost certainly been softened and sentimentalised.

Rooms 22–27 contain small or fragmentary sculptures. Rooms 22–24 are late classical rather than Hellenistic. The reconstructions of the vivid work from the Asklepion at Epidauros date from the decade beginning 365 BCE. The funerary sculpture in Rooms 23–24 come from the 300s BCE. The steles in particular illustrate the greater realism that will be a hallmark of Hellenistic art and even more so of Roman art.

Room 28

Unknown sculptor
Youth of Marathon, Exhibit 15118, bronze, 350 BCE

The half-life-size bronze in this room is another find from a shipwreck off the coast near Marathon. The posture is a little puzzling, because we now have no idea what the exquisite boy was holding in his left hand, nor why he was gesturing as he is with his right. Whatever it was, it allowed him to stand in the contrapposto position, taking the weight of the body on one leg and thus curving from hip to shoulder to head. The inlaid eyes have been preserved, giving us an idea of some of the realistic detailing of ancient sculpture.

Attributed to Euphranor
Bronze from Antikythera, Exhibit 13396, large bronze, 340–330 BCE

The experts' guess at the identity of this imposing bronze, found undersea near Antikythera, is that he is Paris, shown here holding an apple as a gift for Aphrodite who helped him seduce Helen. There are of course other possibilities. The face is softly Classical, saved from effeminacy by the penetrating inlaid eyes. The detailing of the anatomy is that of an ideal male build. Both this figure and the *Youth of Marathon* put their weight squarely on the left leg. The Marathon figure trails his right leg fairly straight behind him, whereas Paris's posture is more feminine.

An excellent collection of small bronzes is in Rooms 36–39.

Unknown sculptors
Small Archaic and Classical bronzes

The small bronzes include a delightful naked athlete from 600 BCE, Exhibit 6445, and a martial Athene Promachos with daunting helmet from about 480 BCE, Exhibit 6447. Both are from the Acropolis. Interestingly, the small bronzes, such as the running girl, Exhibit 24, from about 530 BCE, may be more animated than their larger companions.

The rooms upstairs contain displays of the frescoes from Thera, or Santorini, which we've already seen on the first visit, as well as a collection of vases from the Geometric to the late Classical periods. The National Museum has a comprehensive collection of vases from every era. Those from the Neolithic period to Mycenean times are displayed in the relevant sections of the general collection. Unfortunately, many from later periods (those we think of as specifically Greek vases) were housed in Rooms 49–56, which have been closed for some years for repair. Some prime examples, however, are exhibited throughout the National Museum, and in virtually all the museums you will visit. For a general commentary on vases, refer to the introduction.

This medieval manuscript illustration shows the persistence of Greek myth into the Middle Ages. Theseus makes a triumphal entry into Athens. French school illustration. 14th century CE. (The Stapleton Collection.)

TRAIL 3:
In and Around Athens

This Trail takes you to several museums and a monastery. Two of the museums are in central Athens. The first is the exceptionally fine Goulandris Museum of Cycladic and Ancient Greek Art. The second is the Byzantine and Christian Museum of Athens where you are close to works that are harder to see in churches. After visiting this museum you can continue the Byzantine theme by visiting some Byzantine churches in central Athens. Other museums worth visiting are also mentioned, although a detailed guide to them is beyond the scope of this Trail.

The third museum is at the end of the Metro in the port of Piraeus and exhibits bronzes retrieved from shipwrecks. Finally a short bus trip takes you to the Dafni monastery to see Byzantine mosaics and paintings placed in a church.

The Trail is set out in a suitable order for visiting, but any convenient order would do. Allow four days—one for the Goulandris Museum, one for the Byzantine and Christian Museum and the churches in central Athens, one for the trip to Piraeus, and one for the Dafni monastery. On the Trail you will see Cycladic, Geometric, Archaic, Classical, and Byzantine art.

Goulandris Museum of Cycladic and Ancient Greek Art

Location: Neofytou Douka 4, Kolonaki. This runs off Vassilissis Sofias. The Evangelismos Metro station has an exit on Vassilissis Sofias. Consult the area map at the Metro exit. The museum is signposted, across the road towards the city.

Contact details: Tel. +30 210 722 8321/3; www.cycladic-m.gr

IN AND AROUND ATHENS

Opening hours: 10:00 am–4:00 pm Mon., Wed., Thurs., Fri.. 10:00 am–3:00 pm Sat. Closed Tuesday and Sunday.
Admission: Low range (Euro 1–4).
Other information: An agreeable cafeteria enables you to stay a long morning or a full day.

This beautifully presented museum, which has friendly and helpful staff, features Cycladic art and vases from Archaic and early Classical times. The ground floor has a display outlining the history of Cycladic art; the first level, the Goulandris collection of Cycladic art; and the second and fourth levels, the Archaic and Classical pieces. Also there, in a new wing (the entrance is from the cafeteria), is a recreation of a noted 19th-century Athenian mansion.

The collection is annotated in English and arranged chronologically. Art from the Cyclades is divided into Early and Middle periods. In this museum, the most significant works come from the early Cycladic period. The museum uses the following chronology:

Early Cycladic I: 3000–2800 BCE
Early Cycladic II: 2800–2300 BCE
Early Cycladic III: 2300–2000 BCE

The Trail follows this chronology, starting in the first room of the Cycladic collection.

Cycladic Sculpture

Ashmolean Museum Master

Syros phase figure, Exhibit 206, Case 1, 2800–2300 BCE, Early Cycladic II
Obsidian from Melos, Exhibits 315–320, Case 2

Unknown artists

Human Figure, Between Cases 2 and Case 3, Exhibit 828, before 3000 BCE, Neolithic period

In Case 1 is a work (Exhibit 206) that typifies the best of Cycladic art in this and other collections—a minimalist female figure with a markedly sloping head, graceful neck, squared shoulders, small breasts, and a quite abstracted idea of body shape. The figure has little depth and was perhaps made to stand against a surface or to lie down. Attribution to the Ashmolean Museum master indicates that experts find close similarities between this and a work in the Ashmolean Museum in Oxford.

In Case 2 are blades of obsidian, the volcanic glass found on Melos and used to work marble and other stone.

Between Cases 2 and 3 is a human figure dating from an earlier period. Its strong rounded thighs are more like a real body than is the Ashmolean piece. Neolithic sculptors clearly worked within less-abstracted conventions about representing body shape.

In general, authorities suppose that Neolithic and Cycladic figures represent divinities rather than the spirits of ordinary individuals. The ample proportions of this Neolithic figure make it plausible that she represents an earth goddess, the source of fertility. The breasts and hips of the Cycladic figure do not suggest an image of fertility. The abstraction may indicate that she is a generalized, perfected spiritual being—possibly a divinity, possibly a spirit that is invoked at the time of death.

We must take care not to associate these ancient works with our own religious or theistic traditions. Cultures can and do imagine the spirit of a person or their group and hence accept a spirituality that does not depend on god figures. We have no real evidence about the purpose of either Neolithic or Cycladic figures. They may not be specifically religious images but rather good luck charms, spiritual friends, servants or token sacrificial offerings to spirits.

Unknown artists

Various figures, Case 3, Early Cycladic 1, 3200–2800 BCE
Shovel-shaped figure, Case 5, Exhibit 961, *violin-shaped figure*,
Exhibit 1065, and *figure of the Plastiros type*
Marble jar, Case 6, No exhibit number, from Early Cycladic I

Some of these very abstracted shapes are dubbed "violin" figures although others look more like miniature hearth shovels than violins. The shovel shape is said to represent torso, neck, and head, and the violin shapes hips, waist, neck, and head. A reason for abstracting these figures might be that marble or stone, though attractive, is harder to work than clay. However, it is also possible that abstraction was the preferred style of a time when portraying gods or spiritual beings in a specifically human form was uncommon.

From the same period, in Case 5, there are versions of the Plastiros type, named after the site of a cemetery on the island of Paros. Although it is from the same general period as the violin figures, it is from a locality that favored more realistic figuration.

This is also the case in what we know of the subsequent phase of Cycladic art (Early Cycladic II).

The marble jar in Case 6 illustrates the very early making of truly elegant stone vessels. In virtually all periods, a lot of pottery is found. Case 6 shows that some Cycladic marble and stone vessels had similar purposes to pottery pieces but the marble achieves greater elegance. A jar like this was probably shaped with hammer and chisel and then hollowed and polished with the use of an abrasive.

Unknown artist
Marble figures, Syros phase, Case 10, Exhibits 252, 253, Early Cycladic II, c. 2800 –2300 BCE

"Canonical" styles emerged in the Early Cycladic II period. Canonical works obey rules that admit only limited variety, and these figures, from the island of Syros, illustrate the canonical style of the phase. The figures are mostly female: arms are folded with the left arm above the right; feet slant downwards; the head is tilted back; and the artists observe body proportions that do not match reality.

Exhibits 252 and 253 are especially interesting because they show vestiges of color. In Exhibit 252, we can see that features were painted; Exhibit 253 has traces of painted clothing. Whether or not painted features would make the figures seem less abstract is a moot point, as we have neither examples nor direct knowledge of the originals. If they represented the dead, the painting perhaps added to their reality. If the figures were images of the spiritual or generalized identity of the beings represented, the painting may have added to their unreality.

A bowl below contains a brilliant blue azurite in powder form and gives an idea of the vivid colors that might have been used.

Unknown sculptor
Marble figures, Syros phase, Exhibit 311, Case 12, Early Cycladic II, 2800–2300 BCE

There is some debate about how these figures were originally posed and what they depict. If they were meant to lie down, this could explain the tilted-back position of the head on some and the tilting down of the feet on many others. These factors, along with the folded arms, lend weight to the idea that the figures represent dead people arranged in sleeping positions, presumably in anticipation of waking in another world, or, if they believed in reincarnation, in another time. Considering the plain backs and the difficulty of carving a head in a tilted-back position, it seems likely that if they were not recumbent, but instead were leaning against or attached to a surface. Except for the very big figures, the standing hypothesis seems unlikely. These sculptors were skilful; if their figures were meant to be standing, we would expect clear evidence of how that was done. Perversely, the mystery surrounding their function now adds to their attraction.

A difficulty with the explanation that such figures represented the spirits of dead people is the predominance of female figures—unless of course all souls were conceived of as female. A difficulty with the idea that they were gods lies in the fact that they are depicted in sleep or death.

Unknown sculptor
The Toast, Case 17, Exhibit 159, Early Cycladic II, 2800–2300 BCE

This is a comparatively rare Cycladic sculpture in three dimensions. Two other three-dimensional figures are the harpist and the flute player in the National Museum.

This seated figure shows a mastery of three-dimensional work. The seat helps to make the design a freestanding piece, but the real attraction lies in what the figure seems to express. Calling it *The Toast* is a modern fancy. However, the tilt of the head and the downward thrust of the feet—both of which are common to other Cycladic figures—are used here in dramatic action. The figure is confident and assertive, ensconced on his chair, making a large gesture. What it is about? Is it a libation—a forerunner of later funeral practices? Since figures have been found in houses and burial places, is it possible that they were possessions during life and then buried with their owners? If not connected to some ritual, is it a decorative object? Once again, we can only speculate.

Unknown sculptor
Figure, Case 20, Exhibit 308, Early Cycladic II, 2800–2300 BCE

After an earlier canonical phase in the Early Cycladic II period, detail that might formerly have been painted is incised into the stone. This male body is differently proportioned from those of the earlier canonical phase. His arms are folded right over left; incised detail shows the fingers of his right hand; he wears a cape, indicated front and back and with an incised hem. The sculptor has detailed ears, eyes, mouth, and eyebrows, as well as a headband and signs of a hairdo. The clothing and hair are features of stone sculpture that were to have a long history in Greek art. As with other Cycladic figures, we are left with the question: who or what is he?

Unknown sculptor
Large female figure, Case No 26, Exhibit 211, Spedos variety, Canonical Early Cycladic II, 2800–2300 BCE

This is the largest of the statues (5.5 feet/1.4 meters) in the room. Since the sculpting followed rigorous conventions to do with proportion and posture, it takes a while to see the variations. In this figure, each part of the body has a firm outline and the proportion of the parts to the overall figure is pleasing even to the modern eye. The modeling gives the figure some solidity though it still seems to be meant to be viewed front on.

Many smaller figures in nearby cases were found in graves but this one is too big for a grave piece. It is more likely to be either a figure for worship or one situated in a place of worship. If that is so, the artist would have fashioned it with reverence, making sure that the proportions and features were correct and perhaps that appropriate rituals were observed as s/he worked.

There is some ambiguity in the stance. Though at first sight it is frontal and somewhat abstracted, the figure takes its weight more on the left leg. The higher line of the hip carries through to the left shoulder and is subtly emphasized by a tilt of the head. The sculptors of the great Archaic kouroi achieved their effects with similar subtleties, suggesting a body poised to move but not yet in motion.

Spedos is the site of a cemetery on Naxos.

Unknown sculptors
Six figures of the Spedos variety Case 22, Exhibit 257; Case 23, Exhibit 598; Case 27, Exhibit 284; Case 28, Exhibit 280; Case 29, Exhibit 282; Case 30, Exhibit 304, Canonical Early Cycladic II, 2800–2300 BCE

Grouped around and behind the large figure are six companions floating in their perspex cases as though in another dimension. Despite their radically different origins, these figures undoubtedly appeal to modern sensibilities, echoing 20th-century abstract and primitivist movements. Whatever Cycladic cultures were actually like, this art makes one feel that it was peaceful—in love with beauty and sharing common ideas about elegance, grace, and virtue that were eloquently expressed by their sculptors. They belong to our dream of the Greek islands, the rocks white in the sun and the "wine-dark" seas nearby.

Exhibit 22 was long ago broken at the knees and repaired by shortening the statue—putting feet where the knees would have been. Exhibit 30 has indications of a headband, cap, and curls that can be seen from the back. There is paint on the left eye.

The heads of all the figures taper back, suggesting a hairdo or headpiece, as in Exhibit 30. Exhibit 23 is a slender figure with a very long neck whereas Exhibit 28 has the proportions of a thicker figure, with fattened thighs, a short torso and a neck as thick as the head. Exhibit 27 has a particularly long, pyramid-shaped nose. Relative to Exhibit 23, Exhibit 29 is very short from the shoulder to the folded arms.

These differences suggest that the canons adopted by various workshops of sculptors reflect differences in physical types in the real world and/or differences in the way the human form is idealized in the spirit world.

Goulandris Master
Male figure, Case No 25, Exhibit 281, 2800–2300 BCE

This torso of a standing male is a more robust and rounded figure than typical figures. The slightly parted legs and the penis are different and, though it is a fragment, the piece acquires a strong presence. This and several pieces nearby (e.g. Case No 25, Exhibit 281) are identified as the work of a particular sculptor who has been dubbed the Goulandris Master. Experts see enough similarities to conclude that groups of works can be traced to workshops, studios, or even individual master craftsmen. Since these schools or individuals have no known names, they are named after a collection with a notable example of the type. The same naming conventions apply to vases of the Archaic and Classical periods.

At this point, climb the stairs to the next floor.

Early and Classical Greek Vases

The third level (second floor for British readers) of the Cycladic Museum is a good spot to see some black-figure and red-figure vases well displayed.

The Swing Painter
Black-figure vase Athene and Hermes, Case No 19, Exhibit 116, 540–530 BCE

The use of black figures on a red background was a common technique of vase painting in the 500s BCE. This vase demonstrates two popular themes: gods and figures of mythology—on one side Athene and Hermes accompanied by two mortals; on the other Dionysos, god of riot, drunkenness and ecstasy flanked by two satyrs. Athene has her helmet and great round shield. Hermes has his courier's staff and fancy footwear. Even though the drawing is quite vigorous, especially of the satyrs, the characterization is conventional. Both scenes remain static and the supplementary decoration is close to rudimentary.

Unknown potter and painter
Black-figure vase horseman, Case 23, Exhibit 115, 560–550 BCE

A horseman in vigorous action, flanked by two athletes and, further back, two old men, indicates that vase painting developed secular subjects. (So, possibly, did wall painting, but this is hard to confirm because very little wall painting has survived.) Athletes, horsemen, and hunters were favorite subjects for vase painting, possibly because they involve young men, strong action, dramatic and interesting poses and were seen as aspects of the good life among the elite. Athletic activities were also facets of religious festivals.

The Phineus Painter and others
Chalcidian black-figure vases, including Exhibits 128 and 130, Case 26, 550–525 BCE

The half dozen vases in this case are from the vastly productive potteries of southern Italy and Etruria, major centers of Greek pottery. Greek settlers made some; Etruscans imported others. Two of the smaller ones could be imitations of their bigger neighbors, both by the Phineus Painter. In all, three of the six—including

Exhibits 128 and 130 and the large (unnumbered) piece between the two—are identified as the work of the Phineus Painter. On one side, the large vase shows a series of riders, apparently taking part in a race and on the other side, a lion and a sphinx looking back over their shoulders. The *kylix* (bowl) with the big eyes seems sinister, but the eye is often a sun symbol and there may be no connection with magic.

Villa Guilia Painter
Red-figure vase: The Seduction, Case 28 Exhibit 148, 450 BCE

Vases with red on a black background are characteristic of the 400s BCE. This *hydria* (water vessel) presents a scene from the lives of the gods. Eos, the winged dawn goddess, is seducing a youth by tickling his chest with a branch. Whether the youth is willing is hard to say. The museum note says he is refusing her but he is both walking away and looking back. His posture is ambiguous. The gesture of his right hand suggests that he is reaching out to her. In neoclassical Europe, erotic behavior in classical clothing was dubbed Arcadian.

Painter of the Louvre Centauromachy
Red-figure vase, Case 29, Exhibit150, 450–44 BCE

This amphora shows a secular scene—a warrior being farewelled, presumably by his parents. He is mostly nude, and armed. As part of the ritual of farewell, his mother has poured a libation from the jug she holds. His father appears to be bidding him farewell, perhaps with words of advice.

Unknown painter
Red figure vase, a bell krater: scene of revelry, Case 31, Exhibit 152, 430 BCE

A bell krater is a sort of large mixing bowl, for drinks. The revelers are returning from an ancient form of carousing known as a symposium. The men are naked, the woman dressed. Probably the woman was hired to play the flute for them. The man on the left dances very much in the manner of modern Greeks. The man behind the flautist seems to be attempting a form of hokey-pokey. The last reveler on the right looks as though he has tried to dance and is losing his balance. It is a complex scene to fit on a vase with such economical means. Close by, in Case 34, an amphora shows musicians with a double flute and a lyre in another Dionysiac procession.

Unknown painter
Red-figure amphora: erotic scene. Case 32, Collection Number 1115, 480–470 BCE

Today, we would say this was pornographic art. At the time, male nudity was standard, not only among gods and heroes but, for instance, among athletes who competed naked. Female nudity was only suggested by the treatment of drapery in sculpture, on pottery and probably on wall painting. On vases, explicitly sexual scenes appear, involving men and boys or men and women. In this case, men with erections are cavorting with naked women. It may be seen as a scene depicting ordinary life—men frolicking with prostitutes—or, more likely, the painter used a Dionysian framework to depict sexual activity. The mythological overtones of this scene are reinforced by the image, on the other side of the vase, of Europa and the bull (the form Zeus adopted for his coupling with Europa).

The Charles Polites Collection

On the fifth floor (fourth floor for English readers) is the Charles Polites collection. Polites was a diplomat, plastics manufacturer, pianist, and patron of the arts.

Unknown potters and painters
Various Geometric vases, Cases 6–10, 900–700 BCE

Among this selection are vessels used for water, wine, and oil, and as grave markers. On the various shapes, the contrast of dark colors against clay is truly elegant. Case 9 (Exhibits 55–63) has vases for various uses but Case 6 has examples of funerary vessels (Exhibits 49 and 51). The largest of these (Exhibit 51) is an amphora decorated with basic geometric shapes of crosses within concentric circles on the body and hourglass shapes within concentric circles on the shoulder. In Case 10, Exhibit 50 still has the little holes made by the point of the compass that drew the concentric circles. There are also examples of hatching, meanders, and the swastika. Though no examples of weaving survive from this time, some of the patterns are common in weaving and could have originated in that craft.

The benchmark vase for the Geometric style is the amphora by the Dipylon painter in the National Archeological Museum. This and works at Kerameikos demonstrate the development of elegance and taste in this style.

The Lysippides painter
Black-figure hydria, Herakles Leaves for Olympus, Exhibit 30,
Case 8b, 525 BCE

Herakles (known to the Romans as Hercules) was a favored subject for the Lysippides painter, who depicts him on works in collections outside Greece. This is the moment of Herakles's ascent to Olympus. From the left, Athene, shown with a spear, prepares to act as charioteer; Herakles, next to her in his lion skin, holds a hefty club; in the center are Dionysos and Hebe; and on the far right, Hermes in his hat, is making ready. A count of the horses' legs shows that the chariot is a quadriga, i.e. drawn by four horses. As a hero, the child of a god, and a mortal, Herakles performed many labors and wonders and after death was granted immortality and a life among the gods. There he would marry Hebe, Hera's daughter. At the moment of ascent, Herakles is accompanied by gods, but it is the sprightliness of the horses that gives the scene its drama. Below is a line of sirens and panthers; on the shoulder of the vase, warriors who carry dipylon shields in the shape of double axes engage in heated battle.

The Stath Artos

The new wing of the museum is accessible through the cafeteria on the ground floor. The mansion that houses it illustrates the revival–and long-term survival–of classical motifs in modern European architecture and decoration: pediments, pilasters, half columns, the Doric order, mosaic floors, and the use of interior light wells. There are many fine examples in the public buildings bordering the Syntagma. This mansion has the typical coloring but a lighter domestic touch. The use of a city mansion to display objects identified with its great past is a reminder of the commitment that many citizens have to their city and its history, and also to the patronage that individuals and families have bestowed on the city and its achievements.

Three vases, Cases 1, 2, and 8

Cases 1, 2, and 8 display some lovely vases. The fountain scene in Case 1 (Exhibit 1104) from 530 BCE is boldly executed. The big hands on the women filling their jugs are striking, and the birds above are feeding quite aggressively.

Equally bold is the 580 BCE crater in Case 2 (not numbered) of a Dionysian scene by the Three Maidens Painter. Under the handles, the circle of panthers, goats, and the sirens ensure that the scene is wild.

In Case 8, there is a bowl with a lid from the late Geometric period, about 750 BCE, with patterns of meanders and diamonds. The handles are four horses and the mirror shows a rosette on the base.

Byzantine Art in Athens

The excellent Byzantine and Christian Museum of Athens is close to the Museum of Cycladic Art. You might want to visit both on the same day, but the Trail is arranged so that you make a day of visiting the Byzantine museum to see the work at close quarters and then go to a selection of Byzantine churches in the heart of Athens. At the end of Trail 3 (after a trip to Piraeus) we return to Byzantine art in the monastery of Dafni.

The Byzantine and Christian Museum

Location: Vassilissis Sofias (Street), close to the Evangelismos Metro. Consult the street map outside the station to see the exact location.

Contact details: Tel. +30 210 721 1027; www.culture.gr

Opening hours: 8:30 am to 3:00 pm Tues. to Sun; closed Mon.

Admission: Low admission fees (Euro 1–4).

Other information: There is a ground plan of the museum in the leaflet you get with your ticket.

This new, handsome museum is organized on two levels. Level I is at ground level. It provides an overview of the transition from the ancient world of Greece and Rome to Christianity and the empire of the Byzantines. Level II is underground, and contains mostly painting. Within the levels are numbered galleries. Level I is briefly described here, but more detailed coverage is given for three galleries on Level II.

Byzantine painting conforms to theological canons. Its distinctive style persisted for centuries and to some extent continues today in the Eastern churches. The earliest surviving material, mainly in mosaic form, is as decorative as fine jewelry and conveys a powerful sense of its underlying theology. Mosaic, frescoes and painted panels (generally called "icons") are of very high quality throughout the Middle Ages and into the 15th century.

For an account of common themes and their placement in churches, see the notes on the monastery of Dafni at the end of this Trail.

Level I

The displays on ground level explain the scope of the Byzantine Empire and illustrate the transition from the pagan art of antiquity to early Christian art during the 3rd and 4th centuries of the Christian era. The most telling are in Gallery I.1, which show that the popular Greek image of the shepherd carrying his sheep was adopted as the Christian image of the Good Shepherd who goes in search of the lost sheep (Exhibits 1 and 2). On the Sidarama Sarcophagi (Exhibits 5–8) we see recognizably Roman forms adapted for Christian uses.

Gallery I.3 illustrates the use of Roman basilica architecture for Christian worship after Christianity became the official state religion in 323 CE. From this century through to the 6th century, early Christian art had a great flowering, especially in Ravenna from which the Empire was ruled for a time before the center shifted definitively to Constantinople. The art of this period remains Roman in its forms but is infused with a new light and grace. The marble church decoration and the jewelry of the period (illustrated in Galleries I.3 and I.4) testify to this renewal.

Now descend to Level II. Some galleries on this level contain useful explanatory material which make detailed coverage here redundant, so we offer detailed coverage for Galleries 3, 6 and 8 only.

Level II, Gallery 3: Worship and Art

This large space is dominated by a dazzling display of icons. They are suspended in three rows (not counting the lone one just inside the entrance to the gallery.) Further icons and some frescoes are on the walls. Begin with the fresco on your right.

Unknown painter(s)

The Dormition from Palaio Panagia Monastery in Laconia, BXM 1015, 1200–1300 CE

The Dormition refers to a legend that enjoys great status in Christianity. Mary, the virgin mother of God, summoned apostles and others to her deathbed. At death, she was taken to heaven in order that her mortal remains would not be left to decay on earth. In the west, the concept of the Dormition was gradually replaced by the image of the Assumption, which paralleled the Ascension of her son Jesus. The Eastern church, however, retained the imagery of the Dormition.

This scene shows the apostles and others gathered around the reclining Mary with angels who are waiting to receive her when she falls asleep (hence the word *dormition*, which means sleeping). The obvious meaning is that death is but a sleep from which she will wake in paradise, where she and her son will occupy unique places of honor. Mary is in a fairly palatial building, which apparently has no roof. The perspective, too, is strange. Even if artists of the time could not handle perspective, they could give an accurate frontal view of a building. In this case they have not done so, perhaps because the odd perspective of the building focuses attention on the scene.

Lettering on Byzantine paintings often consists of abbreviated words. Here the lettering in the painting identifies Mary as the Mother of God. Above Mary, some ghostly blue figures break through the line of the building and there is a Mary with child in the top left corner. These are scenes from an earlier work that has been painted over so that a single moment replaces the earlier series of scenes. Later still, the whole picture was covered over and then repainted. Note a rectangle of small pebble rendering on the right.

The Dormition fresco is on the wall leading to Gallery II.4 where further frescoes are placed in settings that imitate their original positions in the church. Return then to II.3 and the icons.

Icons are generally painted in tempera on wood. They are most commonly used to decorate the sanctuary screen or are placed in a position of devotion in the church itself. Icon painting adheres to strict conventions that are still applied today. Among other rules, the use of three-dimensional figures is restricted. Rules also apply to the placing of paintings and icons within a church. As with the frescoes, the names of the people portrayed are often written alongside them.

In the first row, on the left, you will find:

Unknown painter(s)
Double sided icon, on one side a *Crucifixion scene*, 900–1200 CE
and on the other *a Virgin*, identified as the *Virgin Hodegetria*,
BXM 995, 16th century CE

In this Crucifixion, the visible painting is from the 13th century,
but traces of preceding works go back nearly four centuries. The
layers indicate that essentially the same subject was being painted
over, or, perhaps, just freshened and slightly altered. The bird-like
archangels Michael and Gabriel are identified above to the left and
right and the figures of Mary and John (the apostle) standing on
each side of the cross are also identified in writing. The stars on the
background are from the 10th-century version. Both the figures of
John and Mary show over-painting. A forearm and hand near
John's thigh belong to another figure, which has disappeared into
him. The vase on Mary's shoulder catching the stream of blood that
comes from Jesus's side is from an earlier version. Some features of
Christ's body are outlined but, because the painting is flat, the
body, with its arms extended on the cross, looks emaciated. The
conventional curving of the body is graceful, following from the
tilted head to the rather elegantly placed feet, but a sense of
suffering is communicated, especially because of the way in which
he looks out of the painting at the viewer.

The Virgin on the other side of the icon shows greater rounding
of figure and face but ecclesiastical painting in Greece was to
remain traditional and would never move into the more realistic
styles followed in Western Europe. Hodgetria, meaning "to guide,"
is used in relation to the Virgin Mary in a similar way to titles such
as "Guiding Star" applied to her in Western Christianity.

In the second row, on the left, there is:

Unknown painter(s)
The Virgin Glykofilousa, BXM 984, 1100–1200 CE

This work was found under a later 18th-century one depicting the
same subject. The subject is one of the common themes of icons,
in which the child is shown making an affectionate gesture with
his left hand on his mother's face ("*Glykofilousa*" means sweet kiss)
while his right holds a scroll. The Virgin's head is tilted to receive
the kiss. The child's torso is shown frontally and his head and legs
are turned across the line of the body.

On the wall, left of the row, locate:

Unknown painter(s), perhaps from Mount Athos
Raising of Lazarus, displayed in a case, BXM 980, 1100–1150 CE

Here Lazarus emerges from his tomb, his winding sheets coming loose. The story is taken directly from the Gospel of Saint John (Ch. 11) in which the sisters of a dead man beg Jesus to bring him back to life. The scene has been imagined with the two women still at the feet of Jesus, their attention focused on him while their brother, his eyes re-opened, prepares to leave the grave. Jesus, in the center of the image, gestures towards the once dead man and is clearly the miracle-worker. The red ground confers timelessness on the event.

In the second row, right of *Glykofilousa,* is:

Unknown artist(s)
Mosaic *The Virgin Episkepsis (Visitation)*, BXM 990, said to be from Constantinople, 1300–1400 CE

Though still unmistakably in the same style as the painted icons, the use of mosaic to depict the Virgin and Child has provided fresh possibilities. The background, haloes, and folds in the garments are in gold and sparkle in the light as you look at it from different angles. The gold-lined folds in the garments work to unite the figure of the mother and child.

In a niche on the wall, on the right, you can see:

Unknown painter(s)
Virgin and Child, BXM 989, 1200–1300 CE

In this work, both figures are upright and facing out. The child's right hand is in the teaching gesture, that is, with the hand facing out, two fingers raised and the thumb turned in. He holds a scroll in his left hand. It is contrary to all expectations of an infant that he would be the teacher. Showing him in this role emphasizes his uniqueness and reinforces the notion that he was the Messiah and the Incarnation of God. Mary's right hand gesture presents the child and his power to the world. In contrast to the *Glykofilousa,* her face is severe, acknowledging that the child belongs to the world. Both woman and child communicate to the viewer but with no interaction between them.

In the third row, on the left, is:

Unknown painter(s)
Double sided icon, on one side *Preparation of the Throne* and on the other, *a Virgin and Child with panels showing the life of Christ*, BXM 1002, 1300–1400 CE

The subject is the preparation of the throne where Christ will sit when, as ruler of the world, he comes to judge all people and send them to heaven or hell. Christians believe that the judgement will take place at the end of time, following the terrifying events of the Apocalypse. This throne is rather a simple-looking, wooden structure, but there is no doubt about its purpose, as there is a text leaning on it with its name written alongside. Jesus's crown of thorns hangs from the cross piece at the top and two angels hover nearby. You can still see the face of one on the right peering out from among its many wings. In some Byzantine churches, the *Preparation of the Throne* is used in place of the image of *Christ Pantocrator*.

On the wall, to the left, are some frescoes:

Unknown painter(s)
Frescoes from Saint George at Oropos: Three Fathers of the Church, A Deacon, and *Three Church Fathers*, BXM 1004, 1005, 1006, 1200–1300 CE

All but one of these figures is a Father of the Church—a common image in Byzantine churches. The middle figure in 2228 is Saint Gregory, presumably Saint Gregory of Nyssa. The fathers are bearded and the deacon is shaven, emphasizing the venerability of the fathers and the junior status of the deacon or acolyte. Their features and clothing follow conventions for depicting such dignatories. They stand frontally, holding books signifying their learning and role as teachers, and wearing church vestments with large black crosses signifying authority. All have haloes, which means that they are saints and hence worthy subjects of art.

They are large figures and would have dominated the interior of Saint George. Their function is not so much to excite devotion as to convey the idea that people's faith is supported by learning, wisdom and tradition. The teaching of theologians was the essence of intellectual life at the time.

To the right of the exit is:

Unknown painter(s)
Crucifix, BXM 981, 1300–1400 CE

Angels hover above the two arms of the cross. On the painting, we can read Pontius Pilate's words "Ecce Homo" meaning "Here is the man." On the crucifix is written "King of the Jews." A group of women stands at one side, headed by his mother. The men, including the beloved John, who gestures towards the dying man, are on the other. This is recognizably a portrayal of suffering lifted outside time and made glorious. The god-man dies against a golden background and angels hover at the arms of his cross ready to go with him to heaven.

Level II, Gallery 6: Franks and Latins in Byzantium

Unknown painter(s)
Double-sided icon, on one side *Saint George* and on the other *Saints Marina and Irene*, BXM 1108, 1200–1300 CE

Saint George is carved in high relief as a Roman soldier. The relief emphasizes his status as a significant hero: it makes the head and body stand out boldly from the scenes from his life, and his two hands are shown clearly. A tiny figure at the saint's feet is said to be the female donor of the icon. On the other side, St Marina is all in red and St Irene on the right wears jewels and a crown. Above the two women is Christ, identified as usual with the initials IC XC. (IC are the first and last letters of Jesus in the old Greek alphabet and XC, the first and last letters of Christos.) The power of their faith is shown in the gestures with which the two women indicate their God. Note that Irene is depicted quite differently from her companion. Her facial features are more delicate, her skin tones lighter, her clothing more ornate.

Level II, Gallery 8: The Final Flowering

A number of works in this last gallery illustrate the merging of late Byzantine art with late medieval painting as it developed in Italy. The trend, however, did not have a strong hold in Greek church art, which continued to adhere to Byzantine conventions.

Unknown painter
Archangel Michael, BXM 1353, 1300–1350 CE

The inscription on the upper part of the work identifies the subject as the Archangel Michael the Great. Matching his title, he is imperious, with wings folded. He stands outside time in a golden space, with a golden halo and carrying a staff and an orb that may represent time itself. His reputation would be known to the viewers. He is an awesome figure.

Archangel Michael, 1300–1350 CE. (Museum of Byzantine and Christian Art Athens).

Unknown painter from Constantinople
Double sided icon, on one side *a Crucifixion scene* and on the other side *Mary*, BXM 1354, 1300–1350 CE

This stark scene has the cross rising out of a fortified Jerusalem. The symbolism of the crucifix growing out of Jerusalem and towering over it recalls surrealist painting. Here the isolated figures of John and Mary are bereft of all comfort. The painting of the drapery is elegant and renders them as good people who should never have been subjected to this situation.

Piraeus: The Archeological Museum

The ancient port of Piraeus was essential to Athenian sea power and has been inhabited since 2000 BCE. A port of both ancient and modern Athens, it disappeared during Turkish rule and even its name was lost. In its early days, between 470–460 BCE, the original port and its surrounding area were developed under the care of Hippodamos, recognized as one of the world's first town planners. The distinctions he made between private, public and religious spaces are still significant in European and European-influenced cities. Along the harbor are countless tavernas where you can feast on fresh seafood. The trip needs a short half-day.

Location: 31 Trikoupi, Piraeus. The Metro goes to Piraeus, as does the 040 bus from Syntagma Square. The Archeological Museum is well signposted and easy to find from the station.

Contact details: Tel. +30 210 452 1598; www.culture.gr

Opening hours: 8:30 am–3:00 pm Tues.–Sun. Closed Monday).

Admission: Low range (Euro 1–4).

At the museum, go upstairs to view the four grandiose bronzes found in storage in Piraeus. These treasures are from the 4th, 5th and perhaps 6th centuries BCE but were warehoused prior to being shipped, presumably to Rome, in the 1st century BCE. The warehouse was destroyed by fire and the bronzes rediscovered in the 20th century. Three are from the mid- to late-4th century BCE—as is the *Bronze Boy* from Marathon in the National Archeological Museum in Athens.

One of the advantages of bronze sculpture is that the inlaid eyes often survived. However, bronze statues were so easily melted down and recycled that many did not survive at all. References to them in written accounts that do survive give us some idea of what was lost.

Bronze Statues

Unknown sculptor
Athene, Exhibit 646, c. 350 BCE

The massive Athene, recognizable from her helmet and, originally, the spear that she would have held in her left hand, is bigger than life-size and filled out by densely packed drapery. The drapery is indicative of the taste for elaborate fabric sculpting in the 4th-century BCE but one can still discern the shape of the body beneath the folds. Indicative also of the taste of the period is the softened, somewhat wistful expression on the face, assisted by the slight tilt of the head.

Even though size works against it, the aim of the sculptor in this period was to make the goddess look sympathetic. A 5th-century Athene, such as the one which inhabited the Parthenon, is an imperious and fearsome figure, apparent even in the somewhat wretched marble copy in the National Archeological Museum. In Phidias's chryselephantine original, she would have been a wild and terrible figure from another world. In this bronze, she is a big, armed, but amiable woman—more of the guardian-angel type than the vengeful, meddling Athene of Homer.

There is some speculation about whether this is an original 4th-century work by Kephidotos or Euphranor, or a Hellenistic work imitating earlier styles.

School of Praxiteles
Artemis, Exhibit 4648, Late 300s BCE

This smaller of the two bronzes of Artemis is said to be of the school of Praxiteles, who was the most prestigious Greek sculptor of the late 4th century BCE. The quiver on her back and the hand that would have held her bow identify Artemis. She appears in many friezes alone or with her brother Apollo and had many of her own sanctuaries. Like Athene, she has been somewhat softened by 4th-century BCE ideology. As the goddess who reigned over the animal kingdom and was herself a hunter, she was earlier portrayed with wings and had lions for companions. By the 4th century BCE, she is a rather boyish-looking young woman. Unfortunately, this statue has been considerably damaged.

Attributed to Euphanor
Artemis, Exhibit 4647, c. 350 BCE

This larger-than-life-size figure is attributed to the sculptor Euphranor. Quiver and bow are missing but crossed ties on the upper body indicate the presence of a quiver. As with Athene, the sculpting of the garments is dense.

As the eye takes in the lines of drapes, the crossed bands, the fall of the shoulder, and the tilt of the head, the slight S-curve of the body, with the balance more on her right than her left leg, is emphasized. This position replaced the frontal posture of Archaic works and survived as a favorite posture for figure sculpting and painting in later periods of Western art from Gothic through to Romantic Classicism.

Unknown sculptor
The Piraeus Apollo, Exhibit 4645, c. 520 BCE, perhaps later

At over six feet, this is a large cult statue of Apollo. Apart from the hands, which held a bow in the left and some sort of offering vessel in the right, the general style is of a kouros of the late 6th century BCE. (Most kouroi had their arms at their sides, like Irish dancers.) However, unlike kouroi, he looks down. He is sculpted in the round, the back a nice study in large and small curves with especially attractive buttocks.

Various Vases

Next to the room with the Apollo is an illuminating display of pottery with sections of the cases devoted to various periods: Mycenaean 1400–1100 BCE, Geometric 900–700 BCE; black-figure 600–500 BCE and red-figure 500–300 BCE. Sit on the convenient bench to note the continuities and differences. For more discussion of vases, see the Introduction.

The Mycenaean on the whole favored bold and simple geometric shapes. Some human, animal, and vegetable shapes were added rather late in the Mycenaean civilization. The vases from this period often feature fine, freely drawn decoration.

The Geometric period—especially in its late phase, about 700 BCE—produces gems such as the large vase in the center of the Geometric case, adorned with rings of meanders, horses, sea horses, swastikas, waves, and checkerboard panels alternating with scenes of girls holding hands and probably dancing. These dancing girls are shown with bodies front-on but faces in profile, in the Egyptian manner. Their waists are narrow, their eyes big and their hair long. The handles of the vases are in the form of goat's head and horns. The lowest panel is a procession of charioteers with double-ax shields and warriors with round shields. The warriors have characteristic long noses and helmets. The horses are irresistible, with thin elongated bodies, long necks, and legs.

Why an art based on geometric shapes developed is a puzzle. Earlier work, such as the Mycenaean, used natural shapes and represented natural objects in their decoration. The makers and painters of Geometric vases are at least their equals in skill but their whole approach is different. We can only speculate about what happened artistically during the so-called Dark Age of some 200 years between the end of the Mycenaean world and the emerging society that produced the Geometric vases. Perhaps the disasters that brought down civilizations led to iconoclastic ideas. As time went on, they adopted motifs from nature in the manner of Egyptian and Middle Eastern work.

Archaic and Classical vases are broadly grouped into black figure on a red background and, from later times, red figure on black backgrounds. There were also white vases. Examples here show typical variations between the three types.

Look, for example, at the black-figure work on the vase where a goat is sacrificed. There are Archaic-looking figures with pointed beards and fairly spare line drawing within the black mass. The red figure allows for more drawing within the silhouette; stances are freer and there is more detail. The white background vase, on the top right, features the equivalent of pen-and-wash technique as in watercolor.

Behind you, grave monument sculptures form another important part of the museum's collections. Remains from infant and child graves can still evoke sadness.

Monastery of Dafni

Location: The Monastery of Dafni is 7 miles (11 kilometers) outside of Athens. To drive there, take Iera Othdos out of central Athens and follow it until it dead ends at Dafni. You can also take the A15 or B16 buses from central Athens to Eleusis, and get off at Dafni. You can also get there on buses 860 and 880 leaving from Penepistimiou, close to Omonia.

Contact details: Tel. +30 210 581 1558; www.culture.gr

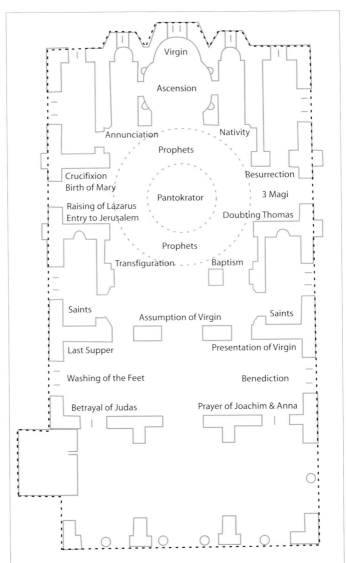

Virgin

Ascension

Annunciation   Nativity

Prophets

Crucifixion   Resurrection
Birth of Mary
                        Pantokrator   3 Magi
Raising of Lázarus
Entry to Jerusalem   Doubting Thomas

Prophets

Transfiguration   Baptism

Saints   Saints
              Assumption of Virgin

Last Supper   Presentation of Virgin

Washing of the Feet   Benediction

Betrayal of Judas   Prayer of Joachim & Anna

The layout of images and stories from the lives of Christ and Mary
is typical of the prescribed iconography of the Byzantine era.

DAFNI: BYZANTINE ICONOGRAPHY

When Pausanias followed the Sacred Way from Athens to Eleusis he passed a temple to Apollo Daphnaios on the site of the monastery of Dafní. The place name refers to Apollo's love for the nymph Daphne who turned herself into a laurel tree to escape him. The temple was in a grove of laurels. One Ionic column from the temple is in the colonnade of the narthex (the double gallery as you enter the church). Lord Elgin helped himself to the other columns left over from the temple's destruction in 395 CE.

The present octagonal church dates from 1100 BCE. It is dedicated to the Dormition of the Virgin. Within it, the big attractions are the marvelous mosaics which have lasted from the 11th century and cover most of the interior, principally with scenes from the lives of Mary and Christ. The figures are still and solemn but able nonetheless to convey emotion, as does the Virgin grieving in the crucifixion scene. The lambent, gold background tells us they are looking into heaven. Dominating all from the central dome is Christ as the Pantocrator, the Almighty. Pairs of letters on each side of him identify him in the conventional way: IC, the first and last Greek letters for Jesus and XC, for Christos. Other scenes and figures are also identified by name or key words.

Although the arrangement of figures and stories in Byzantine mosaics and frescoes vary, the conventions are consistent enough to take Dafni as an archetype for most churches. In religious discussion, an icon is a picture. The picture might be of God, Christ, Mary, an angel or a saint. It might also be of a scene from the Bible or the Gospels. The word "iconography" refers to the way pictures are made, the subject matter, the meaning and their overall arrangement in a sacred building.

Iconoclasm means the breaking of icons. Attempts were made in the 8th and 9th centuries to ban any kind of picture within churches. The argument was that pictures of Christ and the saints would become idols, worshipped in their own right. The movement failed, and sacred images came increasingly to use the human form. However, opposition to creating images that looked too much like human beings continued to some extent in the Byzantine churches.

Byzantine art at its peak observed fairly strict rules of iconography. The diagram of the church shows the order of the images and stories in the monastery of Dafni, which resembles a typical iconography in a Byzantine church. Other arrangements occur in other churches but variations are not great. The figure of Christ, usually as the Pantocrator or Almighty, is central. Mary, the great prophets, the apostles, and scenes from the lives of Christ and Mary are always in prominent positions around the central image, while saints and learned leaders of the church will be at lower levels. These figures frequently have their name or an abbreviation of it worked into the picture. Also, the patron saint of the church will feature in frescoes, mosaics, and painting. The succession of scenes in a section of the church may go through a full cycle, from the Annunciation to the Ascension, although this doesn't happen at Dafni.

Use the diagram to guide you as you walk around this important Byzantine church.

Other Museums

Athens has a number of private and specialist museums. Of those housing fine private collections, the Benaki and the Kanellopoulos are well worth visiting. The Numismatic Museum is of specialist interest to coin enthusiasts and is one of the few of its kind in the world.

Benaki Museum

Location: Corner of Koumbari Street & Vassilisis Sofias Avenue, near the Cycladic Museum, and the Metro Evangelismos or Syntagma.
Contact details: Tel. +30 21 0367 1000; www.benaki.gr
Opening hours: Mon., Wed., Fri., Sat.: 9:00 am–5:00 pm; Thurs. 9:00 am–11:00 pm; Sun. 9:00 am–3:00 pm, closed Tuesdays.
Admission: Euro 6; Euro 3 discount.

The Benaki is a very well-managed and enterprising foundation. It has both a permanent collection and a program of special exhibitions. The permanent collection gives a panorama of Greek art and history from prehistoric to modern times. Among its Byzantine pieces is one of El Greco's icons from his youth in Crete, the *Adoration of the Magi*. There are also astutely chosen items of Coptic and Islamic art. The special exhibitions, which are advertised in advance on the museum website are wide-ranging and imaginative.

The twelve rooms on the ground floor of the Benaki's permanent collection have items from all the periods covered in *Art for Travellers*. A handsome guide book, economically priced at 15 euros, gives a careful and engaging account of each of the periods with comments on specific works. Although the items of the collection do not generally rank with the masterpieces in parallel collections, they provide a very discriminating and accessible introduction to the range of Greek art. On the upper floors, the collection extends to modern times. Art travellers might find the Benaki an agreeable way to introduce themselves to the range of Greek art before tackling the larger or more specialized museums.

Kanellopoulos Museum

Location: Panos Street Plaka, Metro Monastiraki.
Contact details: Tel. +30 210 321 2313; www.culture.gr
Opening hours: 8:30 am–3:00 pm Tues. to Sun. Closed Mondays.
Admission: Euro 2.

The Kanellopoulos collection is in a neo-classical mansion just below the Acropolis. It has a permanent collection that covers all periods from prehistoric to Byzantine art. Like the Benaki, it provides a discriminating overview of the span of Greek art, with particular attention to Byzantine works. Some of its important earlier works include a charming terracotta figurine of a young woman holding a lyre from the 4th century BCE and a 2nd-century marble head of Alexander the Great.

The Numismatic Museum

Location: 12 El Venizelou (Panepistimiou).
Contact details: Tel. +30 210 364 3774; 361 2190, 361 2519;
protocol@nm.culture.gr
Opening hours: 8:30 am–3:00 pm. Closed Mondays and public holidays.
Admission: Low range (Euro 1–4).

Heinrich Schliemann's beautiful mansion, the Palace of Ilion, contains around 600,000 coins from ancient Greece, Roman and Byzantine periods, from medieval times and modern times. It is a thematically organized, self-guiding museum with fascinating coins.

TRAIL 4:
Delphi

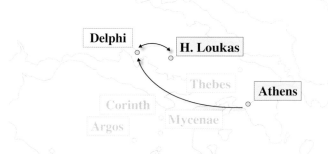

Delphi **H. Loukas**

Thebes

Corinth **Athens**

Mycenae

Argos

Trail 4 | Athens - Delphi

Delphi is the most entrancing and memorable of all ancient sites. Renowned for its oracle, it was, with Olympia, a Panhellenic sanctuary, open to all Greeks no matter what their local loyalties. Delphi flourished from Archaic to Roman times. This Trail takes in the site, explores the museum, and ends with a visit to the nearby Hossios Loukas monastery. The periods represented are the Archaic, Classical, and, at Hossios Loukas, the Byzantine. A considerable number of art works found on the site are in the museum near the entrance.

The buildings, impressive as they would have been, would still have been dwarfed by the superb landscape. Above the site is Mount Parnassus, sacred to Apollo, the god of the sanctuary, and his muses. Beyond the ruins, framed against blue skies and grey slopes, you can

Left: Treasury of the Athenians, Delphi

DELPHI

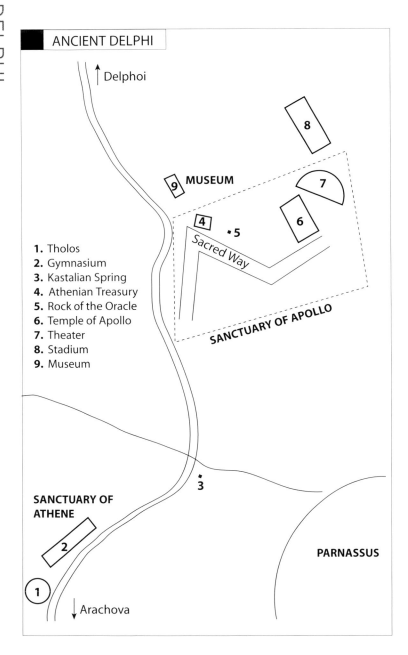

ANCIENT DELPHI

↑ Delphoi

8

MUSEUM

9

7

4 • 5

6

Sacred Way

1. Tholos
2. Gymnasium
3. Kastalian Spring
4. Athenian Treasury
5. Rock of the Oracle
6. Temple of Apollo
7. Theater
8. Stadium
9. Museum

SANCTUARY OF APOLLO

• 3

SANCTUARY OF
ATHENE

PARNASSUS

2

1

↓ Arachova

look down far below to the port of Itea and the celebrated olive groves of Amphissa.

To get to Delphi by public bus from Athens, catch the 024 bus outside the National Gardens to the long distance bus terminal (Stathmó Leoforíon) just off Liosion Street. Once there, look for the bus to Delphi. Alternatives to the public bus are tour buses or car, both more expensive. If you take a tour bus, get one that goes via Hossios Loukas so that you can take in the monastery there.

It's best to allow two days. If you want to do the trip in a day, be at Stathmó Leoforíon in time to catch the earliest bus at 7:30 am to get to Delphi at 10:30. Take about four hours to see the museum and site. You can then return on a 4 o'clock or 6 o'clock bus. However, the area is so beautiful and the site itself so spectacular that Delphi is suitable for an overnight trip. There are plenty of hotels of all grades in Delphi and a youth hostel as well. Taverns are plentiful and prices displayed so you can choose what suits you.

Ticketing arrangements allow you to go to the site or museum or both. The combined ticket can be used over two days.

The Site

Location: The site and museum are on the edge of the modern town, within easy walking distance of the bus stop.

Contact details: Tel. +30 226 508 2312; www.culture.gr

Opening hours: 7:30 am–7:30 pm Mon.–Fri., 8:30 am–2.45 pm Sat.–Sun. During winter (Nov 1 to Mar 31) hours are 8:00 am–3:00 pm.

Admission: High range (Euro 9–12). The ticket admits to both site and museum and is valid for two days.

Delphi is dedicated to the god Apollo. Although, like most Greek gods, Apollo can be quite ruthless, he is also associated with many of the essentials of Greek life expressive of harmony and order, such as music, poetry, purification, law, and prophecy. The immensely powerful faculty of prophecy was exercised through the Delphic oracle, who added considerable political clout to what was already a key religious center.

Greek mythology identifies Delphi as the center or navel of the earth— the Omphalos. It was the legendary place where two eagles met, having been released by Zeus from opposite ends of the earth. As well as being a religious center dedicated to music and harmony, it had a three-month winter season when the riotous Dionysos occupied the sanctuary. Apollo, as god of music, had a retinue of muses living on nearby Mount Parnassus.

The legends of Delphi portray the oracle as well as the site as extremely ancient. Before Apollo took over, the oracle was dedicated to Gaia, the Earth Goddess, and guarded by the dragon Python. Apollo, whose home was on Delos, transformed himself into a dolphin and with the aid of a Cretan ship landed on the coast below Delphi, climbed up to the oracle, killed the Python, and renamed the sacred site Delphi (derived from dolphin). The earlier name is retained in the Pythian games.

The main temple on this Parnassian site is, naturally, the temple of

The Delphic Oracle

In the ancient world, innumerable far-reaching political decisions were taken on the basis of the ambiguous utterances of the Delphic and other oracles. One of the best known of these is reported by Herodotus in The Histories *(translated by Aubrey de Selincourt, Penguin Classics.) The oracle, he says, promised Croesus, the King of Lydia, that if he made war on Persia, he would "destroy a great empire." Croesus promptly attacked, but instead of adding to his empire, he found himself captured and imprisoned by the Persians. His days of ruling an empire were over. Thus, says Herodotus, "the oracle was fulfilled; Croesus had destroyed a mighty empire—his own."*

The fame of Apollo's shrine at Delphi spread far and wide. Plato esteemed Apollo's wisdom above all the other gods in matters of religion and morality. In his Republic, *he proposes that Apollo should lay down the basic laws of an ideal society. The Delphic oracles were consulted before any major enterprise—especially before founding new cities or colonies. A priestess or sybil, in a trance, delivered the Delphic prophecies from inside a cavern obscured by smoke and fumes. The prophecies, notorious for their ambiguity, were then interpreted by priests. As in many other cultures, the Greeks went out of their way to justify even the catastrophic outcomes of perverse prophecies.*

The Romans were not greatly interested in Delphic prophecy and the Christian emperors looked to their own sources. When the Byzantine Emperor Julian the Apostate (361–363 CE) made a final effort to revive the oracle, it gave its last prophecy: "Tell the king: the great halls have fallen down. Apollo no longer has a chapel, nor a laurel tree to aid prophecy. There is no spring. The waters that had so much to say have dried up."

The site was finally closed down by a decree of the Emperor Theodosius. (379–395 CE).

Apollo; there have been a succession of temples built to Apollo here. Monuments to Athene have lesser stature. The majority of ruins are treasuries and votive statues erected by cities and communities to honor and thank the oracle.

Delphi was probably at its peak in the Archaic period of the 6th century BCE. Over the next several centuries it continued to accumulate shrines and treasuries to house the various offerings made generally to Apollo. It survived attacks from barbarians. Even the Romans, who took the sanctuary and its powers less seriously than the Greeks did, continued to endow the sanctuary, but Pausanias claims they also did some looting. "Delphi," he wrote, "has also to suffer its share of the universal arrogance of Nero, who stole from Apollo five hundred different bronze images of gods and of men."

The site as we see it today is essentially that of the 5th and 6th centuries BCE but settlement dates back to Neolithic times and there was a substantial settlement during the Mycenaean period 1600–1100 BCE. There are local finds from most periods through to Christian times and they indicate its continuous use as a sacred site. With the spread of Christianity, Delphi was abandoned, except for some parts that were reused for Christian buildings. One such church is just within the entrance to the site. Greek and French archeologists uncovered the ruined and buried site from 1892 onwards.

The ancient site extends on both sides of the highway to the town. The upper side, above the museum, is Apollo's, the lower side, below the road, is Athene's. The diagram of the site is numbered in the order in which the Trail is described. Begin at the smaller, lower site, which is set within an olive grove and contains the remains of a couple of temples to Athene, some treasuries and a cylindrical building in the Doric order called the **Thelos (1)** which has been partly restored. It would have been an important building, although we don't know its function—note the multicolored stone and the relief decoration.

Away from this site through the olive groves are the sites of the **gymnasium (2)** and an area for track events. The site contained several buildings and two areas: the upper one for running and the lower one containing the pool and baths.

Next, along the road from the Gymnasium to the upper site, is a gorge containing the **Kastalian Spring (3)**. The spring ran with purifying water used in the main sanctuary. Steps, bronze spouts and fountains were built—one in Archaic times and the other by the Romans. The Archaic arrangement is the one on the left near the road. Above the Roman fountain, note the niches cut into the rock. It is thought that these were where offerings to the nymph Kastalia were left.

You can now proceed to the larger upper site, which was dedicated to Apollo and was the more important. Pausanias rightly described it as being "on a steep slope from top to bottom." It is dotted with the remains of treasuries, dedications and temples. When the site was in use, treasuries and votive monuments wound up the hill on both sides of the road.

From the bottom of the hill, the main entrance marks the beginning of a **Sacred Way**. This still zigzags up the hill, with two sharp turns, to the main temple of Apollo.

The first section of the Sacred Way was lined with many treasuries and votive statues, generally donated by cities or communities to thank the oracle or keep in her good books. Pausanias found the Way

The Pythian Games

The Pythian Games were held every four years at Delphi and were second only in prestige to those held at Olympia. The Nemean and Isthmian Games (on the isthmus of Korinth) were held every two years. Celebrations in Greek cities usually involved games, but these four brought together all Greeks and therefore served a particularly high purpose, reflected today in the international Olympiads.

The Pythian Games eventually included all the events of the Olympic Games (see Trail 7 for more detail). The Games may have

DELPHI

crowded with these when he toured Delphi in the 2nd century CE, but relatively little remains now. Splendid material from the treasury built by the island of Siphnos is in the museum. Just after the first turn the impressive Doric **Athenian Treasury (4)** has been reconstructed using a technique known as anastylosis, which reuses all the original bits from the building and fills in the rest with a clearly distinguishable material. Original sculptures from this treasury plus a wall of hymns to Apollo are in the museum. Pausanias records that the Athenians built it to celebrate their victory over the Persians at Marathon (in 490 BCE) but there is scholarly argument over its date.

Next to this treasury as you ascend is the ruin of the Delphi council house. Immediately after this a pile of rocks marks the place where the Python kept guard over the oracle—this is called the **Rock of the Oracle (5)**. A sanctuary to the Earth Goddess Gaia was behind these rocks.

begun, however, as musical contests inspired by Apollo. Pausanias says: "The most ancient contest the Delphic people remember, and the one where a prize was first offered, was for singing a hymn to the god." Subsequently the flute-song was abolished "because it was an unlucky sound." Prizes were replaced by wreaths for victors. One of the victors of the games donated the bronze Charioteer (which is now in the museum) to commemorate his success the Greek lyric poet Pindar (518–438 BCE) wrote odes to the victors in the games at Olympia, Delphi, Nemea, and Korinth. Of these renowned athletes he wrote:

So great a share of the lovely things of Hellas
Is theirs, let God not envy them
And change their fortune.
Though God alone never tastes woe,
Yet that man is happy and poets sing of him.
Who conquers with hand or swift foot
And wins the greatest of prizes
By steadfastness and strength
And lives to see
His young son in turn, get garlands at Pytho.

(From Pindar, *The Odes Pythian X*, translated by
C.M. Bowra, Penguin Classics, 1969)

Opposite: *The Tholos in the sanctuary of Athene Pronaos, c. 380 BCE.*
(*Bildarchiv Steffens*).

As it approaches the temple, the so-called Polygonal Wall dominates the second section of the Sacred Way. Built in the 500s BCE as a retaining wall for the temple of Apollo, its massive, irregularly shaped stones are crowded with inscriptions, mainly from Roman times, granting freedom to individual slaves.

The second turn in the Way leads to a steep rise and the **Temple of Apollo (6)**. To your left at the top of the steps are the foundations of the altar to the god, known as the Altar of the Chians, a construction in black and white marble. To your right is a cylindrical pedestal. According to Pausanias, this held "a tripod of gold standing on a bronze snake" which "the Greeks dedicated in common from the spoils of the battle at Plataia." The bronze, he noted, was still there but the gold had not been left "in the same condition." The bronze, which consisted of a column of intertwined snakes culminating in three heads that supported the gold tripod, was long admired as a masterpiece and transferred by Constantine to stand before Hagia Sophia in Constantinople. It was later erected as a fountain at the Hippodrome (which also contained the bronze horses looted by the Venetians for San Marco) and spouted wine, water, and milk from its three mouths.

The temple ruins we see today are from the 4th century BCE, the third temple on the site. The previous two were destroyed by fire and earthquake. Apollo's home was a massive Doric construction, on the general pattern of other temples such as the Parthenon. The prophecies were made from within the inner building or from a cavern that could be approached from the inner building. Some sculptures from the temple are in the museum.

On an area above the front end of the temple, there was, in Delphi's heyday, a building that Pausanias calls a clubhouse, where Delphians "used to meet in ancient times both for old tales and for serious conversation." He gives a lengthy and illuminating description of the paintings by Polygnotos that adorned the walls—narrative paintings "of extraordinary beauty" based on Homer's epics. All are gone, unhappily.

Above the temple is the **theater (7)**, which dates from the 4th century BCE but was rebuilt in Roman times. It would have accommodated about 5,000 spectators for the dramatic performances and music contests that were part of the Pythian Games, hosted by Delphi every four years.

If you are feeling fit, make the climb up to the **stadium (8)**. The present one dates from the 2nd century BCE. Track, field, boxing, and wrestling events for the Pythian Games were held here. Horse and chariot racing took place on the present-day Plain of Chrisos. From here you will go to the **museum (9)**.

The Archeological Museum

The museum is light and airy, a consistent reminder of the world just outside and the first home of the works exhibited. It has recently been refurbished and extended, but the changes should not substantially affect the order of the main works of art covered on this part of the Trail.

At the head of the stairs as you enter is a recreation of the Omphalos, which symbolizes Delphi's position at the center of the world. It represents a cone inside a mesh and the original would have had a couple of eagles on top.

Start in the large room to the right of the vestibule.

Unknown sculptor
Naxian Sphinx, c. 569 BCE

This large piece sits on the remains of an Ionic column that would have been about 32 feet (10 meters high), and was dedicated to Delphi by the inhabitants of the Cycladic island of Naxos.

Sphinxes are not easy to relate to and are not meant to be. They are monsters and for Greeks, basically foreign monsters borrowed from the Egyptians. Among other things, the sphinx was associated with death and gained some popularity because it was linked with the story of Oedipus.

An interesting feature of the *Naxian Sphinx* is that the variety of treatment gives it plausibility. The lion, the bird and the woman are in three layers: the lion looking as though it is ready to bounce into action; the middle section of the bird stylized by turning wings and feathers into clear geometric lines; and the woman's head rounded and pleasant-looking even though the smile of the sphinx is supposed to make the face enigmatic. Given its originally great height above ground, it rightly gets its presence from bold lines: the feline curves at the rear balancing against the semicircular curve of the wings and the front legs, chest, and head holding a strong vertical. The restrained molding of the Ionic column suits the *Naxian Sphinx* neatly.

Unknown sculptor
Caryatid from the façade of the Siphnian Treasury, 525 BCE

This young girl—the one next to her survives only as a head— did the same job as the famous ones on the Erechthion on the Athenian Acropolis: that is, she held up the roof of a porch on

DELPHI

The Naxian Sphinx: a crouching sphinx on an Ionic votive column. From Naxos c. 560 BCE. (Archeological Museum Delphi)

her head. Caryatids are a further illustration of the rather flamboyant nature of Greek architecture and one that is sometimes lost in the bleached and tumbled-down ruins with which we are familiar.

This one has a sweet face. Some of the sweetness might be the result of the broken nose, which leaves only her more rounded features. Her smile—like that of her neighbor—is very charming. Signs of additional flamboyant touches can be seen in the holes that would have contained some sort of bronze diadem and the traces of visible color. The features of the face and hair as well as the drapery were painted, all of which would have given the caryatid a worldly air, in keeping with her public job.

Unknown sculptors
Pediment of the Siphnian Treasury, 525 BCE

On the left of the sphinx but past the entrance to the room is the pediment from the Treasury of the Siphnians (Siphnos is a Cycladic island). Treasuries were simple versions of temples with a vestibule and a closed chamber. They had a pediment (the triangular bit above the columns) and a carved frieze front and sides. Like temples, they were not places of worship. Rather, they belonged to the god, were made beautiful out of respect for the god and designed to show off the wealth and good intentions of the donors.

The Siphnian treasury is one of the most decorated of its kind. The pediment shows Herakles and Apollo having a brawl over a tripod used for oracles. Herakles wanted to take the tripod and set up his own oracle. The god figure in the center seems to be helping Apollo, who is also getting a hand from others, such as his sister Artemis. The lower part of the sculpting is in relief and the upper part in the round. The legs of the two main figures are in very high relief, while the legs of others are noticeably less rounded. These remains of the pediment illustrate the strength of Greek sculptors of the period in using a dramatic moment and filling it with movement and action.

Unknown sculptors
East frieze from the Siphnian Treasury, 525 BCE

Below the pediment is a scene that encapsulates a lot of the Greek attitude to their gods. It is close to intact and the whole work can therefore be viewed much as it was intended.

In this, the gods watch a battle from the Trojan War from their equivalent of the corporate box. On the left are the gods who support the Trojans—Ares with a shield, Aphrodite trying to get Artemis's attention, Apollo turning to make a point to Artemis and a headless Zeus. On the right are the patrons of the Greeks. Poseidon is missing but we see a line up of women—Athene, Hera, and possibly Demeter.

In the battle scene, heroes are locked in combat—Aeneas with Hector and Menelaus with Aias. On the left of the battle is a Trojan chariot and on the right a Greek chariot. The battle continues over the top of a dead warrior. The contrast between the violence of battle and the apparent banter among the godly spectators shows that the gods are both interested in the doings of heroes and mortals and somewhat indifferent as to the outcome. There are remains of red on the shields.

Unknown sculptor, presumed to be the same artist as the east frieze
North frieze from the Siphnian treasury, 525 BCE

This frieze shows the battle between the gods and the giants. The giants were the sons of Uranus, the heavens, and of Ge, the earth. As soon as they were born, they attacked the Olympians, hoping to replace them. To get at the Olympians, the giants put one mountain on top of the other and used this added height to hurl stuff at their rivals. Only mortals could kill them so Zeus recruited Herakles.

In part of the frieze, on the left hand side, we see a lion savaging a giant. At first glance, he may look as though he is crying out in anguish, but his face is actually covered by a helmet. The lion is drawing a chariot driven by Cybele and behind her, with his lion skin draped on his shoulders, is the hero Herakles.

Return to the entrance vestibule and on the left, before you go into the room containing *The Twins*, find a bronze warrior.

Unknown artist
Bronze Youth, 625 BCE

This figure has the elongated look of earlier sculpture but is approaching more natural proportions. The slender-waisted youth may be a warrior. Warrior figures were popular at the time, at least partly because of the extent to which the Greek states kept fighting one another. His left leg is slightly forward, a movement that would become even more pronounced in Archaic sculpture. His arms are held at his sides and his fists clenched—somewhat like Egyptian figures. His face is triangular with a long nose and large eyes, the hair is decorative but in horizontal lines, and the top of the head is flattened.

With the entrance behind you, ahead of you are two impressive kouroi.

Polymedes of Argos (?)
Twin kouroi: Kleovis and Biton, 610–580 BCE

There is some disagreement as to whom these figures represent and who made them.

A sculptor's signature on the base of the one to the right is incomplete. It reads "...medes from Argos" and is interpreted by some as Polymedes from Argos but the fragment may not justify the conclusion. The twins might be the Dioskouroi (Castor and Pollux, sons of Zeus out of Leda) or the two sons of a priestess from Argos. If the latter, they are Kleobis and Biton. Herodotus says that the lads one day yoked themselves to their mother's chariot because the oxen failed to turn up, and pulled her about 5 miles (8 kilometers) to Hera's sanctuary. As they rested from their exertions, the goddess rewarded them with the gift of eternal sleep. The reward seems ambiguous, except that it preserved their youth for all time.

They are a powerful-looking pair, shoulders squared by their arm positions, the thumbs placed appropriately for standing at attention. The less damaged one on the right still has an exquisite curve incised sufficiently on the rib line to be plausible but sufficiently bell shaped to be decorative. The pubic hair is decoratively incised. The faces convey the eagerness of youth and would seem even more so were the eyes not now sightless. Standing side by side they represent youthful strength and brotherly companionship.

The room to the right of *The Twins* contains what might be one of the biggest surprises to admirers of white Greek marbles of perfected human figures.

Unknown artists
Chryselephantine Statues, 6th century BCE

Imagining the paint and inlays of which we see many traces on marble statues in no way prepares you for what the great Phidias of

Parthenon fame actually preferred by way of materials: chryselephantine, or work of gold (*chryssos*) and ivory (elephant tusks). Chryselephantine work was mounted on a wooden core and the exterior of face, body, and garments was of ivory for the flesh and gold for hair and garments. Phidias's famous statue of Athene inside the Parthenon was a 40-foot (12-meter) high effort in this medium.

In the case on the left are some unique examples of this work. The display cases contain fragments of two statues. The larger one in the center is Apollo and the smaller one on the right is Artemis, his sister. Though the faces of Apollo and Artemis are quite different, they both have the Archaic smile. Their gold work is elaborately hammered into panels depicting mythical beasts and wild animals.

To the right of this case is a larger-than-life size assemblage of a bull that was made of gold and silver leaf and attached to a wooden frame. It had been damaged in the 5th century BCE and put into storage with other damaged precious objects where it remained to be dug up in 1939.

Work of this kind—obviously highly prized by the most noted of Greek artists—is light years away from the Romantic visions of austere white statues amidst ruins with which we are nowadays more familiar.

Return to the entrance room and go left.

Unknown artists
Metopes from the Athenian treasury, 5th century BCE, in an early phase of the Classical period

The Athenians built a treasury at Delphi to thank Apollo for their victory over the Persians at the Battle of Marathon in 490 BCE. What are left of the metopes depicting the labors of Herakles and the labors of Theseus may be fragments but they make the clear point that Athens is associated with victors and heroes. This political message calls for no subtlety and is plain in both subject matter and execution.

On the right as you come into the room is Herakles. On your left as you exit are several scenes of Theseus. The Greeks universally admired Herakles (the Romans called him Hercules) as an ideal of strength, courage and tenacity. Theseus was a favorite of the Athenians. General mythology claimed him to be mortal, but the Athenians claimed that Poseidon fathered him and Athens often used his exploits to press home claims about their connections with various parts of the Greek world. His greatest feat was slaying of the Minotaur in Crete, thus saving the Athenians a regular tribute of seven youths and seven maidens to be eaten alive. Herakles can usually be identified by the Nemean lion skin around his shoulders.

In each case, the faces have a lot of the Archaic in them—the broad nose, high cheeks, smiling mouth, and carefully styled hair. The bodies are in the positions of vigorous action that are typical of friezes.

In the next room (Room 7), there are two things to note. The fragments of the old Temple of Apollo also depicted the battle of the gods and the giants. On the right, before the entrance into the rear room, is a large block of marble incised with hymns to Apollo—part of the Treasury of the Athenians. The significance of this is the insight it gives into ancient Greek music. Between the lines are letters of the Ionian alphabet in various positions that were used as musical notes.

In Room 8, as well as more fragments from the Temple of Apollo is a Winged Victory.

Unknown artists
Winged Victory, from 510 BCE

This nike has lost her main wings but retains one winged ankle. The figure is in the Archaic style, balancing geometric form with human form. The off-center lines of the garments as they fall down the body suggest forward movement. This pose is the conventional one of Winged Victories, often used as statues on the front of a temple roof (the *acroterium*). The satisfaction of victory is in the imperious face.

A lion's head, acting as a waterspout from the roof, is nearby: it is an example of an ancestor of the medieval gargoyle.

From here, head for:

Unknown sculptor
Charioteer, c. 470 BCE

Noted bronze sculptors such as Pythagoras, Kalamis, and Kritios have been suggested as makers of this masterpiece, essentially because it is such a fine piece of work. The figure was part of a much larger ensemble containing four horses, a chariot and maybe a groom. The groom and more particularly the fact that the charioteer is wearing a crown of victory impart the suggestion that he has pulled up to be admired as the victor. Symbolically, the victory honors the donor as well as the athlete.

The lines of the belt on the chiton, the long garment, give a sense of the body held in a proud but calm posture. The chariot race was a long (about 9 miles/14 kilometers) and violent contest with many falls, but here we have the inner calm of the victor

Bronze charioteer of Delphi (detail). c. 470 BCE. (Archeological Museum of Delphi)

with the clash and speed of the race behind him. Like many athletes, he makes an extremely demanding activity appear essentially graceful. In the words of Pindar's Olympian Ode I he "breathes a delicious and serene air / When he remembers the Games." The grace of the body is emphasized by the symmetrical folds in the chiton from the belt down. It is a reminder that difficult physical feats are performed by young people for the pleasure of everyone else.

It is our great fortune that the eyes are preserved in place. The lighter whites contrasting with the inner depths of his eyes hold and reflect the intensity of his moment of victory.

In a small case on the left, the only other exhibit in the room is:

Unknown potter
White kylix, 480 BCE

This is a plate shaped rather like a small fruit bowl with a painting of Apollo playing his lyre and pouring out a libation of red wine. The black raven perched near the edge might refer to Apollo's love for the mortal Coronis, daughter of the king Phlegyis. She was Apollo's lover but betrayed him with a mortal and he had her killed. Later, in remorse, he turned the raven that had warned him of her deed from a white bird into a black bird.

Like photographs today, decorated vases and dishes pictured scenes whose images were both familiar and powerful for their audience. The impact was captured, as it is here, in poses, attitudes, actions, and symbolic details.

As you return from *The Charioteer's* room, note on your right the very early small bronzes, a couple (Exhibit 3495 top left and 7730 center) reminiscent of Cycladic forms. There are also Mycenaean pottery figurines, which demonstrate the longevity of the site.

On your left there is statuary typifying the move to secular subject matter and the flamboyance of style of later Roman times.

As you leave this most important of all Panhellenic sites—more so even than Olympia—you have several choices. Your ticket is good for two days, so an overnight stay and another visit are a good idea. Alternatively you could stay in Delphi overnight and go back to Athens via the splendid monastery of Hossios Loukas.

Hossios Loukas

Location: Hossios Loukas monastery, now a national monument, is a shortish trip from Delphi on the road between the towns of Distomo and Livadia.

Contact details: Tel. +30 226 702 2797; www.culture.gr

Opening hours: Open daily from 8:00 am–7:00 pm (closing at 6:00 pm in winter.)

Admission: Low range (Euro 1–4).

The monastery is an 11th-century Byzantine masterpiece rich in mosaic and fresco. Situated on the slopes of Mt Elikon, it takes it name from its founder Hossios Loukas (Blessed Luke), a hermit who died in 953 CE, credited with miracles of healing and a gift for predicting significant events. The nearby village of Stiri takes its name from the ancient site on the mountain.

The exterior is a wonderfully colored and decorated jumble of buildings. Stone from the acropolis of Stiri has been reused among the ornate Byzantine brickwork. The complex of churches present very early examples of Byzantine ground plans: one is cross-shaped with four central columns supporting a lantern, while the larger main church is octagonal and domed.

Inside the walls, there are four areas to visit: the main church, or Catholikon; the crypt beneath it; the older Church of the Virgin, which is connected by a portico to the right of the main church entrance; and the refectory, within the monastery.

The main church, the Catholikon, was built in the 11th century after Loukas's death. It is built over the crypt. The Church of the Virgin (Theotokos), originally called St Barbara's, is said to have been begun during the lifetime of Hossios Loukas and finished shortly after his death. There is wonderful stone and brickwork inside and outside the old church.

The refectory (monks' dining room) was destroyed during World War Two and has been restored to house Byzantine sculpture.

The buildings will repay leisurely inspection from outside and in. The ornate brickwork includes pieces from ancient buildings, which are fascinating, while the paving and sculpting of marble within the main church is wonderful, elegant, and detailed.

The Catholikon

The finest ensemble of original mosaics is in the narthex of the main church, the Catholikon. As soon as you enter the main, west door of the church you are in the narthex.

Unknown artists
Byzantine mosaics and frescoes in the Catholikon, 11th century BCE

Opposite the entrance in the arch, or *tympanum,* above the door leading deeper into the church, is an expansive mosaic of the delicately outlined Christ the teacher. He holds a book of the gospels, which he points towards with his right hand. He is a serious, but not forbidding, figure. His identity is affirmed by the IC (for Jesus) and XC (for Christos) on the gold ground.

Above Christ, on the ceiling within circles set in triangles, are the figures of Mary, John the Baptist, and two angels whose names are hard to read on the work.

Around the narthex, there are about 40 more figures of saints and martyrs (identified in writing) and four scenes focused on the death and resurrection of Christ. The sequence begins with Christ washing his disciples' feet. He begins, we suppose, with Peter. Behind Peter, John is taking off his sandals.

Next in sequence is the crucifixion. This is given a simple, calm treatment, in which the bleeding Christ charges his two most beloved people, Mary and John, to look after one another as should a mother and son. The only element of landscape is the tiny hill of Golgotha with its skull beneath the cross.

The next scene is Christ descending into the underworld. It is identified by the Greek word for the resurrection H(The) ANÁSTASIS (read C as S). Beneath Christ's feet hell has broken open. Sepulchers have sprung open and from one, Christ leads Adam and Eve as representatives of humanity, by the hand to bring them with him to Paradise.

The final scene is the meeting with doubting Thomas, the apostle who would not believe Christ had come back from the dead unless he could put his hands on Christ's wounds. In this representation he is about to put his finger into the wound made by the Roman soldier's spear. Believers look on.

Past the narthex and within the main nave of the church there is a mix of mosaics and frescoes. Early work in some parts was destroyed by earthquake, and some of the frescoes, for example of the Pantocrator surrounded by saints, angels, and prophets in and beneath the large (30-foot/9-meter) dome, are replacements from the 16th and 17th centuries.

In the quadrants supporting the dome are mosaics comprising scenes essentially from the life of Mary: but the Annunciation is no longer extant. There is the birth of Christ, his presentation in the temple, and his baptism in the Jordan by his cousin John the Baptist. The scenes are full of activity. The nativity packs in all the expected detail: the child is in the crib and a beam of heavenly light illuminates him as angels sing of his coming. His parents, shepherds, and sheep cluster around. The landscape is rocky and mountainous. In the presentation and the baptism, the focus is firmly on the central action. In presentation Mary, backed by Joseph, holds up her child for Simeon and Anne (two of the attendants at the temple) to see. The figures dwarf the temple. In the baptism, Christ is immersed in the river as John performs the baptism attended by angels holding a robe.

In the apse at the east end of the church above the altar, Mary is enthroned in a gilt hemisphere holding her infant son. The child is in a teaching posture enveloped in the still figure of his mother. Around the nave is a host of saints and monks.

Crypt

There are more frescoes in the crypt: the entrance is within the main church.

Unknown artists
Byzantine frescoes in the crypt, 11th century BCE

The crypt underneath the main church provides foundation for the church and a place for the tomb of Hossios Loukas. The frescoes on the walls and ceilings of the crypt are from the same period (early 11th century) as the mosaics in the Catholikon. Cleaning has revealed varied images of lively scenes in clear colors. Again, there are many images of saints, as well as a range of scenes from the passion and death of Christ: his entry into Jerusalem with palms spread at his donkey's feet, the last supper with his apostles, his death, and his burial by his mother and friends. The burial scene is in double time: on the left the body is laid in the tomb, whilst on the right an angel indicates to the women visiting the tomb that he has risen from the dead.

Coming up from the crypt, to the right as you face the altar the
Catholikon is joined to the older Church of the Virgin. On a
tympanum on the arch leading to the older church is an imposing
mosaic of the founder Loukas, identified in the lettering. The drafting
is rigorously geometric—especially in the beard and cloak. In the older
church are more frescoes, including this particularly famous one, Jesus
of Navi.

Church of the Virgin

Unknown artists

Jesus Navi in the Church of the Virgin, 11th century BCE

At the beginning of the old church, on a wall that would originally
have been external, a 10th-century fresco of Jesus as a soldier was
uncovered in 1965. When the churches were joined, the image was
covered with marble lining. The lettering calls him Jesus Navi and
indicates that he is addressing Michael the archangel.

At this point you may wish to visit the refectory to view the Byzantine
paintings housed there, or you can take a bus back to Athens to begin
your journey south on the next Trail.

The Sacrifice of Iphigenia. *Roman copy, in Pompeii, of a fifth-century BCE fresco by the Greek painter Timanthes, first century CE. (Museo Archeologico Nazionale, Naples, Lauros/Giraudon/Bridgeman Art Library)*

Trail 5:
The Homeric Trail

Men from Argos and Tiryns with its massive walls
And from Hermione and Asine that stand over the deep gulf
From Troezan and Eionae and vine-covered Epidauros
And men from Mycenae, the mighty walled citadel.

Homer, *The Iliad* Book 2

Mycenae, where I was raised.

From Euripides, *Iphigenia in Aulis*

This Trail goes south from Athens to the Peloponnese and starts at the site of ancient Corinth, famous in antiquity and in early Christian times, and then on to the Argolid, to Mycenae, Argos, and Epidauros. You should allow at least three days, although if you are travelling by car, the trip may take less time. The periods represented on this Trail are Helladic, Mycenaean, Geometric, Archaic, Classical, and Roman.

Homer's epics are set in Mycenaean times. Stories of the Trojan Wars, Perseus, and Herakles originated in the countryside around Mycenae and are full of dreadful events and chilling acts. There are many examples: Perseus, who slew the Gorgon and used its head against his enemies, also killed his own grandson; before Herakles went off to complete his twelve labors, he either lost his temper or went mad and killed his wife and all of their children; Agamemnon, chief commander of the Greek army and King of Argos—or perhaps Mycenae—appeased the gods by sacrificing his daughter Iphigenia before leaving for Troy.

This Trail takes travellers to the source of the epics. The undoubted highlight is the ancient site of Mycenae. In nearby Argos, the museum has an excellent and accessible collection. The town of Argos is on the edge of a plain that gives its name to the province known as the Argolid and the term Argive, much used in Homer.

Further along the coast is Nafplio, where the museum also has some fine exhibits. It is then a short bus trip to the world heritage site of ancient Epidauros.

Trains from Athens leave from the Peloponnisou station, which is close to the Larissis railway station and shown on the map of the area outside the Metro at Larissis. Buses leave from Terminal A in Athens. Both trains and buses run through to Corinth, Argos and Nafplio. Catch local buses from Argos to get to Mycenae and from Nafplio to reach Epidauros. If you can't manage the entire trail in one go, Corinth is about 50 miles (80 kilometers) southwest from Athens, and frequent trains and buses from Athens make a day trip to Corinth feasible.

Ancient Corinth

This Trail to Corinth goes to the ancient site and its accompanying museum. Corinth was a great trading and political center from Archaic through to Roman times. Homer described it as "Korinth, the luxurious." It owed its trading eminence to having ports both on the Aegean Sea and on the Gulf of Corinth, which gave access to the Adriatic. The impressive canal cut through the isthmus nowadays provides access from the Aegean to the Gulf. In the Greek period it was

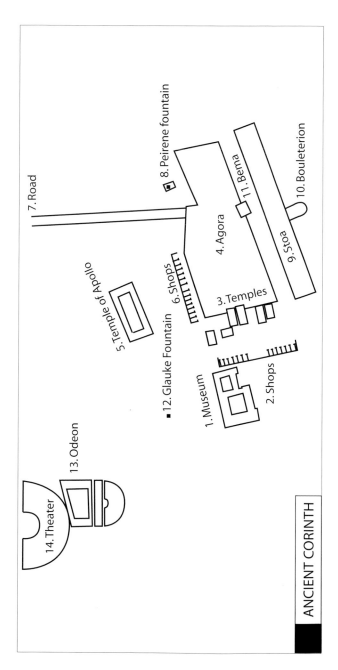

ANCIENT CORINTH

1. Museum
2. Shops
3. Temples
4. Agora
5. Temple of Apollo
6. Shops
7. Road
8. Peirene fountain
9. Stoa
10. Bouleterion
11. Bema
12. Glauke Fountain
13. Odeon
14. Theater

noted for its distinctive pottery. In Christian literature, it is strongly associated with the disciple Paul.

Location: 4 miles (7 kilometers) outside Korinthos (modern Corinth). A bus leaves for ancient Corinth from the bus station opposite the Corinth railway station.

Contact details: Tel. + 30–274 103 1207; www.culture.gr

Opening hours: Site and museum 8:00 am–7:00 pm in summer, 8:00 am–5:00 pm in winter.

Admission: To site and on-site museum is mid-range (Euro 5–8).

The Archeological Site

Visit the site to get the flavor of the place before going to the rather modest museum. The diagram shows the layout of the entire area. From the entrance, you pass the **museum (1)** on your left. A little further on, you reach the main excavation of Ancient Corinth. Immediately past the museum are the remains of a row of **shops (2)**, then a row of **Roman temples (3)**, and then the square or main **agora (4)**. To your left on the north is the **Temple of Apollo (5)**. The square of the agora was completed to the east by a basilica.

Start on the north side, at the temple.

Unknown architect
The Archaic Temple of Apollo, 550 BCE

Seven Doric columns survive from the Temple of Apollo (5), which is on the highest part of the site and presides over a wide, evocative view. On a sunny day, you will see the blue of the Gulf and the mountains of the mainland that stay capped with snow for much of the year. From where you stand, the Doric columns are outlined against the sky. The temple is of the Archaic period and the style of the columns allows the building to be dated to about 550 BCE. The columns each appear to have been carved from a single limestone block. They are stout but their twenty flutes lighten them. Tapered, they fan out into plain but gracefully proportioned capitals. There were six columns on the short sides and fifteen on the long sides. All that was visible before the excavations, which were initiated by Greek archeologists and continued during the 20th century by the American School of Classical Studies, were the seven columns and parts of the rampart walls.

Temple of Apollo at Corinth in the Doric order, from the sixth century BCE.
(Bridgeman Art Library.)

Below the temple is a series of openings, the remains of the northwest **shops (6)** of the Roman agora. The basic shape of the agora goes back at least to the 4th century, but there were continual additions and many of the remains are Roman. The shops and buildings would have been behind colonnades, some with Ionic columns and some with Corinthian columns.

Towards the eastern end of the north side is the old **road to the port of Lechaion (7)**, which would have been framed on the agora side by a monumental arch, and lined with buildings, public baths and lavatories, votive statues, and inscriptions. The limestone paving is original.

Look back to see the huge bulk of Acrocorinth, the hilltop and acropolis of Ancient Corinth. It was a citadel within the city ramparts but dramatically higher and intended for defensive purposes. Today, it is a very steep climb to the remains of medieval fortresses built by Byzantines, Franks, Turks, and Venetians with only slight evidence of ancient fortifications.

On the east side of the road, close to the agora, is the **Peirene Fountain (8)**, a spring enclosed in a two-story arcade under the patronage of Herod Atticus and modified during Byzantine times. In one story, Artemis accidentally killed Peirene's child and she wept until she was changed into the spring. In a quite different story, Sisyphus was given the spring in exchange for information about Zeus's abduction of a young woman.

Opposite, on the south side, were shops fronted by a **stoa (9)**, built in the 4th century using Doric and Ionic columns to make an arcade, behind which were rooms used as places to stay or places of entertainment. A vaulted building in the middle of the stoa was a **bouleuterion (10)** (meeting house) of the later Roman senate.

Below the stoa was a row of shops. In the middle of the row of shops, in front of the stoa, was the rostrum **bema (11)** where St Paul may have spoken. On most days, you see large groups following in the steps of Saint Paul. Paul wrote two of his influential epistles to the church in Corinth, where he lived for eighteen months spreading the new Christianity, especially among Gentiles (non-Jews). In Corinth, Paul worked with Jewish tent-makers and argued with Jews and Greeks, converting some and antagonizing others. His brush with the law is recounted in the Acts of the Apostles 18:12–16:

When Gallio was pro-consul of Achaia [the province of which Corinth was capital], the Jews made united attack upon Paul and brought him before the tribunal, saying "This man is persuading men to worship God contrary to the law." But, when Paul was about to open his mouth, Gallio said to the Jews "If it were a matter of wrong-doing or vicious crime, I should have reason to bear with you, oh Jews; but since it is a matter of questions about words and names and your own Law, see to it yourselves. I refuse to be a judge of these things." And he drove them from the Tribunal.

From here go to the museum.

The Museum

There are two rooms: the first to the right displays earlier works; the second to the left displays later works. This arrangement was greatly disrupted by a notorious theft in 1990 in which several hundreds of items were stolen and a guard wounded. The theft considerably depleted the collection in Room 1. When a little under half the stolen goods were recovered in April 1999, they were displayed in new cases in Room 2. This event highlights the value placed on smaller museum exhibits in the international art underworld.

The site is popular, so the museum is often crowded with large groups moving through rather briskly. Displayed in the vestibule is:

Unknown artists
Griffins attacking a horse, 460 BCE

This is a piece from a mosaic floor. The space is dominated by a griffin, its strong lion muscles outlined, a huge wing spread back over its body, and its cruelly shaped beak sinking into the horse's neck. Yet it seems to stand still. The horse is pulling back under attack, its knees buckling. The scene is a mixture of realism and decoration.

Room 1

Look at the first few shelves on the left of the room.

Unknown artist/s
Long spouted jugs, Early Helladic, First case on the left (unnumbered), c. 2500–2000 BCE

Jugs of this shape are sometimes called sauceboats, because they resemble modern objects of that name. The elegant spout and asymmetrical handle have been shaped by hand. The curve of the body to a comparatively narrow base lightens its appearance overall.

Between the first two cases, you will see:

Unknown artist/s
Mycenaean krater, Exhibit C48–164, 1200 BCE

Warrior figures, in helmets and wearing animal skins, are driving a chariot. The body of the horse is very elongated and the mouth, mane, and bridle are quaintly stylized. The warriors are driving towards geometric trees, and between two of them is a grotesquely elongated black warrior. The curve of the vase and the shapes created seem to invite the use of elongated figures. The coloration is black on white—the clay used in Corinth was off-white rather than the terracotta red that is characteristic of Athenian pottery. Here, the drawing is mainly dark lines on a clear background with dark banding above and below.

Unknown artist/s
Mycenaean goblet, Case 8, Exhibit CP 112, 1500–1180 BCE

It is instructive to identify the elements that make this piece so elegant. The outline shape takes the curve of the goblet swiftly down to its narrow base. The plain, vegetal design on the body follows the proportion and echoes the goblet shape, but the greater mass of the lighter-colored background defines the overall shape. The handles continue the outward curve of the body before bringing it up into the rim.

Nearby, in the top left of Case 9, is a tall-stemmed goblet of a somewhat later period (c. 1180–1060 BCE) of delicate shape, design and color. In the next case is:

Unknown artist/s
A large long-necked amphora, Case 10, Exhibit T2412, c. 800–750 BCE
A wine pitcher on a tripod, also in Case 10, c. 750–725 BCE

The large amphora is decorated with big birds and meanders. The decoration, which features water birds with plants around them, is concentrated on the shoulder. Vertical lines that could represent reeds separate the birds from each other. The neck is decorated with a simple meander and the body with concentric lines that can readily be produced as the pot spins on the wheel.

The wine pitcher on the tripod is copiously decorated, every surface filled with a different motif. The figurative motif is of a grazing animal with exaggeratedly long, thin legs so that when the animal's neck is bent to the ground, it too is long. Since a grazing animal must reach the ground, the image is following the logic of the long neck. However, painted in this way, a combination of factors pulls off a triumph of design, which makes the most of the pitcher's long neck. Although the neck of the pitcher and the drum of the tripod are about the same height, the narrowing and decoration make the graceful pitcher look taller than the base.

Unknown artists
Early Corinthian alabasters, Exhibits C40 259 and C40 266, Cases 13 and aryballos, c. 500s BCE

Pottery was important to the Corinthian economy. Between 725 and 550 BCE, Corinthian vases dominated the Mediterranean art market. Corinthian vases, e.g. Exhibits C40 259 and 266, are, in general, black figures on the whitish background of the local clay. Animals such as owls and roosters, as well as mythological animals such as sphinxes and griffins, are the favored motifs, with leaves, flowers, and trees in the spaces making an intricate overall pattern. A favored shape among Corinthian vases is the thick-handled aryballos (scent bottle). One here shows a dancer identified as Pyreias who jumps high in the air, arms aloft, to the music of a double-flute player. Many vases are imported—evidence that Corinth was an important center of trade.

Unknown artists
Miniature Altar, Case 24, 500s BCE

Opposite Case 13, on the left-hand side of Case 24, is a fragment of a miniature altar indicative of the painting style of the 500s BCE. One side shows a prancing lion, its mane represented in a saw-tooth pattern, its tongue dangling. The other side shows a man wielding a club and grasping the long neck of a bird, which is towering over him. The drawing of the red and black figures is very like the drawing on the vases. Figures are presented in silhouette, to which fine lines add detail.

Room 2

Room 2 now features material recovered from the 1990 robbery. Immediately inside the room, on the left as you enter, is a display of attractive Byzantine plates. One shows a boat in the central part of a round plate—an example of how simple line can capture the essence of a shape and, despite the limitations of the space, give a clear sense of movement and tension. Another has a princess sitting on someone's lap. Despite the abstraction in the drawing, the scene is human in a way that Byzantine church painting was not, suggesting that in the secular world, an artist could be freer.

Unknown artist/s
Early Corinthian wine pitcher, Exhibit 6 in the fifth case from the foyer, c. 600 BCE

The body of this vessel carries successive bands of decoration that establish its roundness as it curves up to the spout. At the base, geometric shapes and a broad, dark band support the line of lions, sphinxes, and bulls that move in a world of rosettes and dots. Above is a band of zigzag lines and another band of animals fitting into the shoulder of the jar and coming up to the darkly painted bands of neck, mouth, and handle. There is a sense of movement

THE HOMERIC TRAIL

in the work, which is very assured.

Unknown artist/s
Kylix with black- figure work, Exhibit T 2827, 2828 in the fifth case, c. 500 BCE

The underside of the bowl (kylix) shows a charioteer going full pelt and on either side in the same zone, a sphinx with thin bird's legs, the haunches of a lion, and an elegantly curved tail. The white-gowned charioteer is bent forward, his whip high over his head. A flurry of reins and the multiple legs of his two horses—one white, one black—express excitement and speed.

At the back of the room are interesting copies of marble statues, in particular, the copy of a head by Polykleitos and on the other side, some examples of Roman floor-mosaic work, which is by turn colorful, decorative, and vigorous, exemplifying the control that artists of the time had over this medium. Both in decorative borders and portraits, there is effective, controlled use of color to achieve a three-dimensional effect.

After you have visited the museum, behind it you can find the Glauke Fountain (12). The Glauke Fountain is named in honor of Glauke, wife of Jason the Argonaut. The story is that Medea gave Glauke a gift of a chiton that she had poisoned and the bride tried to soothe her burning wounds in the cool of the fountain.

Further on are the Odeon (13) and the Theater (14). The Odeon was used for concerts over 200–300 years, and the Theater dates from 500 BCE. In Roman times it was renovated for gladiatorial contests.

Mycenae

Location: From Athens or Corinth, train or long-distance buses go to Argos; from there it is a local bus trip. Buses from Athens stop only at Fichti where another bus goes to the modern village of Mykines and a mile or so (3k) beyond, to the site of ancient Mycenae. By car take the National Highway E65 and turn at the village of Fichti.

Contact details: Tel. +30 275 107 6585; www.culture.gr

Opening hours: Summer 8:00 am–7:00 pm; winter 8:30 am–3:00 pm. Open every day.

Admission: Mid range (Euro 5–8).

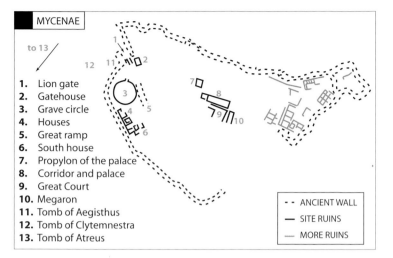

MYCENAE

to 13

1. Lion gate
2. Gatehouse
3. Grave circle
4. Houses
5. Great ramp
6. South house
7. Propylon of the palace
8. Corridor and palace
9. Great Court
10. Megaron
11. Tomb of Aegisthus
12. Tomb of Clytemnestra
13. Tomb of Atreus

- - ANCIENT WALL
— SITE RUINS
— MORE RUINS

THE HOMERIC TRAIL

Other information: The Treasury, or Tomb, of Atreus is about quarter of a mile (400 meters) from the entrance to the main site along the road to the village. You may wish to walk there and come back by bus.

In the 19th century, the eccentric Heinrich Schliemann used Homer's text to find the sites of Mycenae and Troy. At Mycenae, he made astonishing finds of gold and precious artifacts in graves and did not hesitate to identify objects with legendary figures. Stunning pieces taken from this site are in the National Archeological Museum in Athens. Others were sold or bequeathed by Lord Elgin and others and are overseas.

That such prizes survived in the earth for over three millennia challenges our notion of history. Perhaps there was a fairly rapid collapse and decline in population that allowed the ancient citadel to be covered by soil and growth and remain undisturbed. Or, the area may have been revered and therefore protected until eventually its purpose was forgotten and what could be seen no longer invited exploration.

The diagram shows the layout of the site. From the entrance to the site, you are quickly in sight of the **Lion Gate (1)** and climb to a fortified citadel at the top of the hill, which contains the remains of tombs, palaces, walls and ancient roads.

Unknown sculptor/s
The Lion Gateway, c. 1250 BCE

Looking at it now, it is hard to imagine that the Lion Gate remained buried up to the lintel until Schliemann's time. It is a fitting place for the giant heroes and cataclysmic deeds of the great epics. There is not a single other place in Greece that carries such an air of raw power and invulnerability.

The story is that Perseus, son of Zeus, came here to establish a new city. He commissioned the Cyclops—legendary giants—to be his builders. As you see, the walls are huge blocks, hewn to fit together without mortar, in a style now known as Cyclopean building. The stone was dragged into place, fitted and worked on as the wall was built. The blocks around the entrance ways, both here and at the tholos tombs further on, are smoothed and fit together without the smaller stones inserted along other parts of the wall.

The gateway, made of four solid blocks, is not quite square—a little over 10 feet (3 meters) high, not quite 10 feet (3 meters) wide and tapering very slightly on the sides. The lintel and the threshold each weigh over 20 tons. An arch of greenish limestone blocks in

The Lion Gateway, the entrance to ancient Mycenae, 15th century BCE.

the form of a triangle above the lintel transmits the weight of the wall. Within the triangle are the famous lions that give the gate its name. (Some scholars now think the figures are griffins). In this part of the world, a lion has often been a symbol of strength and authority. This symmetrical pair was made to guard the world within the walls. (Griffins were also guards.) They have both lost their heads but they probably faced outwards and kept an eye on all who approached. They stand on either side of a dais supporting a central column that symbolizes the palace they protect. Their posture—common now in heraldry—allows the relief carving to show the ribs and the curl of belly and thigh, which is further emphasized by shadow. Taking in the whole, the silent strength of the gateway and enclosing walls invite images of mighty battle and conquest, like those of *The Iliad.*

The double gates opened inwards. The outer edges of the jambs and lintel protrude; thus the opened gate was prevented from swinging out. The holes on the inner side of the door, jambs, and lintel are from Mycenaean times and housed the workings of the gate. The round holes on the lintel and the threshold, beside the jambs, held the hinges. On each jamb and just inside the entrance is a square hole into which the bar was slotted to secure the gate from inside. Near the inside edge of the jambs are small recesses for handles, thus allowing the gate to swing right in when the bar was taken down. Other markings on the thresholds may be from later periods.

Immediately through the entrance on the left is a small, low-ceilinged **room (2)** once thought to be a guardroom, but comparison with other sites now suggests it was a sanctuary. The ramp that continues through the gate goes up to the palace.

On the right, you soon come to **Grave Circle A (3)**. Schliemann's most spectacular excavation was of five of the six royal shaft graves here. The Grave Circle dates from 1350 BCE and when first in use, was outside the first ring of walls. The second ring, dating from 1250 BCE and containing the Lion Gate, enclosed this Grave Circle. Buildings within the citadel later covered them—one reason why they remained untouched by looters until Schliemann turned up. Fortunately, he passed on the spectacular finds to the state and they are in the National Archeological Museum collection. He made extravagant claims for the finds. Having first trusted in Homer to find the site, he drew on Homer's characters to identify specific objects, such as the gold *Mask of*

THE HOMERIC TRAIL

Agamemnon (in the National Archeological Museum) and the Tomb of Clytemnestra (just outside the walls).

Six graves were in the circle, which has been excavated and is fully visible. They were rectangular rooms, about 10 feet (3 meters) by 12 feet (3.5 meters) and used to bury royal families. The walls were of rubble, and the roof was made of slabs or branches covered in clay. The site of each tomb was marked with a stele. (An example in the National Museum is decorated with a horse-drawn chariot and spirals.) There are signs that a banquet was held over the grave at the time of the burial. Within was a lavish pile of funeral objects. The dead were buried fully clothed and much ornamented. Some had gold death masks over their faces (also an Egyptian practice.) Overall, there was an estimated 34 pounds (15 kilograms) of goldwork found in these graves.

Below the grave circle are a number of **houses (4)**. The famous Warrior Krater and frescoes now in the National Archeological Museum were found nearby. **The Great Ramp (5)**, of original Cyclopean masonry, provided pedestrian access to the higher levels. From the top of the ramp, to the south, you look down on the remains of a row of **houses and temples (6)**, also the source of Mycenaean frescoes. Follow the path towards the site of the palace. The original Mycenaean buildings were destroyed by fire and later built over with Archaic and Hellenistic temples. Take the path up to the **propylon or entrance to the palace (7)** and continue towards the right, up into the north **corridor of the palace (8)**. On your right, you enter the almost square **Great Court (9)**, which overlooks a wonderful southern view of the Argive plain. Left, to the east of the courtyard, are the main rooms of the palace called the **Megaron (10)**, including a porch and a vestibule that lead into a main chamber. At floor level are outlines of the walls of the porch and vestibule. The main room—a public room like a reception room rather than a living area, and about 40 foot (12 meters) square—had a hearth in the middle. You can see the footings of four pillars. In the northeast corner, you can climb a short distance to a little room where Agamemnon was allegedly murdered by his wife's lover. Whether or not the story is true, there is no evidence to identify this as a murder site.

Similarly baseless speculation has led to the naming of several remarkable tombs—The **Tomb of Aegisthus (11)**, of **Clytemnestra (12)**, and **Atreus (13)**—which you can visit now if you go back out to the Lion Gate, down the ramp and to your left.

Unknown architects and builders
Tholos tomb known as *The Tomb of Aegisthus* (11), c. 1500 BCE
and nearby,
the *Tomb of Clytemnestra* (12), c. 1220 BCE

The Tholos (circular) tombs, which come from a period following that of the Circle Graves, were for royal use. Non-royals had chamber tombs. This tomb was therefore built to hold a royal corpse, which is some small justification for using the name of Aegisthus who appears in stories as Clytemnestra's lover. However, if this had actually been his tomb, he was buried nearly 200 years before the Tomb of Clytemnestra was built, so at least one of the names is wrong. The 27-yard (22-meter) entrance is lined with a substantial rock wall. It ends at a tall doorway whose corbelled arch makes a triangular shape above. Inside the now empty space are the elegantly curved walls of a chamber 16 yards (13 meters) in diameter.

Further along is the so-called tomb of Clytemnestra, which is larger, better preserved, and later than the tholos tombs. There was originally a sculpted façade on both the existing doorway and the triangular arch above. Inside, impressive unmortared stonewalls climb up to a height measuring much the same as the chamber's diameter. The beehive-shaped interior, with the outdoor light streaming in through the doorway, is impressive. Walk around the perimeter to appreciate the height of the building and its strength.

Next to the Tomb of Clytemnestra is Grave Circle B, which contained both royal shaft graves and graves for others. These graves did not have as many precious objects as Grave Circle A, but were nevertheless substantial and had remained undisturbed until modern times.

Outside the main enclosure and about a quarter of a mile (400 meters) down the road towards Fichthia is the largest of the tholos tombs, known sometimes as the Treasury of Atreus (based on a remark by Pausanias) and sometimes as the Tomb of Agamemnon.

The Treasury of Atreus (13) c. 1250 BCE

A large section of the hill was taken out to create a space for this great monument, which comes from the same period as the Lion Gate. Slightly bigger again than the so-called Tomb of Clytemnestra, it has a large chamber to the side. The tomb was raided in ancient times so we can gain no more detailed understanding of the building, although the given name suggests that great riches were found. Even though there are not enough for reliable reconstruction, fragments of the entrance provide a few clues as to how the façade was sculpted and decorated. The green marble half column in the Athens Archeological Museum suggests that the façade was visually rich. Inside, courses of conglomerate stone accurately fitted together, speak volumes for the skill of the workmen and the exacting standards of those responsible for the design and execution of the building.

There are a number of similar tombs nearby but they are not so accessible or well built as the three indicated here.

You can now return to Argos by local bus.

Argos Archeological Museum

Of the three museums that can be visited on this Trail—Argos, Nafplio and Epidauros—Argos is the most rewarding. Although all three are near the major Mycenaean sites of Mycenae and Tiryns, their Mycenaean collections are limited because of the concentration of Mycenaean works in Athens. The Argos has lovely material from Neolithic through to Roman times. The collection is concentrated in three rooms and under a portico in the garden.

> **Location:** Argos is in the Peleponnese between Corinth and Nafplio. It is also the closest town to Mycenae. The museum is in Olga Street on the central square.
> **Contact details:** Tel. +30 275 106 8819; www.culture.gr
> **Opening hours:** 8:30 am–3:00 pm, closed on Mondays.
> **Admission:** The price is in the low range (Euro 1–4).

The first room is upstairs to the right of the foyer. It has an absorbing and imposing collection of Mycenaean and Geometric works. Displays are arranged chronologically, beginning with the cases on the left of the entrance. Two of the three prime Geometric pieces are displayed in the middle of the room and one in the right-hand corner immediately after the entrance.

Mycenaean, Geometric and Archaic Works

Unknown artist/s
Various Geometric vases, c. 800–700 BCE

Taken together, these vases provide an encyclopedic range of the motifs used in the Geometric period. The period holds a particular fascination for the modern eye accustomed to abstraction and symbolism. The colors are usually red, brown, and black on a clay-colored surface covered with decoration. The most prominent part of a vase, usually the shoulder, most often carries recognizable figures. The treatment of figures involves a great deal of elongation and simplification. The female waist is exceptionally pinched. Males and horses are nearly stick figures but have prominent muscles. Women are shown with their hands upraised or joined. Some are thought to be dancers, which could be an extrapolation from present times when dancers are sometimes in similar poses. They may be wailing and grieving. Common natural elements include horses, fish, and birds, flowers, leaves, and snakes. The horses may be led by men, fighting each other or grouped heraldically. The men are often recognizable as warriors, and there is a pair of wrestlers who look more like stick insects than human beings. Water birds and game birds are sometimes sketched in naturalistic silhouette, sometimes distorted to make repetitive patterns. The range of geometric patterns is wide: meanders, parallel lines, waved lines, circles, dots, chevrons, swastikas, wheels (presumably meant to represent suns), spirals, and patterns derived from natural objects such as birds and leaves. The surface may be broken into areas independent of each other but because the overall style is maintained, the use of juxtaposition, overlapping, and apparent discontinuity does not fragment the total pattern.

What is most striking is how much lively detail is contained within this lavishly decorative framework.

Middle Helladic and Mycenaean Finds

Art from the Middle Helladic (2000–1600 BCE) and Mycenaean period (1600–1100 BCE) are in cases on both sides of the room, finishing near the back with a Mycenaean suit of armor and a case of weapons.

The Middle Helladic, belly-shaped pieces are in characteristic grey and brown. Nearby sites, such as Lerna, are notable for the finds of Minyan pottery, the first wheel-made pottery. Schliemann named

THE HOMERIC TRAIL

this pottery after Minyas, a legendary king descended from Poseidon and ruler of central Greece. The pottery is the most characteristic artwork of the Middle Helladic period, which has not been particularly rich in art finds. The vases are monochrome (first gray and later yellow) and the surface is smooth and shiny. In contrast, the hand-made works of the same period have a matt finish and are decorated with very simple lines. The hand-made pottery of this period ranges from long-spouted jugs to very big storage jars or pithoi like the four just inside the entrance to the room.

There is more work from this period in the Lerna collection in Room 3 downstairs.

Past these first cases are cases holding objects from the Mycenaean period, including some interesting and evocative human and animal figures from graves at sites close by Argos.

Unknown artists
Finds from Mycenaean sites near Argos, c. 1550–1100 BCE

Many of these objects come from tombs and cemeteries in and around Argos. There is no compelling evidence that Mycenaeans had a cult of the dead so we can look to simpler explanations for the preservation of these objects. They were of durable material, such as metal and baked clay, and they were buried and hence more protected than objects on the surface. The figures are small but appealing, especially the animals which are often caught in an alert pose, noses up, sniffing the air. The female figures belong to common types. One is of a mother nursing a child, known as a *kourotrophos*, phi type—a Madonna and Child of its time. Possibly it marked the spot where a mother and child were buried. The head has painted features and a long nose which the potter probably made with a pinch. The eloquent red flowing lines on the body emphasize the cradling of the child in its mother's arms, the swelling of her breasts, and her stance. The whole expresses a special unity between mother and child.

Among the female figures, another common type represented here is known as the psi type, which features upraised arms and a mantle covering the body to the waist. In comparison with the *kourotrophos*, the red lines emphasize her height and the openness of her stance. The head is modeled in the usual manner with a long, thin face, and she wears a strongly shaped headdress or crown. The psi type may represent goddesses or priestly figures. While these human figures follow apparently prescribed conventions, the animal figures seem to be freely conceived and even playful.

Beyond the fourth case, which contains vases of the very early Geometric period (c. 1100–900 BCE and often called the Dark Ages), is some bronze armor from a later time. This was undoubtedly made for an early Argive warrior, well before the time of the *Iliad*. The anatomy of the small torso is outlined in the Archaic style: the helmet comes well down over the forehead and sidepieces protect the cheeks, but the face and the back of the neck are exposed. The crest on the top of the helmet is shaped like a horseshoe. It is plainer but still similar to that often worn by Athene.

In the following case, there is a fragment of late Geometric pottery.

Unknown potter/s and painter/s
Fragment with panels of dancing women, birds and geometric decoration, c. 800 –700 BCE

This assured work features successive bands of geometric patterns that leave no space undecorated and move upwards to the broadest part of the vessel. Here, panels separated by vertical lines feature repetitive figures. The stately women, who may be dancing, are in an upright stance, with ax-head-shaped bodies, shapely waists, and bell-shaped skirts, and the sashes or ribbons that trail to the ground over their hips suggest special or ceremonial costuming. Each holds a branch aloft. Between them are V-shapes that may represent background trees or shrubbery. Above and below are lines of water birds, their legs trailing strangely before them (perhaps as seen refracted in water), their necks uniformly bent.

Past these cases is a model of Ancient Argos showing the theater built into the side of a hill above the old city with its stoas, shops and temples. Some of the remains lie under modern Argos and have not been excavated.

Set into the end wall are four cases, essentially of Archaic period pottery. A gem among them is in the middle of the second case from the left.

Unknown potter/s and painter/s
Polyphemus blinded by Odysseus and a companion, c. 700–600 BCE

The fragment is of a simple narrative, depicting the essential action rather than any preamble or consequence. The composition is cleverly based on a triangle. Polyphemus the giant, and obviously the most powerful creature, is lying on the longest side of the triangle formed by the stylized rocks of his cave. Odysseus and a companion are smaller figures on the shortest side of the triangle, holding a pole, which forms the upper line of the composition. They are in the act of thrusting the pole into Polyphemus's one eye. He is being undone by the cunning of the mortals who have contrived to intoxicate him and devised a weapon large enough to put out his only eye. Their well-founded fear of him is shown in the distance they keep from him.

The Lerna Collection

The door at the end of the Mycenaean room leads to a downstairs room in an old mansion with a display of early material, mainly pottery from Lerna. Lerna, some 6 miles (10 kilometers) south of Argos and on the coast, was inhabited in Neolithic times and flourished as a center from about 2500–2200 BCE. It had several large buildings within defensive walls. The best known of the big buildings was a large two-story building now christened the House of Tiles because of its terracotta tile roof. One of the tiles is in the case at the end of the room. When the building was destroyed by fire about 2000 BCE, roofing tiles disappeared from building for 1500 years. The site continued to be inhabited into the Middle Helladic period (2000–1600 BCE) but not into Mycenaean times, so the objects in this room come from the period of transition from the Stone Age to the Bronze Age and consist mainly of pottery typical of the period, including some gray Minyan pottery – a name given by Schliemann to the first wheel-made pottery.

Of special interest is a small headless statuette displayed in a case on its own on the left of the room

Unknown sculptor
Neolithic statuette of a female, c. 3000 BCE

Most archeologists speculate that figures such as this are idols—not representations of real people but figures of gods or figures with some ritualistic significance. What is really interesting about this statue is that it is fairly naturalistic compared with work of the Mycenaean period. The sculptor had an eye for beauty. There is a strong but graceful flow down to the hip. The breasts are well formed, the thighs rounded and strong, the buttocks firm and prominent, the hands clasped in front of the body in an apparently ritualistic pose. The contrast between this naturalism and later, more abstracted work illustrates that style and convention rather than levels of skill dictate how artists work. One period will value some degree of naturalism, whereas another—perhaps later, perhaps earlier—will insist on various degrees of abstraction.

The room upstairs contains sculpture, mostly copies, of the Roman period and a floor mosaic of decorative patterns. Outside, in the garden under a portico, are some fascinating Late Roman floor mosaics.

Unknown artists
Mosaic floors from a house site, c. 500 CE

Mosaics on secular themes are an especially charming aspect of Roman art and perhaps indicate the subject matter of the prolific but now largely vanished painting of Roman times in domestic and public buildings. The mosaics displayed here are from a much later time than the works in the museum. They include a calendar of the year's economic activity, scenes of hunting, and Dionysian revelry. Their size and the subject matter suggest a wealthy rural holding.

The months, as was common during the Middle Ages, are personified and associated with largely rural activities. Mostly the men are in a similar posture in which their weight is carried on one leg and the other bent ready to step forward. They have Latin names written in the Greek alphabet (in which, for example P sounds as R, C sounds as S, H sounds as I).

The symbols are still clearly recognizable. March takes its name from Mars, the god of war. An armored soldier stands near the cooking pot, a symbol of hearth and home, holding a weapon in his right hand and indicating a dove, often a symbol of peace, with his left hand. April, the month most associated with spring and new birth, is the good shepherd, a figure of virtue in earlier times and taken up in the Christian tradition. May is harvesting fruits and nuts. June is harvesting grain. The hunting scenes pay particular attention to the lively activity of the dogs, which leap about, eager for activity. The huntsman's crouch suggests the sort of stealth adopted during the hunt, even when there is no one watching.

A typical scene of Dionysian revelry is appropriately even more animated. Dionysos's extraordinarily long right arm reaches out towards the female dancer. Both her tunics and skirt swirl about and she is caught at a moment in the dance when she has both feet off the floor.

The Trail goes next to Epidauros, but to get there you first travel to the major town of Nafplio, so, if you have time, stop there and visit the museum to see more Mycenaean finds). You may also wish to visit Tiryns, which is nearby. (See *Elsewhere in the Argolid* at the end of this Trail.)

Epidauros

Location: 19 miles (30 kilometers) from Nafplio by local bus or car. The bus takes you to the ancient site.

Contact details: Tel. museum+ 30–275 302 2009; www.culture.gr

Opening hours: 8:00 am–7:00 pm daily (5:00 pm in winter).

Admission: Mid-range (Euro 5–8).

Epidauros is associated with *Asklepios*, the god of healing, who was particularly popular in late Classical times when there was an *asklepion* (place of healing) on the Athenian Acropolis. He was recognized as the son of Apollo and Coronis. Abandoned by his mother, he was suckled by a goat and protected by a dog, animals that sometimes appear in representations of him. He learned medicine from the centaur Chiron. After his death at the hands of Zeus, Asklepios changed into a constellation. He is associated with the underworld and with serpents.

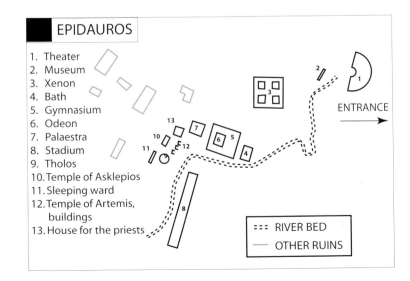

EPIDAUROS

1. Theater
2. Museum
3. Xenon
4. Bath
5. Gymnasium
6. Odeon
7. Palaestra
8. Stadium
9. Tholos
10. Temple of Asklepios
11. Sleeping ward
12. Temple of Artemis, buildings
13. House for the priests

ENTRANCE

::: RIVER BED
— OTHER RUINS

The theater at Epidauros, attributed to Polykleitos the Younger 370–330 BCE.
(Bridgeman Art Library)

THE HOMERIC TRAIL

Asklepios and Medicine

The symbol of Asklepios, snakes curled around a staff, is still used today by pharmacists. Two of his daughters were Panacea, meaning cure all, and Hygeia, meaning health. Hippocrates is said to have been one of his descendants. The preamble to the Hippocratic Oath invokes Apollo, Asklepios, Hygeia, and Panacea thus:

"I swear by Apollo the Physician and Asklepios and Hygeia and Panakeia calling all gods and goddesses to witness, that I will keep this oath and this bond to the best of my power and judgement ... "

(A. R. Burn, *The Pelican History of Greece*, Penguin Books, p 272.)

The site of ancient Epidauros is justly renowned for its wonderful theater, which is hardly a ruin since it is still used for its original purpose. The site is also fascinating as the ruins of the ancient sanctuary of Asklepios. Epidauros is also famed as the place where Greeks declared their independence from the Ottomans on 13 January 1822. The diagram shows the layout of the entire site. First, you come to the **theater (1)**.

Attributed to Polykleitis the Younger
The theater at Epidauros, probably 370–330 BCE

The path from the present entrance leads first to the theater. You pass along a tree-lined path that suddenly opens into an extraordinary space, impressively large but contained within the most simple and elegant geometry. Epidauros is the best surviving example of a Greek theater, but above all it is an overwhelming piece of architecture, memorable for the way it embodies the ancient aesthetic virtues of clarity, simplicity and harmony. The diagram shows the layout of the original.

You enter the theater at ground level between a restored doorway and the footings of the skene (or stage building from which actors entered and exited) and proskenion (the front of the stage). Immediately beyond is the circular orchestra and rising above is the theatron, (viewing area) tiers of seating that have made the slope of the hillside into a regular, inverted cone. Spectators entering in ancient times would have had this view

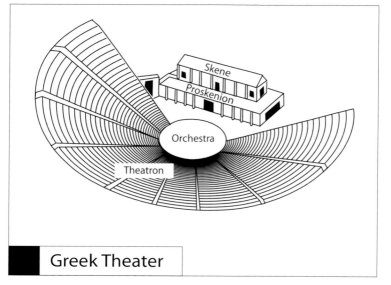

Greek Theater

blocked by the skene until they got inside. The circular effect would have been even more breathtaking.

Greek architects, like philosophers and many thinkers after them, saw mathematics, and especially geometry, not merely as an instrument but also as a way of glimpsing the divine order of the universe. The circle represented the perfection of the supernatural world and carried some of its power. The shape of the seating bound spectators to the circle, and within the circle, players would act out and reflect on the ways in which mortals interacted with their gods and their own destinies. The pure geometry of the building demonstrated the human capacity to reach out to and comprehend the divine.

The intellectual life of Classical Greece is perhaps best known by the works of the tragic dramatists of the 5th century, Aeschylus, Sophocles, and Euripides, as well as the 4th-century philosophers, Plato and Aristotle. However, architects, sculptors, and painters were also highly respected and influential citizens and integral to the intellectual life of those extraordinary times. They drew their subject matter from the same body of myth and narrative, but more importantly, they explored and brought to dramatic life the universal preoccupations of the ancient Greek world.

Like the statuary of both Archaic and Classical styles, drama was enacted by characters who were both individuals and representatives of ideal types. The figure was human but the face was masked, just as a statue was recognizably human but not an individual portrait. Classical sculpture possibly owes its sense of the dramatic moment in a narrative to the influence of theater. More generally, art and drama share a dread that humans must struggle against irrational and violent forces and, consequently, express a longing for harmony and rational order.

Early in the 5th century, playwrights would direct, choreograph, and perhaps perform their own works. Much of the dialogue was given to a chorus of about twelve who recited on the orchestra, where the leader occupied the place of the former altar. A poet named Thespis had introduced the idea of having an actor (called a hypocrit). Aeschylus used two actors and Sophocles brought in a third. The three, all men, played all characters, using masks to change their persona, and high heels and vertical stripes to look taller.

Beyond its splendor, the importance of Epidauros is the precise view it gives of the shape of Greek theaters compared with its famous but more altered counterparts in Athens and Delphi. The centerpiece is a dancing area or orchestra. At Epidauros, the skene has not encroached on the orchestra, as it often has elsewhere. The orchestra is a circle at ground level, a little over 22 yards (20 meters) in diameter and marked at the center where the altar of Dionysos (the thymele) would have been. The thymele is a reminder of the primacy of the Theater of Dionysos on the slopes of the Athenian Acropolis. Greek theater developed out of rites associated with Dionysos, including musical performances and sacrifices. In Athens, these performances evolved into the tragic drama of Aeschylus, Sophocles and Euripides and the comedies of Aristophanes. Frequently, an indoor Odeon was built nearby for recitals of poetry and music. It is unknown how much of the vast Athenian repertoire, now mostly lost, might have been performed in Epidauros.

Despite the size of the theatron, the slope looks comfortably graded. Halfway up is a walkway that underlines the circular geometry of the whole and marks the limit of Greek building of the 4th century. The rows above are a little steeper, which helps to contain the space even more elegantly. The front seats were for dignitaries. The lower 34 rows held about 6,000 spectators. The extra 21 rows added in Roman times doubled the seating capacity.

On the outer edge of the orchestra are the remains of the skene. At each end, the frame of a doorway, called a parodos, has been restored, but only some foundations remain from the skene and proskenion. In the beginning all the action took place on the orchestra and the skene provided back rooms and support for painted sets. Late in his career, Aeschylus moved the actors into the proscenium, leaving the orchestra to the chorus. Millennia later, European theater put all the action behind the arch of the proscenium with the orchestra, if required at all, out of sight below the stage.

The skene was deep enough to carry revolving sets. It had a flat roof, reserved for placing the gods, and cranes and other machinery to make them move about (hence the phrase *deus ex machina,* used in modern theater to mean an arbitrary intervention to resolve the plot).

One of the spectacular attributes of Epidauros is its acoustics. When the theater is empty, someone standing in the middle of the orchestra tearing a piece of paper can be heard clearly and without distortion all over the theater up to the top row. Presumably, the acoustics hold true for a full house.

From the theater, the path descends to the **museum (2)**, which can be left until last. From there, signs point you towards the ancient site. As with many Greek sanctuaries, the key points of this site are the theater, the games area and the temple area. As you enter the site—a flat area beyond the museum and over a dry riverbed—the first buildings you come to are mostly concerned with the sporting elements of the cult. In most cases, only foundations of buildings remain.

The very first **(3) the Xenon**, was a 4th-century hostel for pilgrims. The foundations indicate that the rooms were built around four internal courtyards. According to researchers, it was a double-story brick building with 160 rooms. Opposite its west side is a small **building (4)** thought to have been baths (it contained tubs and basins) serving both the pilgrims' hostel and the adjacent **gymnasium (5)**. A large stone and mud-brick building with colonnades, courtyards, and rooms, the gymnasium was a place for young men to train their bodies and cultivate their minds. The word gymnasium means a place to exercise naked, which is how athletes both trained and competed. Games had a role in the religious ceremonies of the sanctuary—the site of the most famous games, Olympia, was above all a sanctuary to the top god Zeus. At Epidauros, where people came to be cured, taking part in theater or sport was sometimes prescribed. The games complexes include stadium, gymnasium, baths, and quarters for athletes. Within this area was a Roman **odeon (6)**. This was a semicircular auditorium used for music and poetry: the outline of its seating can still be seen.

Next to the gymnasium is a smaller building **(7)** from Roman times, thought to have been a **palaestra or wrestling school**. The **stadium (8)**, an essential part of this complex, is outside the fence on the other side of the modern road leading to the entrance.

The next set of ruins, directly ahead as you pass the sports buildings, make up the sanctuary of Asklepios. The most prominent building today is the circular **tholos (circular domed building) (9)** which is being reconstructed.

Attributed to Polykleitos the Younger
Tholos, 360–330 BCE

The function of the building is unknown but it is taken for granted from its style and position that it had a sacred role. The outer circle of the tholos consisted of a colonnade of 26 Doric columns. The remains of the basement, comprising three concentric circles, show an outer colonnade about 72 feet (22 meters) in diameter. The white marble walls, resting on the second circle, were penetrated by a sculpted doorway facing east and reconstructed in the museum. Inside, the walls were decorated by the painter Pausias (Among the pictures, says Pausanias, was one of Eros and one of Methe, in which you could see a "glass cup and the woman's face showing through it.") The innermost circle supported a colonnade of fourteen Corinthian columns (see below). Within was a trapdoor giving access to the basement. The concentric circles of the basement are broken in the manner of a simple maze to allow for circulation. Archeologists speculate that these underground passages were built to house Asklepios's snakes.

To the right of the tholos, set a little further back, is the **Temple of Asklepios (10)** and behind both is a long narrow building **(11)**—an **abaton (sleeping ward)**. The temple of Asklepios stood in a sacred grove of olive trees, to which men were not allowed to go to die nor women to give birth.

Theodotos and others
Temple of Asklepios, 490 BCE

Very little is left of this temple. There are a few fragments and some copies of sculpture in the museum and some more substantial pieces in the National Archeological Museum in Athens. The architect Theodotos worked on it for five years for an annual fee of 350 drachmas. The remains indicate that he used the Doric order for six columns at each end and eleven on each side. A local sculptor, Timotheos the Epidauran, sculpted the pediments following the common themes of battles with the Amazons and the Centaurs. The statue of Asklepios was a gold and ivory (*chryselephantine*) construction by Thrasymedes of Paros. As usual the statue of the god was hidden inside the temple, in the inner room, or cella, and as was customary for statues of gods of healing it was sunk about two feet (0.60 meters) below floor level. Setting the statues in a sunken cavity may have symbolized Asklepios' association with the underworld.

Within the grove and to the right of the temple of Asklepios was a **Temple to Artemis (12)** and a **house for priests (13)** that stood on the site of an earlier temple and altar to Apollo, father and patron of Asklepios. The temple area was heavily furnished with votive statuary and treasuries from grateful pilgrims and communities.

The practice for pilgrims to the sanctuary was to make sacrifices and offerings to Apollo, Asklepios, and probably Hygeia, and to undergo a ritual of purification. They then spent the night in the abaton, or dormitory, lying on the skins of sacrificed animals. These rituals alone might suffice to cure them. Failing that, Asklepios might appear in their dreams from which the priests of the temple could interpret cures. The cures ranged from taking baths to doing physical or mental exercises in the sporting, musical or dramatic facilities. Many might pass muster today as alternative therapies. That they worked for many ancients is attested by the offerings, often in the shape of the cured body part, left at the sanctuary much as votive offerings at shrines are still left at Christian healing sites.

Return to the museum, which you will pass on your way out. While there, you may care to view the fine column described here. Elsewhere in the small museum are inscriptions (first room) and plaster copies of statues (second room). The inscriptions describe therapies and aspects of the building of the temple and the tholos. Plaster casts include an offering from someone cured of an ear complaint.

Traditionally attributed to Kallimachos
The Corinthian column, Copy of a 4th century BCE work

Vitruvius attributes the Corinthian column to the Athenian architect Kallimachos. Vitruvius' story is that Kallimachos saw acanthus growing among the momentos left on a young Corinthian woman's grave and based his innovative design on this natural arrangement. The acanthus bush, which has been greatly stylized to make the design, has a broad, dark-green, serrated leaf and a bell-shaped flower. This very fine example of such a column is said to be a copy of an original by Polykleitos the Younger, who, if he was indeed the architect, used the Corinthian order in building the colonnade of the tholos. There are a few remains of the original tholos nearby.

Elsewhere in the Argolid

If you have more time in the Argolid, the city of Nafplio and its museum, and the site of ancient Tiryns are the pick but the area teems with ancient sites such as Asine and Lerna (see Argos museum).

Nafplio, with its Venetian center and coastal setting, is often said to be the most attractive city in Greece. Two rooms in a Venetian palace house its museum collection of Helladic and Mycenaean finds from the area (in the lower room) and material from the Geometric to the Classical periods in the upper room. The Mycenaean finds include some fragments of fresco from Tiryns.

A few miles along the highway from Nafplio to Argos are the ruins of the great center of Tiryns. Like Mycenae it is a citadel with Cyclopean walls but built on a low rise in the middle of a plain. The thick walled Cyclopean tunnels are of interest but the finds from the site are to be found in the National Archeological Museum in Athens and the Archeological Museum in Nafplio.

TRAIL 6:
Olympia

Delphi

H. Loukas

Thebes

Athens

Corinth

Mycenae

Argos

Olympia

Nafplio

Epidauros

PELOPONNESE

The fame of the Olympiads in the Games of Pelops
Overlooks the wide earth.
There a man's strong prime endures its toils,
And the victor all his remaining days
Breathes a delicious and serene air
When he remembers the Games.

Pindar, "Olympian I" from *The Odes* translated by
C.M. Bowra, Penguin Classics

OLYMPIA

Many are the sights to be seen in Greece, and many are the wonders to be heard; but on nothing does Heaven bestow more care than on the Eleusinian rites and the Olympic games.

From Pausanias, *Description of Greece*.

Introduction

Olympia, in the western Peloponnese, is an important site, home not only to the ancient Olympic Games but also to one of the seven wonders of the ancient world, Phidias's statue of Zeus. The site today consists of the ruins of the sanctuary to Zeus and a notable museum, with material from prehistoric to Roman times. It is listed as a world heritage site.

It can be reached by road, bus or a combination of train and bus from Athens. Allow two to three days for the Trail, depending on how you travel.

Periods represented on this Trail are Helladic, Mycenaean, Geometric, Archaic, and Classical.

Location: Trains from Athens leave from the Peloponnisou station, which is close to the Larissis railway station and shown on the map of the area outside the Metro at Larissis. Buses leave from Terminal A in Athens. They go to the modern village of Olympia, which has plenty of accommodation faciliaties. The ancient site is signposted from the modern village of Olympia.

Contact details: Tel. +30 262 402 2517; museum: 402 2529; www.culture.gr

Opening hours: Site 8:00 am–7:00 pm daily; museum: 8:00 am–7:00 pm Tues. to Sun.; noon–7:00 pm Mon.

Admission: Site and museum in the high range (Euro 9–12).

Wonders of the Ancient World

The seven wonders, finally codified in the Middle Ages, were the statue of Zeus at Olympia, the lighthouse at Alexandria, the Colossus of Rhodes, the mausoleum at Helicarnassus, the Temple of Artemis at Ephesus, the hanging gardens of Babylon and the great pyramid at Giza.

OLYMPIA

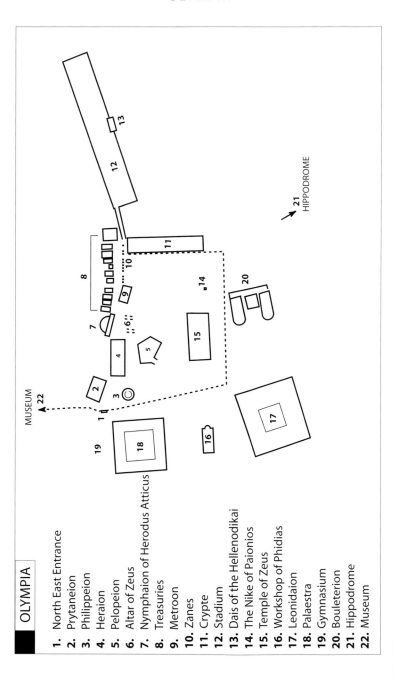

MUSEUM

HIPPODROME

OLYMPIA

1. North East Entrance
2. Prytaneion
3. Philippeion
4. Heraion
5. Pelopeion
6. Altar of Zeus
7. Nymphaion of Herodus Atticus
8. Treasuries
9. Metroon
10. Zanes
11. Crypte
12. Stadium
13. Dais of the Hellenodikai
14. The Nike of Paionios
15. Temple of Zeus
16. Workshop of Phidias
17. Leonidaion
18. Palaestra
19. Gymnasium
20. Bouleterion
21. Hippodrome
22. Museum

OLYMPIA

Archeological evidence shows this site continuously occupied since about 2000 BCE. The first Olympic Games were held in 776 BCE and thereafter for just over 1000 years, to 393 CE. Emperors and earthquakes demolished much of the sanctuary that was slowly covered with sand from the flooding of nearby rivers. German archeologists—mainly responsible for bringing it to its present condition—began excavating the site in 1875.

Panhellenic Games and the Olympic Truce

I pray you may walk exalted
All these days of your life.

> Pindar, "Olympian I" from *The Odes* translated by
> C.M. Bowra, Penguin Classics

The Olympic Games, held every four years, were Panhellenic, that is, open to all Greeks. Athletes came principally from the elite classes and competed as individuals. The Games thus reinforced Greek identity and male values. The main prize was the glory of excelling, but athletes also earned wreaths and awards of value.

To ensure that all Greeks could get to the Games, a truce that guaranteed safe passage to competitors and spectators was observed in all Greek states even if a war was currently being waged.

The Sanctuary

The Greek art traveller Pausanias visited Olympia in the 2nd century CE when the sanctuary was intact. It was, he wrote, in the province of Elis between the "large and very pleasant river" Alepheius and its tributary the Kladeos. The legend was that a hunter Alpheius fell in love with a huntress Arethusa, who, unwilling to marry, "turned from a woman to a spring". Still in love, Alpheius also changed into a river and mingled his waters with those of his loved one.

The modern entrance to the sanctuary (which was the exit in Pausanias's time) is close to some of the oldest buildings. Our description follows the numbers on the diagram of the site.

Inside the **northeast entrance (1)** is what's left of a group of three

OLYMPIA

buildings: on the left, the **Prytaneion (2)**; on the right, the **Philippeion (3)**; and straight ahead, the **Temple of Hera, or Heraion (4)**.

The Prytaneion was the headquarters of a group of priests (the prytaneis) responsible for running the sanctuary. The cylindrical Philippeion to the right was erected by the Macedonian King Philip II to commemorate his victory over the Greeks at the battle of Chaeroneia in 338 BCE. It consisted of eighteen Ionic columns surrounding a cylindrical cella (inner room), built, says Pausanias, "of burnt brick" within which "are set statues of Philip and Alexander [Philip's son], and with them is Amyntas, Philip's father." These works too are by Leochares, and are of ivory and gold, as are the statues of Olympias and Eurydice [Philip's wife and mother]. The Temple of Hera is directly in front of the entrance.

Unknown architect
The Temple of Hera, c. 600 BCE

The Heraion is a long narrow Doric temple built about 600 BCE. The inner columns were originally of wood, as earlier temples probably were, and gradually replaced by stone columns—Pausanias saw one oak pillar about 800 years later. As the temple of Zeus was a focus for male competitors in the Olympic Games, so the Heraion was for competitors in the separate female games. Pausanias gives us the details:

Every fourth year there is woven for Hera a robe by the Sixteen Women, and the same also hold games called Heraea. The games consist of foot races for maidens. These are not all of the same age. The first to run are the youngest; after them come the next in age, and the last to run are the oldest of the maidens. They run in the following way: their hair hangs down, a tunic reaches to a little above the knee, and they bare the right shoulder as far as the breast. These too have the Olympic stadium reserved for their games, but the course of the stadium is shortened for them by about one-sixth of its length. To the winning maidens they give crowns of olive and a portion of the cow sacrificed to Hera. They may also dedicate statues with their names inscribed upon them. Those who administer to the Sixteen are, like the presidents of the games, married women. The games of the maidens too are traced back to ancient times; they say that, out of gratitude to Hera for her marriage with Pelops, Hippodameia assembled the Sixteen Women, and with them inaugurated the Heraea. ...

From Pausanias, *Description of Greece.*

Inside the temple were numerous statues, some in gold and ivory, and others in marble, of varying antiquity, in Pausanias's opinion. To judge from the space he devotes to its description, the most prized object was a lavishly carved cedar chest known as the *Chest of Kypselos*. Kypselos was a ruler of Corinth. The carving and decoration in gold and ivory was something of an encyclopedia of Greek mythology.

To the right of the Heraion was a sacred enclosure—now little more than a mound—called the Pelopeion (5).

Pelopeion c. 1100 BCE

Dedicated to Pelops, the legendary god-king associated with Olympia (from which came the name Peloponnese), this ruin dates from 1100 BCE and was embellished through to Classical times. Beyond is the temple of Zeus, which we pass later. Pausanias notes that the Pelopeion "is far enough removed from the temple for statues and other offerings to stand in the intervening space." "Sacrifices in this enclosure used a black ram," says Pausanias. "No portion of this sacrifice goes to the soothsayer, only the neck of the ram it is usual to give to the 'woodman' as he is called. The woodman is one of the servants of Zeus, and the task assigned to him is to supply cities and private individuals with wood for sacrifices at a fixed rate, wood of the white poplar, but of no other tree, being allowed."

The **Altar of Zeus (6)** is not far.

Altar of Zeus

Pausanias described the altar:

Some say that it was built by Idaean Herakles, others by the local heroes two generations later than Herakles. It has been made from the ash of the thighs of victims sacrificed to Zeus, as is also the altar at Pergamus ... The first stage of the altar at Olympia, called prothysis, has a circumference of one hundred and twenty-five feet; the circumference of the stage on the prothysis is thirty-two feet; the total height of the altar reaches to twenty-two feet. The victims themselves it is the custom to sacrifice on the lower stage, the prothysis. But the thighs they carry up to the highest part of the altar and burn them there ... The steps that lead up to the prothysis from either side are

made of stone, but those leading from the prothysis to the upper part of
the altar are, like the altar itself, composed of ashes. The ascent to the
prothysis may be made by maidens, and likewise by women, when they
are not shut out from Olympia, but men only can ascend from the
prothysis to the highest part of the altar. Even when the festival is not
being held, sacrifice is offered to Zeus by private individuals and daily
by the Eleans.

From Pausanias, *Description of Greece*

The **Nymphaion of Herodus Atticus (7)**, the **Treasuries (8)**, the
Metroon (9) and the **Zanes (10)** are beyond the altar.

Nymphaion of Herodus Atticus, 150 CE

After the Pelopeion and the altar, on the other side of the Heraion
is a Roman monument erected by Herodus Atticus to honor his
wife Regilla. Little remains of the composition of statuary and
cisterns, whose running water was supplied by the system Herodus
installed in the sanctuary.

The *Treasuries*, the *Metroon*, and the *Zanes*

Immediately after the Nymphaion are the ruins of a row of
Treasuries on your left and, on the right the remains of a small
Doric temple dedicated to the mother of the gods. The Treasuries,
from the 6th century, were built by cities to contain their
dedications of gold, silver, bronze, and ivory. The Metroon was a
small temple in the Doric style, built about 400 BCE and dedicated
to the Mother of the Gods. Beyond the temple is a row of stone
pedestals which used to hold bronze sculptures of Zeus. "These"
says Pausanias, "have been made from the fines inflicted on
athletes who have wantonly broken the rules of the contests, and
they are called Zanes [figures of Zeus] by the natives. The first, six
in number, were set up in the 98th Olympiad. Inscriptions on the
images," he says "are a warning to all the Greeks not to give bribes
to obtain an Olympic victory." The nature of the images suggests
heavy fines. Bribery was the most common offence, but one person
was fined for thumping a rival who had won and another for
running away from the opposition.

The Stadium

At the end of the Treasuries is a stone arch known as the **crypte**,

(11), which is what remains of a monumental entrance (*propylon*) and a tunnel that joined the sanctuary to the stadium. The present **stadium (12)** is probably the third. The first Archaic stadium was within the sanctuary about where the Treasuries are. A second stadium, also from the Archaic period, was moved a bit to the east and flanked by embankments for spectators. The present stadium, still further to the east, is from the Classical era, about the middle of the 5th century. Successive shifts of the stadium and the addition of new buildings separated the stadium from the sanctuary and suggest that by the 4th century BCE the games had become more clearly a form of entertainment rather than a set of solemn religious events.

The embankments of the later stadia could hold about 40,000 people sitting on the ground, with a few stone seats for VIPs. One set of seats, known as the **Dais of the Hellenodikai (13)** because it accommodated the games judges (literally, the judges of the Greeks, the same ones who imposed rules and fines), is in the middle, on the right as you enter from the sanctuary. Opposite the dais is an altar to Demeter Chamyne. Demeter, earth mother, and goddess of fertility, has a long association with the site. Chamyne, meaning "on the couch," apparently refers to Demeter's priestess, who was the only non-virginal woman allowed to watch the games. The length of the stadium was a stade, about 200 yards (190 meters). The glamour foot race was one stade, the double foot-race was two stades, and a longer race was about three miles. After the fourteenth Olympiad the all-male athletes ran naked, perhaps because they

Gate-crashing the Games

A married woman caught at the games risked death by being thrown from a mountain. Pausanias tells the story of a widow named Callipateira who, he says, was the only woman caught. She "disguised herself exactly like a gymnastic trainer, and brought her son to compete at Olympia. Peisirodus, for so her son was called, was victorious, and Callipateira, as she was jumping over the enclosure in which they keep the trainers shut up, bared her person. So her sex was discovered, but they let her go unpunished out of respect for her father, her brothers and her son, all of whom had been victorious at Olympia. But a law was passed that the future trainers should strip before entering the arena."

From Pausanias, *Description of Greece.*

OLYMPIA

thought it was quicker, perhaps out of vanity. There was also a race in armor, consisting of at least a shield and a helmet.

The games included wrestling and boxing. Field games—long jump, discus, and javelin—combined with running and wrestling to make a pentathlon. The pankration was a trial of strength involving boxing, wrestling, kicking, strangling and twisting, and few rules.

Chariot races were held on the **hippodrome (21)**, a course about four stades long, to the south of the stadium (outside the site map). The chariots were drawn by four horses and raced about nine miles.

Returning to the sanctuary from the side of the dais, you cross the remains of a Classical era stoa—an arcaded building called the Stoa of Echo because of its acoustics—and come to the principal building, the **Temple of Zeus (15)**. In front is a ruin of a 30-foot (9-meter) high triangular pedestal that held Paionios's 12-foot (3-meter) high marble **Nike of Paionios (14)**. The nike statue is now in the museum.

Libon of Elis
Temple of Zeus, c. 470–456 BCE

This local work was held in its day to be the most perfect example of the Doric style. Its highly regarded exterior sculptures are examples of the early Classical or "severe" style. Significant fragments are in the museum. Pausanias saw it in all its golden glory:

The temple is in the Doric style, and the outside has columns all around it. It is built of native stone. Its height up to the pediment is sixty-eight feet, its breadth is ninety-five, its length two hundred and thirty. The architect was Libon, a native. The tiles are not of baked earth, but of Pentelic marble cut into the shape of tiles. The invention is said to be that of Byzes of Naxos ... At Olympia a gilt caldron stands on each end of the roof, and a Victory, also gilt, is set in about the middle of the pediment. Under the image of Victory has been dedicated a golden shield, with Medusa the Gorgon in relief. The inscription on the shield declares who dedicated it and the reason why they did so ... On the outside of the frieze that runs round the temple at Olympia, above the columns, are gilt shields one and twenty in number ...

He goes on to describe the frieze and pediments that are in the museum. However, the temple's most celebrated feature was the now vanished statue of Zeus, made by the Athenian Phidias for the cella in about 430 BCE. Similar to his statue of Athene on the Acropolis in Athens, Phidias made a 40-foot (12-meter) high assemblage of gold, ebony and ivory on a wooden frame. The head of the god on his throne almost touched the ceiling. Ivory was used for flesh, gold for drapery, beard, scepter and smaller statues. The throne was of all three materials as well as glass and precious stones.

Pausanias describes this wonder of the ancient world thus:

The god sits on a throne, and he is made of gold and ivory. On his head lies a garland, which is a copy of olive shoots. In his right hand he carries a Victory, which, like the statue, is of ivory and gold; she wears a ribbon and—on her head—a garland. In the left hand of the god is a scepter, ornamented with every kind of metal, and the bird sitting on the scepter is the eagle. The sandals also of the god are of gold, as is likewise his robe. On the robe are embroidered figures of animals and the flowers of the lily ... The throne is adorned with gold and with jewels, to say nothing of ebony and ivory. Upon it are painted figures and wrought images. There are four Victories, represented as dancing women, one at each foot of the throne, and two others at the base of each foot. On each of the two front feet are set Theban children ravished by sphinxes, while under the sphinxes Apollo and Artemis are shooting down the children of Niobe... The description then details the many figures and stories carved on and before the throne and the paintings surrounding it. "The figure ... binding his own head with a ribbon", he notes. "is said to resemble in appearance Pantarces, a stripling of Elis said to have been the love of Phidias."

Pausanias concludes:

I know that the height and breadth of the Olympic Zeus have been measured and recorded; but I shall not praise those who made the measurements, for even their records fall far short of the impression made by a sight of the image. Nay, the god himself according to legend bore witness to the artistic skill of Phidias. For when the image was quite finished Phidias prayed the god to show by a sign whether the work was to his liking. Immediately, runs the legend, a thunderbolt fell on that part of the floor where down to the present day the bronze jar stood to cover the place.

The care of the materials used in these chryselephantine (gold and ivory) statues stirred Pausanias' curiosity:

All the floor in front of the image is paved, not with white, but with black tiles. In a circle round the black stone runs a raised rim of Parian marble, to keep in the olive oil that is poured out. For olive oil is beneficial to the image at Olympia, and it is olive oil that keeps the ivory from being harmed by the marshiness of the Altis. On the Athenian Acropolis the ivory of the image they call the Maiden is benefited, not by olive oil, but by water. For the Acropolis, owing to its great height, is over-dry, so that the image, being made of ivory, needs water or dampness ... When I asked at Epidauros why they pour neither water nor olive oil on the image of Asclepius, the attendants at the sanctuary informed me that both the image of the god and the throne were built over a cistern ... And the Greeks in my opinion showed an unsurpassed zeal and generosity in honoring the gods, in that they imported ivory from India and Aethiopia to make images.

From Pausanias, *Description of Greece.*

Past the temple and in front of you is **Phidias's workshop (16)**. The workshop where Phidias made his wonder of the world was built around 440 BCE. After Phidias it was turned to other uses. When Pausanias visited the site, it was a cult building. In Byzantine times it was a Christian basilica, now recognizable in the ruins.

On the south side of the basilica are the ruins of the large and luxurious **Leonidaion (17)** commissioned about 330 BCE by Leonidas of Naxos. Originally meant as a place of entertainment for visiting VIPs, it later became a luxury villa. To the right of the workshop of Phidias; towards the entrance are the **palaestra (18)** and the **gymnasium (19)**. Both buildings are marked by rows of columns and are of the Hellenistic period (3rd and 2nd centuries BCE) and were used for training. Wrestling and boxing might have been practiced in the palaestra and the much larger gymnasium, an early Olympic village, used for field practices and to house athletes. These, like the stadium and **hippodrome (21)**, were outside the sanctuary.

Of the buildings close to the Leonidaion and back towards the stadium, the most significant is the Archaic-period **bouleterion (20)** where the Council (Boule) met and athletes swore on the altar of Olympian Zeus to honor the rules of the games.

Back at the entrance take the path to the **museum (22)**.

Olympia Museum

Olympia's splendid museum is among trees a short walk from the archeological site. It comprises a vestibule and ten rooms of exhibits laid

Johann Adam Delsenbach, engraving from J.B. Fischer von Erlach's impression of Phidias's statue of Olympian Zeus at Olympia, 1721 CE. (The Stapleton Collection)

out, like most Greek museums, in chronological order and occasionally by theme. The prize exhibits are the pieces from the pediments and metopes of the temple of Zeus but there are many other lovely works ranging from Helladic to Hellenistic times. Fine exhibits from the late classical period are the Hermes of Praxiteles, the most celebrated of the 4th-century sculptors, and a Nike by Paionios. An excellent guide to both site and museum, published by the Archeological Receipts Fund, is on sale in the site shop.

Room 1

Of great interest in this room are the works in bronze, which give a comparatively rare insight into the arts of the so-called Geometric period. Taken together with the Archaic work in Room 2, this is one of the richest collections anywhere of bronze work of the period.

The Geometric period is historically obscure, but artistically impressive. It is dated from the end of the Mycenaean age (about 1100 BCE) through to the Archaic era (about 700 BCE) and is effectively the first Greek art. (The Mycenaeans apparently spoke Greek but their art was Minoan in style.)

Unknown artists
Helladic and Mycenaean pottery, Geometric bronzes, 4000–700 BCE

This is a display of fairly small objects, mostly in cases. The first seven cases contain pots ranging from the Early Helladic to the Mycenaean period, the latter primarily from tombs in the vicinity of Olympia. The decorations in brown and red on fawn backgrounds from the Mycenaean period illustrate the interaction of abstract and natural forms that characterized craftwork in Greece for millennia. For example, Π 561, an amphora with four handles, combines birds' heads with geometric patterns that could be derived from bird shapes or from water patterns. Complexity in the overall shape of pots is illustrated by Π 181, a vessel known as a kernos and presumed to belong to a ritual.

A wall case containing Cycladic works found at the ancient port of Pheia on the coast nearby illustrates the spread of this style for trading or cultural reasons.

The handles and decorations from bronze cauldrons are exceptionally fine work. B1240 is a complete tripod cauldron with relatively plain handles. Parts of cauldrons often used human or animal figures as handles or as decoration. The strong focus on the human figure, male and female, belies the term Geometric, which applies more obviously to the magnificent large pots of the period. The function of figures as handles may help to explain why they are so often elongated, but it is also clear that the artists of the period relished the elegant strength that elongation gives to a figure. Two such figures appear on the Corinthian tripod leg B1730, which shows Apollo and Herakles jousting for the tripod used by the oracle at Delphi. Both god and hero would become common figures in Greek art. Here they make an early appearance with Egyptian influence evident.

The lively imaginations of the bronze workers are well served by their taste for monsters. B1690, a cauldron handle, is a siren. Griffins—a mix of eagle and lion, hence of vigilance and strength—appear in several shapes of varying ferocity. Griffins stood guard over the treasure of the mythical Hyperboreans. Apollo rode one.

OLYMPIA

Room 2

Unknown artists
Geometric and Archaic bronzes, 700–480 BCE

The bronzes in Room 2 take us into the Archaic era. The figures are in the familiar Archaic conventions, solid, elaborately coiffed, stepping out. Mythological scenes are entrenched along with depictions of monsters. In one panel, Clytemnestra, the unfaithful wife of Agamemnon, is being run through with a sword by Agamemnon's son, Orestes. Behind him, his sister Electra urges him on. Clytemnestra's lover, Aegisthus, makes his escape on the right. Below, Theseus captures an Amazon warrior under Athena's approving gaze. Shields B110 and B4490 are decorated with various Gorgons, creatures with snakes for hair and a look that turned men to stone.

Unknown craftsmen
Departing warrior and hoplite armor, c. 650–550 BCE

In this period, warriors and battle gear begin to be depicted more often, a sign that the Greeks are flexing their muscles to resist or initiate invasions. M78 has a scene of a departing warrior, focusing on the farewell: this image is also found on vase paintings. As he steps on to the waiting chariot, the warrior looks back and gestures to his wife holding their child. Their eyes meet in a dramatic moment. He is already in armor.

Some of the hoplite armor is well preserved. The word hoplite derives from the word for weapon. Hoplite warriors wore armor from head to toe and carried circular shields. They formed disciplined phalanxes that presented a wall of shields and spears on all four sides. They owned their own, finely decorated armor and their weapons, which implies that that they were men of means and had some sway in their communities. The poet Archilocus, writing in about 650 BCE, suggests that they were stocky, no-nonsense types: "I do not like a tall general", he wrote, "nor a long-shanked one, nor one who is proud of his hair, nor one who is partly shaved. Give me one who is short and bandy-legged to look at, but who walks firmly and is full of courage." (*Penguin Book of Greek Verse*, p130.)

Room 3

Unknown artists
Archaic pediments, c. 530 BCE

As well as more pottery and figurines, this room has fragments of pediments from treasuries dedicated during the 500s BCE. Treasuries were built by Greek cities or states to house the precious gifts made as offerings to celebrate various victories. They are relatively small buildings lining the way from the Heraion to the stadium entrance. The pediment from the Treasury of the Megarons contains a popular scene of the battle between the gods and the giants. The entablature beneath the sculptures demonstrates how triglyphs were spaced. The fragments of the pediment from the Treasury of Gela are a valuable example of the way terracotta moldings in white, red, and black decorated the cornices and other surrounds of a pediment.

Room 4

Unknown artists
Classical sculpture and bronze helmets, 480–300 BCE

A group of clay and terracotta statues—Zeus and Ganymede (T2), a warrior (T3), and a head of Athene (T6)—are excellent examples of the early Classical or Severe style (from 480–450 BCE). The statue of Zeus abducting the boy Ganymede was an akroterion—small statues from pediments.

The myth of Zeus and Ganymede says that Zeus fell in love with the beautiful boy Ganymede when he saw him playing, or in other versions, minding his father's sheep. Zeus abducted him, installed him as a prestigious servant of the gods and granted him eternal youth. The sculpture probably intends to show not only the relative sizes of Zeus and the boy, but also something of their states of mind. Zeus is in action and looking satisfied with the result of his capture of the most beautiful of mortals. Ganymede is in a childish dream, but the fact that he is holding a rooster, a symbol of love, in his left hand suggests that he knows what is happening. In other versions of the story, Zeus sent an eagle to do the snatch or disguised himself as one.

OLYMPIA

Unknown artists
Fragments of a Warrior and Athene, 5th century BCE

Both the reconstructed warrior and the head of Athena show how coloring was used and demonstrate early classical ideals of beauty. The warrior's torso is perfectly muscled and outlined. The face of the goddess is regular and boldly proportioned with large almond eyes, straight nose, high cheeks and full mouth.

Helmets 5th century BCE

Of historical interest are two helmets, B2600 and B5100. The first, with the green patina, is Greek, of the Corinthian type and known as the Militiades helmet because its inscription says that the victor of the battle of Marathon, "Militiades dedicated to Zeus" The bronze-colored helmet is Persian. Its inscription says that the Athenians captured it from the Persians and dedicated it to Zeus.

Also of historical interest is the display of tools and material such as molds found around the site. Phidias might have been among the sculptors who used these. As in modern workplaces, the heavies of the workshop reserved their own mugs. A black, fluted drinking vessel has "I belong to Phidias" incised on its base.

Off Room 4

Paionios of Mende
Nike (Victory), 424 BCE

The Nike of Paionios was on a 40-foot (9-meter) triangular pedestal. The winged creature itself was 10 feet (3 meters) tall. Although the wings and much drapery are missing, the figure remains graceful and impressive. Made towards the end of Greece's great 5th century, it is rich in a kind of realistic detail that nonetheless idealizes the human figure. The swept-back garment serves to dramatize the flight of the nike and to reveal the sumptuous body underneath.

Room 5

This room contains sculptures from the Temple of Zeus (480–450 BCE). When you enter from Room 4 (with the Nike of Paionios behind you), the east pediment of the temple is on the right and the west pediment on the left. Metopes hang on the end walls. The sculptors are unknown, as Pausanias's attributions of these to Paionios and Alkamenes are not accepted now. These fragments have been progressively unearthed since 1876 and pieced together. Scholars regard them as the prime surviving examples of the Severe style marking the transition from the formal Archaic to the freer Classical. Some relate this artistic change to historical events. The war with foreign invaders from Persia ended in 480 BCE and the Greeks must have felt they were entering a new order in which their best ideals could prevail. A temple to the supreme god on the most revered of the Panhellenic sanctuaries would have attracted their best and most innovative artists—even twenty years later, it attracted the great Phidias to make its cult statue.

The new Severe style introduced an unadorned, serious rendering of figures and a dramatic approach to depicting action. Gone were the smile, the studied adornment, and gentle unworldliness of Archaic figures. The subjects were still mainly gods and heroes but were given more human motives and reactions. Some features of figures, such as clothing, hair and eyes would have been bright red and blue; weapons and parts of chariots would have been gilded. The ensemble would have glittered like a gigantic jewel in the Olympian sunshine.

Pelops and Oinomaos prepare for their chariot race, east pediment of Temple of Zeus, Olympia, fifth century BCE. (Archeological Museum Olympia. Bridgeman Art Library/Alinari)

OLYMPIA

First look at the east pediment of the Temple of Zeus. The temple was built on an east-west axis, so the front or east pediment appropriately faced towards the Hippodrome.

Unknown sculptor/s
The chariot race between Oinomaos and Pelops, 470–456 BCE

The pediments are flattened triangles about ten feet (three meters) high at the center and 80 feet (a little over 24 meters) long. The east pediment fits a large group of figures into this awkward space without distorting individual figures. The central figure of Zeus must, by his nature, be the largest. Women are shorter than men; outer figures are either crouching as befits their roles, or in the extremities, lying on their sides.

The subject is the chariot race between the young Pelops and the king Oinomaos. Pelops, son of Poseidon, wanted to marry Oinomaos's daughter, Hippodameia. To do so he had to beat the king in a marathon chariot race across the Peloponnese from Olympia to Corinth. If he lost, he would be killed, like a dozen others before him. This time, Hippodameia had fallen for her suitor, so she persuaded Oinamaos's charioteer, Myrtilus, to weaken his master's chariot. Thus Pelops won the race and the hand of Hippodameia. In the story as told by Apollodoros, Myrtilus, had fixed the race out of love for Hippodameia, but when he later tried to come on to her, Pelops killed him. Myrtilus, however, managed to curse Pelops and his descendants—among them, the much-troubled Mycenaean House of Atreus.

The order of the figures on the pediment is much debated. Essentially it rests on whether Oinomaos or Pelops should be on Zeus's right, rather than as they are now displayed. The current placing follows the basics of Pausanias's description as he saw them before they were brought down by an earthquake, but some argue (a) that Pausanias was not completely clear about whether he meant the statue's right side or the viewer's, and (b) that Zeus had his (missing) head inclined to the right, and hence to Pelops whom he was acknowledging as the eventual victor. But reading Zeus's motives had hazards even for the other Greek gods. The order displayed in the museum seems the better interpretation of Pausanias's description, which follows:

> *... in the front pediment there is, not yet begun, the chariot-race between Pelops and Oenomaus, and preparation for the actual race*

*is being made by both. An image of Zeus has been carved in about
the middle of the pediment; on the right of Zeus is Oenomaus with
a helmet on his head, and by him Sterope his wife, who was one of
the daughters of Atlas. Myrtilus too, the charioteer of Oenomaus,
sits in front of the horses, which are four in number. After him are
two men. They have no names, but they too must be under orders
from Oenomaus to attend to the horses ... At the very edge lies
Cladeus, the river which, in other ways also, the Eleans honor most
after the Alpheius. On the left from Zeus are Pelops, Hippodameia,
the charioteer of Pelops, horses, and two men, who are apparently
grooms of Pelops. Then the pediment narrows again, and in this
part of it is represented the [river] Alpheius.*

(From Pausanias, *Description of Greece*).

Hippodameia is already beside Pelops. He is slim, naked and
youthful. She is adjusting her garment (said to be a conventional
gesture of marriage) and looking towards the horses she will ride
behind with Pelops. Damage to the figures prevents us from
picking up signs of his or her state of mind but what we can see
suggests that most of the protagonists are essentially inward-
looking and somewhat uneasily detached one from the other. The
servant girl (Pausanias says charioteer but it is more likely that
Hippodameia herself would be the charioteer) at Hippodameias's
feet may well know of the plot or at least of Myrtilus's love for
Hippodameia, but she reveals none of that. Nor, on the other side,
does Myrtilus himself. The figure who does betray the import of
the scene is the old man behind Pelops's chariot. Pausanias says he
is one of two grooms, the other being a youth fingering his foot.
Scholars see the old man as a seer who contemplates with some
dismay the meaning of the story of pride, love, lust, betrayal and
murder that is about to unfold. The carving of the seer as an old
man with baggy flesh and bald head marks the beginning of new
conventions of realism in Greek sculpture.

Cross the room to the west pediment.

Unknown sculptor/s
The Battle of the Centaurs and the Lapiths, 470–456 BCE

This is an action scene frequently carved on Greek buildings. The
Lapiths inhabited Thessaly. One of them, Peirithoos, held a
marriage feast to which he invited his friend Theseus and a band of

OLYMPIA

centaurs, who were half-man half-horse. The boorish centaurs got drunk and tried to carry off or rape the young women and boys. The Lapiths resisted and with the help of Theseus overcame the barbarians. The theme was popular because it showed men triumphing over beasts and Greeks belting up barbarians.

The god in the center is Apollo, here in his role as keeper of law and order. Whether he takes sides in this actual scene or is meant to be a godly presence above the fray is not clear. In keeping with the violent action he is gesturing towards the battle on his right, but his upright stance, serene face and decorative coiffure retain some of the spiritual remove of the Archaic style. To his right, Lapith men attack centaurs who abduct Lapith women. The fight is led by (fragments of) Peirithoos immediately to the god's right, who attacks the centaur (identified by Pausanias as Eurytion). Eurytion has made a grab for his bride Deidameia's bared breast. She is trying to wrest his hand away. Further over a kneeling woman in an elegant chiton is being lifted up by her beautiful coiffure. In the far corner women crouch and watch in consternation. "...on the other side," says Pausanias, "is Theseus defending himself against the Centaurs with an ax. One Centaur has seized a maid, another a boy in the prime of youth." (From Pausanias, *Description of Greece.*) Nearby, a centaur in trouble tries to release himself by biting his attacker's arm, and another struggles to hang on to a woman by her leg.

The end walls contain metopes, which are sculpted slabs—here of Parian marble—raised up to the entablatures below the pediments and separated by triglyphs. They are almost life size (5 feet 3 inches, or about 1.6 meters).

These represent the twelve labors of Herakles and are placed as described by Pausanias, starting at the west end of the room with the killing of the Lion of Nemea. Some are easily identifiable, some mere fragments. Substantial pieces of these metopes are also in the Louvre, in Paris. We look at the west wall first.

Unknown sculptors
West wall metopes from the Temple of Zeus:
The Labors of Herakles, 462–457 BCE

Six metopes at the west end are: the lion of Nemea, the Lernaian Hydra, the Stymphalian birds, the Cretan bull, the Keryneian deer, and the taking of the Amazon's belt. Of these, three indicate interesting points of changing styles.

Metope from the Temple of Zeus Olympia. Herakles receiving the Golden Apples of the Hesperides, fifth century BCE. (Archeological Museum Olympia)

There is a lot left of the Lion of Nemea itself and just enough of the rest to see Herakles leaning over the dead animal with his foot resting on the body and his arm on his knee supporting his hand cradling his head. The head, top left, looking down, is of Athene. Hermes was also in the original picture. Both Herakles's posture and face are of a man exhausted by battle. The sculptor has chosen an uncommon moment in a commonly depicted story, and shown the legendary hero expressing an ordinary human emotion.

OLYMPIA

The third in the series—the metope of the Symphalian birds—again chooses a final moment in the labor. Athene, identified by the aegis (a protective cloak or shield) she is holding, receives something from Herakles, presumably one of the dreaded birds that she has helped him kill. She leans back on a rock and gazes equably at Herakles's naked torso. It is an intimate rather than a violent scene.

Next to it, the metope of the Cretan bull contrasts with these two. Whereas they are in the manner of the east pediment, this is like the hectic action of the west pediment. The figure of the man flung across the diagonal forms a cross with the massive bull.

Unknown sculptors
East wall metopes from the Temple of Zeus, 462–457 BCE

The remaining six metopes, on the opposite end wall, are: the Erymanthine boar, the horses of Diomedes, the killing of Geryon, the apples of the Hesperides, the capture of Cerberus and the cleaning of the Augean stables.

The fourth, an almost complete panel of Herakles shouldering the sky with the help of Athene while Atlas, whose job that usually was, brings him the golden apples of Hesperides, is possibly the best known of these twelve metopes. Athene, her trim form visible through her garment, is giving the splendidly built Herakles a hand, without apparent effort, as one might expect of a goddess. The story is complicated. The golden apples belonged to Hera and were kept in the land of the Hyperboreans—a land of perpetual youth and golden memories. Herakles needed Atlas to get them for him from the Hyperboreans, so he volunteered to take the weight of the sky. But when Atlas had the apples, he said he would take the apples to their destination himself while Herakles went on holding up the heavens. Herakles agreed but asked Atlas to hold up the sky briefly while he put a pad on his shoulders. The credulous Atlas put the apples on the ground and took back the sky. Herakles grabbed the apples and left. This is the story told by Apollodoros, many centuries later.

The last two of these six are depictions of strength and determination. In the fifth Herakles braces his body to drag the monster Cerberus from his hellish den. In the sixth he is following a tip from Athene (identified now by her helmet) to divert water from a couple of nearby rivers to flush out the filthy stables. In this scene the diagonal of Herakles's body expresses the feverish effort needed to get the channel dug in the short time allowed for the task.

Praxiteles. Hermes and the Infant Dionysos. c. 330 BCE or else a late Hellenistic copy. (Archeological Museum Olympia)

OLYMPIA

Go through the small Rooms 6 and 7 (Hellenistic sculpture c. 400–300 BCE) to Room 8. Alone in this room is the statue of Hermes by the great master of Hellenistic art, Praxiteles.

Room 8

Praxiteles
Hermes, 330 BCE

Pausanias refers to works that were in the Temple of Hera "among them a Hermes of stone, who carries the infant Dionysos, the work of Praxiteles." The work was in fact found in the Heraion early in the excavations at Olympia; but a lot has since been written about whether it is by Praxiteles or is a copy or is by another sculptor also named Praxiteles. At all events, the pioneer of female nudity in art is here credited with a further examplar of human beauty that would last and be revived through many centuries. The material is Parian marble. The pose is a relaxed S-bend with weight distributed both sides of a central vertical—a pose that persisted in the ancient world, and reappeared in medieval and Renaissance art. No doubt, Hermes is here partly as one of Zeus's many sons—as too is the infant Dionysos who burst from the supreme god's thigh—but also in his role of protector, one who "calms all fear," as Wordsworth says. (*Laodamia*). His soft, still face looks benignly at his very active infant half-brother.

Room 9 has a display of Roman statuary from the site. Room 10 has material from various periods about the Olympic Games. Especially appealing is the boy on his mark ready to go.

TRAIL 7:
To the North—Thebes and Thessaloniki

Vergina   Thessaloniki

Delphi   H. Loukas

Thebes   Athens

Corinth

(Trail 7 | To the North

This Trail begins with a day-trip from Athens to the Mycenaean town of Thebes, where there is an extremely interesting museum. From there, you can spend the night and continue on to Thessaloniki and on to Vergina, a side trip to the spot where the treasure from the tomb of Phillip the Second (father of Alexander the Great) has been moved. The trains and roads north of Athens pass through ancient Thebes (Thiva) on the way to Thessaloniki and Macedonia. The periods represented on this Trail are Mycenaean and Archaic in Thebes and Hellenistic and Byzantine in Thessaloniki. Allow one day for Thebes and at least two for Thessaloniki.

Thebes

Thebes is a little over 50 miles (90 kilometers) northwest of Athens and accessible by car, train and bus. Frequent trains and buses leave from Athens. Trains go from Larissis station, which has a Metro stop. The buses are from Terminal B.

Thebes is named after Thebe, one of the children of the Titan Prometheus and a nymph. At various times in recorded history it has dominated the surrounding region (Boeotia). There are many Neolithic remains and evidence of important settlements from the beginning of the Bronze Age, about 3000 BCE. Archeologists call the period from 3000–1000 BCE Helladic and break it into Early (EH) Middle (MH) and Late (LH) with subdivisions within each. LH, from about 1600–1100 BCE, is effectively the era of Mycenae. EH covers the work of pre-Hellenic peoples from 3000–2000 BCE. Most Hellenic people arrived in the Middle Period (2000–1600 BCE).

Tradition says that Oedipus's ancestors ruled the city. The very large Mycenaean acropolis of ancient Thebes—under the modern town—was probably second only to Mycenae, itself a wild and powerful place. Finds from Mycenaean times provide the greatest feast for art travellers to Thebes. The artworks found here and elsewhere in the Mycenean world are unmistakably Minoan in style. It is not known whether this resulted from the Mycenean occupation and assimilation of Crete or whether Minoan art was already the most prestigious form in the Aegean world before then. However dominant Mycenae might have been politically or dynastically, it was Minoan culture that permeated the Mycenaean world—much as, a millennium later, Greek culture would shape that of the Roman Empire.

Homer's myths and stories were set in Mycenae and became the principal subjects of Greek literature, drama, and art. Some of the exhibits in the museum, notably the painted coffins, come from the same far-off times as the stories.

Location: Pindarou (street), Thiva (Thebes)

Contact details: Tel. + 30 226 202 7913; www.culture.gr

Opening hours: Summer (April-September) Tues.–Sun. 9:00 am–7:00 pm; Mon. 12:00–7:00 pm; winter (October-March) Tues. – Sun. 8.30 am–3.00 pm, Mon. 10.30 am–5.00 pm.

Admission: Low range (Euro 1–4).

Theban plays

Both Sophocles and Euripides wrote tragedies set in Thebes. The first of Sophocles's three Theban tragedies, the dreadful story of Oedipus, starts when Oedipus is a baby and an oracle foretells that he will grow up to kill his own father. He is sent away to avoid this fate but as a young man, returns and unwittingly kills his real father and marries his own mother. When she realises what has happened, she kills herself. Oedipus then blinds himself. In Euripides's version, Oedipus is blinded when he is found guilty of his father's murder. Tradition says that Oedipus washed his father's blood from his hand down by the river near the Hagioi Theodoroi Square, a short walk to the east from the museum.

The modern city of Thiva, including the museum, is built on top of a Mycenaean acropolis (or high city) known as the Kadmeia, which means House of Cadmus. The museum is on an elevated site and clearly signposted for drivers and pedestrians.

The museum has an entrance hall and four rooms. Room A, on the right, has the museum's most important sculptures from the Archaic and Classical periods. Straight ahead in Room D is an extraordinary collection of painted larnakes (larnax in the singular), the coffins or ossuaries found inside tombs, from the Mycenaean site of Tanagra about 12 miles (20 k) away. Room B contains mainly Mycenaean exhibits and Room C later sculpture going into Roman times. For the art traveller, the highlight is undoubtedly the rare collection of 16 painted clay larnakes in Room D, some of which still contain bones. We will visit Rooms D, A, B, and C, in that order.

Go to Room D straight ahead of the entrance. The coffins are numbered 1–16 but they are not displayed in order. Exhibit 1 is the prize.

Room D

Unknown Mycenaean painter/s
Coffin or larnax, Exhibits 1, 2 and 4, 1350–1250 BCE

Exhibit 1, ahead as you come in from the entrance, is the most elaborately painted of the sixteen. There are two scenes on the front. Above, a man slaughters a goat. Below, three young men somersault over bulls. Since these scenes are on a funerary vessel we assume they have religious meaning—for example, that the goat is being sacrificed. The bull jump is a common theme in Minoan art and presumed to have religious connotations. Note that the artist has used only red and black on a white ground whereas much Minoan painting uses many more colors. Both scenes are framed with checkerboards and bars of color that take up the remaining space. The action is vigorous: the large red goat is about to be struck with a sword; the bull jumpers are airborne. They exemplify the Greek talent for picking a dramatic moment.

Both ends of the larnax carry upper and lower scenes. Above, mourning women, painted as silhouettes in red or black, are in the eloquent posture that will be found again and again in Greek art through to the Geometric period.

On balance, female mourners—who play a prominent role at Greek funerals in modern times—are the main motif on the coffins in this collection. Exhibit 2 immediately on your left shows mourners wearing banded skirts, shawls, and wreaths on their heads.

Below the mourners, the body of a recently deceased person is being bent into the coffin. This way of fitting an adult body into the space is possible before rigor mortis sets in.

On Exhibit 4 nearby, the painting shows mourners lifting the body of a child directly into the coffin. However, the painting might not report what happened but symbolize the eventual transfer of the dead person's bones to a final container where they will await grave robbers and archeologists. On the opposite long side, the row of mourners continues across the top half. Below is a symmetrical scene showing two men facing each other, drawn as filled-out stick figures with horse-drawn chariots behind them. Small animals, possibly ponies, fit in around them, perhaps simply to fill the space, but more probably to indicate that they are in the distance. We cannot know whether the scene relates to the life or role of the deceased, or to sports and activities associated with the rites of burial.

Directly to the right of Exhibit 1 is Exhibit 16 and behind, Exhibit 14. Both contain children's bones. Exhibit 14 also contains a couple of broken figurines and a small jar, which might be playthings from this life or for the next.

Unknown Mycenaean painter/s
Coffins or larnakes, Exhibits 16 and 14, 1350–1250 BCE

Exhibit 16 uses black outline on a white ground. One of the long sides and one of the short sides show women in profile, apparently at windows. The other two sides are decorated with net, bar, scroll, and wave shapes. Boldly drawn, the faces conform to a type common in Mycenean painting and the theme of women-at-a-window occurs elsewhere, e.g. in the National Archeological Museum. The obvious supposition is that they are at windows, watching a funeral procession, but they may instead represent the dead watching life from a distance or spirits watching and preparing to receive the recently deceased. The painting differs markedly in style and content from the red-and-black work on Exhibit 1.

On each of the long sides of Exhibit 14 are figures grouped around a freestanding column inside a room. Since a freestanding column is commonly assumed in Minoan buildings in Crete to have a religious function, this larnax reinforces the fact that Minoan culture remained dominant throughout Greece even though Crete was apparently absorbed into the Mycenaean world of the mainland. The four outline figures around the column on one side are crowned or wearing wreaths, (like the female mourners on No 2) and are plausibly female priests. On the other side is another cultural visitor, a sphinx. The Greek version of the Egyptian monster is usually an unpleasant character. The famous one at Thebes, whose riddle was answered by Oedipus, devoured passers-by who did not give the right answer. As on other surfaces, spaces are filled in with animals seen at a distance and larger surfaces covered with net and spiral patterns.

Unknown Mycenaean painter/s
Coffin or larnax, Exhibit 13, 1350–1250 BCE

At each corner of Exhibit 13 stand grotesque birds banded boldly in black and perched on discs, which in turn rest on horn shapes. Most of the decoration on the discs echoes the spiral designs on the box of the larnax below. This is the only one in the collection to deviate from the simple box shape, and the figures on top look as though they communicate a particular meaning. While circles commonly symbolize the natural world, and circles containing squares often stand for the twin worlds of life and death, matter and spirit, we can only guess at the symbolism or intensity of ideas that interested the Myceneans.

As you move around the rest of the larnakes, you will notice the consistent but limited range of red and black, perhaps colors thought

The Riddle of the Sphinx

The story as told by Apollodorus, a Greek writer born in 190 BCE:

During (Creon's) reign, a disaster of no small proportion struck Thebes; for Hera sent the Sphinx. The mother of the Sphinx was Echidna and her father Typhon, and she had the face of a woman, the chest, feet and tail of a lion, and the wings of a bird. She had learned a riddle from the Muses, and seated on Mount Phicion, she posed it to the Thebans. The riddle ran as follows: what is it that has a single voice, and has four feet, and then two feet, and then three feet? Now the Thebans possessed an oracle telling them that they would be freed from the Sphinx when they solved her riddle, so they gathered together repeatedly to seek the solution; but when they failed to discover it, the Sphinx would carry one of them off and devour him. When many had died in this way, including, ultimately, Creon's son Haimon, Creon proclaimed that he would give both the kingdom and the widow of Laios to the man who could solve the riddle. When Oedipus heard of this, he supplied the answer, saying that the riddle of the Sphinx referred to man; for he is four-footed as a baby when he crawls on all fours, two-footed as an adult, and takes on a third limb in old age in the form of a stick. So the Sphinx hurled herself from the Acropolis, and Oedipus took over the kingdom, and also, without realizing it, married his mother (Iocaste).

The Library of Greek Mythology by Apollodorus,
edited by Robin Hard (Translator) 1997.
By permission of Oxford University Press.

suitable for death. All four sides are decorated and there is repeated use of checker, circle, floral, lozenge, net, spiral, and wave designs.

The cases around the walls contain material, mostly vases and statuettes, from the tombs and larnakes of the Mycenaean cemetery at Tanagra. On the end wall are two very small larnakes, about 18 x 9 x 12 inches high (43 x 20 x 47 centimeters). Their size suggests that they were for infants or contained ashes. One on the bottom shelf of Case No 5 is decorated with female mourners, spirals and flowers. Many of the figurines and the vases are in the manner of Minoan figures of the same period.

Go to the entrance lobby and into Room A, which has some truly outstanding kouroi from the Archaic period, interesting fragments from an earlier time and grave steles from 400–100 BCE.

Room A

Unknown sculptors
Two Daidalic works, Exhibits 229 and BE 36, 650–600 BCE

These two exhibits are to the right and left of the entrance. Both are damaged and hence missing a lot of their detail. Found near Tanagra, they belong to the so-called Daidalic style, which sees the human figure emerge after the very schematic representations of the Geometric period and before the more realistic works of the Archaic period. Like their successors, they wear chitons and himations and have elaborate hairdos.

Exhibit 229 on the right of the entrance is female. Some think that BE 36 on the other side is a male figure. The hairdo is characteristic of men of this time: from the back, the hair is coiled horizontally and a tress hangs over each shoulder. The label "Daidalic" derives from the legendary reputation of Daidalus as the earliest sculptor of Archaic works. Such early works are influenced by Egyptian statuary, possibly via Crete. Large-scale representations of the human body, even if formalized as they were in the Archaic period, were a radical departure from the small scale, elongated and stick-like human figures of the Geometric period. Diodorus, a Greek historian who lived in Sicily in the 1st century BCE, extolled the extraordinary realism of statues carved by Daidalos. Those who saw them, he wrote, thought they were like real people who could "see and walk."

Unknown sculptor
Fragment from a temple pediment, Exhibit 10, 520 BCE

The Amazon warrior is recognizable from her helmet and short tunic. Fallen, she fits into the narrow end of a temple pediment, which probably featured the popular theme of the battle against the Amazons. Typical of the finest work of the period, she is shown in a precise moment during the battle. Though wounded and fallen, she is courageously drawing an arrow from her quiver and as she dies, she fights back.

Unknown sculptor
Archaic kouros from the Sanctuary of Ptoan Apollo, Exhibit 3, c. 550 BCE

Exhibit 3, judged to be a little later than 550 BCE, faces you as you enter the room and was found in a sanctuary to Apollo at Mount Ptoan about 12 miles (20 kilometers) north of Thebes.

This life-size kouros is carved from a local marble. It is a masterpiece. Within the tight rules that governed the style and dictated what a figure for a sanctuary would be like, there is a mixture of the beauty and realism most easily associated with a god-man. The face is serene and friendly but inward looking, as though the orderliness of the hair matches the inner order of the person. The flesh is the firm flesh of youth. The ideal is of a slender and unchanging youth. From the back, the buttocks are rounded, firm and high. The whole body seems stilled but ready to step forward. The exaggeration of the abdomen distinguishes it as a male body even while there is an almost feminine grace about the upper body and arm. Within Archaic sculpture, the treatment of this part of the male body is one of the features that we see change over time.

Unknown sculptor

Archaic kouros from the Sanctuary of Ptoan Apollo, Exhibit 1, c. 550 BCE

Immediately behind is another kouros, judged to be a little earlier than Exhibit 3. His arms are at his side, creating a symmetry that emphasizes his long, lean torso. Compared with Exhibit 3, the sculpting has made the abdomen quite prominent; it takes up more space; the space is more stylized; the lines are thicker. Together, abdomen and genitals make a striking image of masculinity. From the back, the long line down to the protruding buttocks indicates how the whole of the body has been elongated.

Unknown sculptor

Archaic kouros from Eutrasis, Exhibit 7, c. 400–350 BCE

Standing opposite is a third white marble kouros found at Eutrasis, between 7 and 8 miles/ 12 kilometers southwest of Thebes. Compared with the previous two, the abdominal area is differently treated, being now more rounded at the top. Also, the body is more solid, the thighs heavier, the back and buttocks strong and taut. The tensions are those of a body in motion—the style is moving towards the naturalism of Classical Greece. Although it is a fragment, enough remains to show that the arms were not held down in the Archaic manner: on the figure's left, you can see where a missing object or a hand was touching near the waist, but there are no signs of an arm or hand touching the body at any lower point. We can assume that the hands and arms were raised or holding some object.

Also in this room are a number of steles.

Unknown sculptors
Grave steles from various sites, 400–100 BCE

The steles are from Classical and Hellenistic periods in the Athenian style, some in marble, some in limestone. They are touching yet do not drift into sentimentality or express a fear of death. The dead person is often seated and being farewelled. Some are with favorite companions or carry symbols of their activities during life. They may be actual portraits or portrait types. However, the figure in one exhibit recalls Hegeso from the Athenian Kerameikos and displayed in the National Archeological Museum. In this collection, the relief carving varies greatly. The dog (Exhibit 44) stands out strongly against a flat background, the fall of drapery gives bodies greater depth, and chairs establish a third dimension building up from a plane behind the figures seated or standing near them.

Room B

Next, Room B has exhibits arranged chronologically from the right as you enter. Exhibits from the acropolis of Mycenaean Thebes (the Kadmeion) are concentrated in Cases 11, 14, 15, 16, 17 and 23. Case 15 holds a notable set of cylinder seals. Do not miss the Geometric vases, especially three pieces displayed on a shelf between Cases 17 and 21, between the entrance and exit to this room.

Unknown artists
Krater displayed on a shelf, 730–700 BCE

Of three vessels on a shelf, from left to right, the first is a krater with late Geometric decoration. In the decorated space, the arrangement of the double-ax-shaped shields of the two hoplites facing each other over a platform seems to refer to the common Minoan symbol of strength and power which also appears independently. A similar motif on the other side shows two hoplites and horses facing each other. Spaces in this upper zone are defined by vertical lines suggesting columns, and filled in with swastikas, disks and a double ax. Below, the narrowing curve of the body is defined by a row of circles and horizontal bands of varying widths. On the base, thinner lines enclose a wide band where a continuous wave connects dots. Without doubt, the potter has assembled his decoration with a view to enhancing the shape of the vessel. It is not so clear what the various elements of the decoration might symbolize, though, as in abstract art of any age, they almost certainly signify universal themes. Swastikas, for example, which revolve around a fixed point, often symbolize regeneration. Straight lines can symbolize earth and wavy lines sea or mountain. Dots represent moon or sun.

Unknown artists
Pithos displayed on a shelf, 730–700 BCE

Pithoi are usually storage jars. This one contained the remains of a small child. Like its neighbor, it has a figurative upper zone with geometric patterning below. On one side, a number of women represented as red silhouettes face another woman, herself a black silhouette. On the other side, a man with a lyre seems to lead a line of dancing figures, two of them children. The fact that this is a burial vessel suggests a religious meaning to the procession, music and dancing as well as the meanders, lozenges, lines and waves. The sequence of the decoration from top to bottom may also have specific meaning.

Unknown artists
Amphora displayed on a shelf, 730–700 BCE

Last on the shelf is a very fine piece of late Geometric design found in excavations for the Thebes railway bridge. Decorative lines delineate both neck and base and give prominence to figurative work at handle height. In this zone, rectangular spaces are elegantly filled with birds whose necks first curve away and then over their bodies, leaving a long beak and a single eye looking out from among the rosettes. Hatching and continuous lines around the handles establish their separate space and function while leaving them still visually part of the whole.

Immediately to the right of the entrance way in Case 9 you will see:

Unknown artists

Helladic period pottery and bronze, Case 9, Early (2800–1900 BCE) and Middle (1900–1600 BCE)

The Bronze Age periods known as Early and Middle Helladic precede the Mycenaean era (which coincides with Late Helladic). Pottery and bronze, which are extremely durable, reveal the art of these millennia.

The vases of the early period are generally hand-made balls and jugs with handles and spouts (sometimes referred to as sauce boats). They are glazed and may be either plain or carry simple decorations in white. Middle–Period pottery is often turned on a wheel and takes on more shapes and larger sizes. Some are plain or carry simple designs but there are also dark glazes.

On the middle shelf, next to a find of bronze tools, is a range of Early Helladic vases from Thebes. One has a frilled band running from the base of the handle; others are plain. The decorated one is a good example of the beak-shaped vase. It resembles the bird shape that occurs elsewhere and probably indicates an interchange that extends eastwards towards Phoenicia. Herodotus in his *Histories* talks of "Cadmus of Tyre and the people who came with him from Phoenicia to the country now called Boeotia" as the founders of Thebes.

Two finely shaped Minyan pieces from the Middle Helladic period are to the right of the early works. Compared with earlier work, these have a different shape, being more sharply edged—perhaps in the manner of bronze vessels—as they were made on a potter's wheel. From this new shape comes a lighter appearance, emphasized when the color remains light and the decoration is built up out of fine lines.

Unknown artists

Pithamphora, Middle Helladic, Exhibit 830, c. 1900–1600 BCE

This piece is displayed in a corner between Case 9 and Case 1. Coming from about a thousand years before the Geometric period, it is evidence of the antiquity of this type of decoration and suggests (as some artists of our own time have done) that the forms and patterns of Geometric art are so powerful that they will emerge in any age.

Case 1 contains finds from Mycenaean tombs and buildings from Thebes and a palace at Orchomenos, about 25 miles (40 kilometers) northwest of Thebes. The top shelf contains a variety of objects from graves, among them a large bronze pin with a crystal head. The middle and bottom shelves contain objects found in a room, including weapons. The right-hand end of the bottom shelf contains some vessels from tombs in Thebes.

Unknown artists
Mycenaean stirrup jar, displayed in Case 1, c. 1500–1400 BCE

Among the Mycenaean tomb finds is a so-called stirrup jar, which has a top handle and spout and is decorated with black zigzags on a brown ground. In the top V-shapes of the zigzag pattern are double axes supported by upright figures. Slight though they are, the figures are prominent on the shoulder. The zigzags follow the wide belly of the vessel and the concentric lines the narrow base (like a top) on which the vessel balances. Each space at the bottom of the zigzags contains an organic shape. Between the V-shapes of the zigzag are upright marks. The positioning of these marks below the figures holding the double axes suggests they might be phalluses, which could in turn mean that the droplet shapes dangling from the A-frame of the zigzags are scrota. If that were so, the zigzag would represent legs. As a funeral piece, it could then be an abstract representation of virility.

Case 2 contains Mycenaean work, found mainly on the hill of Kolonaki in Thebes.

Unknown artists
Amphora in the Palace Style, displayed in Case 2, 1500–1400 BCE

The Palace-Style amphora illustrates the close connection of Mycenaean and Minoan art. The type of vessel and the style appeared in Minoan art before they appeared in Mycenaean work. On this amphora, a palm tree with serrated trunk and umbrella foliage is framed by a double arch and emerging from waves that indicate it is beside the sea. The lines and coloring of the narrower parts of the vase, top and bottom, underline its elegance. It is essentially a heavy vessel but the artist has made it appear light and graceful.

Unknown artists
Mycenaean figurines, displayed in Case 3, 1300–1200 BCE

From among vases, figurines and other objects found in tombs at Kolinaki, the top shelf displays a handful of curious Mycenaean figurines—females with inverted conical hats. Several have their arms raised and are referred to in Greek as psi shapes because of their resemblance to the Greek letter Ψ. Others with arms folded are referred to as tau, which corresponds to the letter T. Large numbers have been found, the rather sketchy design suggesting that they were produced in large numbers, possible for ceremonial purposes. As priestess or god figures, essentially for funeral rituals, they may have been used rather as candles or flowers are used today.

Unknown makers
Storage jars with Linear B inscriptions, displayed in Case 11, c. 1350–1300 BCE

The interest of these jars is that they are labeled with the celebrated Linear B script, which has been incised on the body. They were used for wine or oil. Similar pieces have been unearthed in other Mycenaean centers on the mainland and in Crete. The inscription usually records a name and sometimes a place name. Analysis shows that some were made in Crete and would have been transported to Thebes; others were made in Thebes. Deciphering the Linear B script demonstrates that Cretan civilization had shifted from a Minoan language to an early form of Greek, a change presumably brought about by the spread of Mycenaean civilization.

Room C

Look in the middle of the room to Exhibit 131.

Unknown sculptor
Grave stele of Philotera, Exhibit 131, 400–380 BCE

The carving allows the images of mother and child to sit inside a frame. The effect is to bring them together against a flat ground, which could be this world or the next. The child reaches up towards the mother who gazes down at the tiny figure with grief in her eyes and in the inclination of her head. At the same time, her careful hairdo and the arranged folds of her chiton and himation suggest that she has accepted her death.

Directly behind is a copy of the statue of Artemis.

Unknown sculptor
Roman copy of the statue of Artemis, original from the 400s BCE,
Exhibit BE 63

This copy was found in the cella of a temple of Artemis at Aulis,
dating from its time as a Roman port, northeast of Thebes. It is a
fine piece of work in the original style, suggesting that the original
was quite splendid. The stories say that Artemis becalmed the
Greek fleet in Aulis and that in order to leave for Troy, the Greek
leader Agamemnon sacrificed his daughter Iphigenia. This is the
subject of Euripides's drama *Iphigenia in Aulis*. The statue might be
a copy of the one described by Pausanias. If so, the missing arms
carried torches. Resting the weight of the body on the right foot
provides for an ample curve at the hip. The draped chiton reveals
most of the body: the rounding of the belly and the small high
breast are clearly discernible—as are the navel and nipple. The
folds underline the hip's outward curve.

Unknown sculptors
Grave steles of Boetian warriors charging into battle, Exhibits 54, 55,
56, 240, and BE 43, c. 400–380 BCE

The black marble steles are rare. They were incised in the stone
with lines and dots which would have originally been painted and
easy to see against the dark ground. In a sense, it is like looking at
the plate of an etching, without seeing the print—though the
raised surface would have been painted whereas an etching is
reversed. Move about to where the light gives you the best view.
The draftsmanship is expert. As with Classical works, character is
shown in action at the critical moment of rushing into battle,
shield and weapons poised, face determined. The body is drawn
accurately in perspective, as in Exhibit 54 for example, where the
back leg is thrust forward in side view and the front leg thrust
backwards as seen from the front. In Exhibit 240, the narrow sides
are also used. On one there is a seated sphinx, on the other, a
siren.

Thessaloniki

Greece's second city is an active cultural and commercial center, host to
numerous exhibitions, conventions and trade fairs. Travel agents
suggest that you book accommodation ahead.

Fast train, slower train, bus, and air services are frequent. From Athens, it is six hours by the ordinary train and under an hour by air. A big attraction for art travellers used to be the treasure from the tomb of Phillip the Second (father of Alexander the Great), displayed in the Thessaloniki Archeological Museum. However, because policy is that the treasures of Greece will be shown where they were found, and Phillip's tomb was excavated at the site of Vergina, some 50 miles (80 kilometers) west of Thessaloniki, the treasures are now there. The side trip is well worth the time, so it is mentioned at the end of this Trail, although we do not cover it extensively.

The quality of Thessaloniki's cultural life was recognized when it was nominated as Europe's cultural capital in 1997. The name means "victory (nike) in Thessaly," the name Philip the Second gave to his newborn daughter when he was extending his rule in Macedonia eastwards into Thessaly. The city flourished as a center of pre-Hellenistic art and remained an important center through Hellenistic, Roman, and Byzantine times.

Modern claims that the Macedonians were really Greek can intrude into discussions of archeology and history. However the art was already several millennia old when Greece came into existence, and comes from a period of quite different political organization

Gold wreath of laurel leaves, late fourth century
(Thessaloniki Archeological Museum)

when there was no such place as Greece. What remains clear is that the art of ancient Macedonia has close affinity with Greek art and, subsequently, with Roman art. The later Byzantine art of the region descends directly from the art of the eastern Roman Empire, based on Constantinople.

The Trail includes two major museums. The Archeological Museum, despite the removal of the Macedonian material to be displayed at nearby Vergina, where it was found, has an impressive collection of gold work and finds from other sites. There is also a comprehensive collection of sculpture, jewelry, and ceramics from the Archaic through to the Hellenistic period. The Museum of Byzantine Culture includes examples of various arts from the 3rd to the 13th century CE. There is also a host of Byzantine monuments from which we have selected those with a substantial heritage of art from the richest centuries of Byzantium.

Archeological Museum of Thessaloniki

Location: At the eastern end of Tsimiski (street). Bus No 3 runs along the street. If approaching on foot, use the White Tower as a landmark.
Signage and pedestrian crossings are adequate.
Contact details: Tel. +30 231 083 0538; www.culture,gr
Opening hours: 8:30 am–3:00 pm Tues.–Sun. and 10:30 am–5:00 pm Mon.
Admission: Mid-range (Euro 5–8). Combined ticket including Byzantine Museum is Euro 6.
Other information: Because the renovations and removal of major exhibits to Vergina involve re-arrangement, this guide identifies specific works by their style and catalogue number (if displayed). The room numbers given may change.

Room 9: The Derveni Collection, 350–300 BCE

The exhibits annotated below come from the same period as the finds at Vergina but from sites in and around Thessaloniki. Derveni is regarded as the most important of these sites. It is southwest of Thessaloniki and was excavated in 1962.

The collection comprises material in gold, silver, and clay, and some frescoes. It dates from the time of Phillip and Alexander—a high point of Hellenistic artistic activity when Macedonian power expanded enormously and reached even as far east as Afghanistan.

Unknown goldsmiths
Various gold wreaths representing ivy (M Δ 2579), myrtle
(M θ 7417) *from the tomb of Stavropoulos*, olive (MK 4810),
oak (5151) from the Hellenistic Cemetery of Ancient Europos,
5th–4th century BCE.

These intricate golden wreaths, worn by both the living and the
dead, are unlike any jewelry worn today, including crowns.
Citizens of consequence wore wreaths on ceremonial occasions, at
symposia and finally to the grave.

The wreaths are presented here in an astonishing state of
preservation, shimmering and light. Some, like the myrtle wreath
(7417), include flowers, golden tendrils and leaves. The gold has an
inner glow as well as a dazzling surface light. Because the leaves are
set at different angles, they reflect light from one back to another.
The light gold pieces and their delicate arrangement makes various
parts seem to shimmer and move in the air, taking on something of
the character of the plants they imitate.

Apart from the wreaths, some of the jewelry displays more
general motifs, such as the spirals that recall Celtic ornamentation.

Unknown artist(s)
Derveni krater, Exhibit B1, 330–310 BCE

A large amount of tin in the bronze alloy has given this large urn a
gold color, but there is no gold in it. A combination of techniques
was used—casting for the base and upper parts and repoussé or
hammering through a raised pattern for the body. Kraters are used
for wine and this one features an appropriate Dionysian scene—a
most striking example of Hellenistic art, romantic in conception and
realistic in manner. One side shows a youthful Dionysos with
Ariadne. He is naked with one leg over her knee and she is
beginning to undress. The other side shows a Dionysian orgy with
nymphs being carried off by satyrs. A voyeur at the side of the orgy
and wearing nothing but a boot, has an erection. He is thought to be
the Thracian king Lykourgos. He had offended Dionysos who drove
him mad so that he mistakenly killed his own son. Perched on the
rim of the urn are four figures drowsing or sleeping gracefully while
above the orgy are sleeping couples—the bearded Dionysos and
Silenus on one side; and two maenads (women who take part in the
orgies of Dionysos) on the other. The face of Dionysos figures in the
handles, which are outlined by snakes with corkscrew tails.

Unknown artist(s)
Tomb 11 from Tumulus A at Aeneia, 350–325 BCE

The interior of this tomb for a young woman and her newborn child is painted and decorated as though it were a room. Something of the joy of these young lives is preserved in the design and decoration. The skirting and floor level are painted black and marble. At the top of the painted wall is a frieze and above it a cornice with a white dove and wreaths, ribbons, and a pendant of Aphrodite hanging from nails. Everything is faithfully represented, even the shadows. Thus light and life are preserved in this space, even though when it was closed, the tomb would be in total darkness. The tomb was not sumptuous. It contained a box of bones and a relatively small number of offerings. As with the Derveni urn, the work shows attention to realistic detail: Hellenistic art was a precursor for the ways in which Renaissance painters would treat religious narratives.

Unknown artists
Various pieces of silverware from Tomb B at Derveni, including shallow plates (B15, 16,17), deeper plates (B18, 19), an askos (jug) (B3), and a gilded wine jug (B14), from 330–310 BCE

These silver pieces represent lasting values of good design with their smooth lines and proportion accentuated by their metal surfaces: they could come from our own time. It is noticeable how little the basic design of such objects has changed in thousands of years.

The wine jug and several other pieces feature some gilding. In the wine jug B14, the gilding contrasts with the silver base, handle and neck, further accentuating the lines of the object overall. Nearby ceramic pieces take advantage of their painted and decorated surfaces to emphasize their overall shape.

Museum of Byzantine Culture

Location: Leofórou Stratou (street), beside the Archeological Museum.

Contact details: Tel. +30 231 083 8597; www.culture.gr

Opening hours: Tues.–Sun. 8:00 am–7:00 pm, Mon. 11:00 am–7:00 pm

Admission: Low range (Euro 1–4). Combined ticket including the Archeological Museum Euro 6.

The permanent exhibition here combines art objects, domestic objects and information displays to give a comprehensive account of Byzantine culture. From an art point of view, the most interesting sections are the first four rooms devoted to the early Christian period—from the 3rd to the 7th centuries. The commentary below concentrates on the art exhibits, but the displays about daily life (especially in Room 2) and historical sequences give valuable context.

There is no record of the artists and architects to whom we owe these works.

Room 1

Architectural remains from the church of Saint Demetrius, 5th–6th centuries CE

The arch and piers are decorated with animal and vegetable motifs and, in the corners, winged nikes. The finesse of the carving in marble is typically Byzantine—indeed one of the most attractive features of the style. The nikes serve also as angels, illustrating the easy transition made from pagan to Christian imagery. The political transition had been a century earlier and in the following few centuries, a new culture would be made from the vast architectural and artistic patrimony of the ancients.

Fresco of SS Cosmas and Damian, 6th century CE

The portion of a fresco of two Christians martyred by the Romans similarly illustrates a transition from ancient styles. The figures are not yet fitted into a framework of the Byzantine conventions that essentially require frontal, two-dimensional representation of figures. Indeed they are precursors of later Western imagery. The great debate within Christianity about the propriety of using human figures in ecclesiastical art was yet to rage. Iconoclasm, which branded human figures as "idols" and sought to have them smashed, had brief victories in the 8th and 9th centuries. Its underlying idea continued to have force in the art of Eastern Christianity.

Floor mosaic from church of the Taxiarchs, 6th century CE

The inverted capital re-used for the rim of a well demonstrates the refined variety that Byzantine art introduced to the decoration of columns. The Greeks stuck to their three orders—Doric, Ionic and Corinthian—endowing each with symbolic virtues. The Romans were especially fond of the imperial overtones ascribed to the Corinthian order. Both these tendencies were picked up in western classical revivals. Between times, in the Byzantine east and Romanesque west, capitals became more imaginative (though always delicate) and eventually able to carry complex narrative. Even in this modest, recycled example the elegance of the taste and skill in the stonework is striking.

Elsewhere, mosaic paving and wall painting illustrate the blending of Greek, Roman and Byzantine taste that prevailed in these centuries. Room 2 is a display of urban life in early Christian cities, which is fascinating, but needs little guidance.

Room 3

Room 3 is a large space with fascinating exhibits related to burials and cemeteries. The commentary moves from the left side from the entrance to the center to the right.

Painted tombs, 4th century CE

The first of the burial vessels is a rectangular box adorned with geometric patterns and imitated marble. The other two have barrel vaults. The first of the vaulted ones is known as the tomb of Eustorgios. It contains a scene of the family, parents and two children, at a ceremony. On the side, birds are symbolically overturning amphoras. A crouching person could get into the tomb. The other tomb is decorated on the vault only with plant and bird motifs. Among the birds, the peacocks symbolize immortality. To the ancient Greeks they were a sun symbol, because of their tails. Christians picked up this meaning and extended the idea of the solar wheel to suggest continuity, rebirth and immortality.

Towards the middle of the room, you will see:

Good Shepherd, mid-4th century CE

It is interesting to speculate about the degree to which this engaging image descends from the archaic Greek Moschophoros— the naked countryman with a calf over his shoulders. However, in a pastoral society, the image can arise of its own accord as a powerful symbol of responsibility and care for the weak and the lost, as indeed it did in Christ's parable. The shepherd is a boy; thus innocence in both human and animal equates with virtue.

Next to the shepherd is a sample of low relief carving, and around the area, quantities of small vessels that contained, one supposes, perfumes and oils. In the middle of the room are:

Tombs with frescoes, 4th century CE

The double tomb, each part with a barrel vault, illustrates some of the favored scenes of the times. The left-hand tomb is painted to resemble marble facings. The other is filled with narrative. The themes, from both the Old and New Testaments, are listed on the note beside the right-hand tomb. At the back (of the right-hand tomb) are the expected heraldic birds with amphora. Below is the Good Shepherd. Around the sides and vault the narrative scenes, beginning with Daniel surviving death in the den of the lion, broadly signify the idea of redemption—the release from eternal death. Bold red bands separate the scenes. The front of the tomb, standing separately from it, depicts Adam and Eve.

Displayed around a corner and along the right hand wall are images of plenty and prosperity.

Scenes of plenty, 3rd–5th centuries CE

Presumably these scenes depict the attractions of Paradise, a land of wine and oil, teeming with game. From the 2nd century, we have a fisherman with fish; from the 4th, plump birds, lamb and fish in a Yeatsian "dolphin-torn" and "mackerel-crowded" sea. From the 5th comes the scene of Susanna and the elders. The museum's notes (on its website) suggest that this is an allegory of Jewish and pagan opposition to Christianity.

Room 4

Slabs, 10th–11th centuries CE

The reliefs of a lion, an eagle with a hare, and a griffin illustrate the degree to which Byzantine art moved away from realistic imagery to stylizing shapes and decorating surfaces with abstracted forms. Western art of the Romanesque period showed a parallel but less decorative tendency.

Icon of the Virgin Dexiokratousa, c. 1200 CE

The word Dexiokratousa identifies the icon as one in which Mary holds the child with her right arm. Byzantine painting is here at a long remove from its origins in Roman painting. The subject matter is frequently repeated in a set of conventional poses. Line is favored over mass, which serves to keep the image out of three dimensions even if it is not entirely in two. Even so, the intensity of the mother's gaze and the trusting confidence of the child make a compelling human image.

Room 7

Icons, early 14th century CE

The icons in this room show what has become of Byzantine imagery in its late phase when it is interacting with western art. Giotto was active in Italy at this time, but this painting resembles work of an earlier era in the west, with bodies more outlined than solid and still, rather than dramatic compositions. The very restraint, however, is affecting.

Some Byzantine Churches

At the museum end of Egnatia Street, where it crosses the walls of the ancient city, you are close to the Arch of Galerius and the Rotunda. Following the wall uphill takes you to the museum of Saint Nikolaos Orphanos and the chapel of Hossios David. From there you come back downhill to Saint Dimetrios and Hagia Sofia. Returning to Ayiou Dimitriou, you continue to the walls of the other end of the ancient city to the church of Ayioi Apostoli. Allow a full day to look at all these churches. There are many places to stop for a meal or a drink along the way.

Church opening hours: Churches used for religious activities are usually open every day, but should not be toured when services are on. Visit in the morning, between 7:00 am and 1:00 pm—they often close for several hours over lunchtime and have services between 5:00 pm and 7:00 pm. Sundays and feast days are generally not suitable for touring. One of the churches below (Nikolaos Orphanos) operates like a museum.

Admission: There are no admission charges, but donations are encouraged.

Rotunda

Location: D. Gounari
Contact details: Tel. +30 31 213 627, 204 414, 206 045; www.culture.gr
Opening hours: 8:30 am–3:00 pm.
Admission: No admission fee is charged during the current restorations.

The large domed building, now called the Rotunda, was built in 306 CE in the reign of Galerius, one of the four Tetrachs or administrators of Diocletian's empire. The arch of Galerius, a monumental entrance just within the ancient city walls, is decorated with sculptures glorifying his victories over the Persians. The Rotunda is connected to it via D. Gounari. When built, the two were connected by a colonnaded way wide enough for official processions. Experts are not sure whether the Rotunda was meant to be a temple or a mausoleum. At all events it did not serve the latter purpose and in the 4th or 5th century the vast space was made over into a Christian church, dedicated possibly to the archangels. About 1590, it was made a mosque.

The interior has been damaged in earthquakes and restoration works may make it hard to see its mosaics. They are splendid pieces from an early period in which Roman sensibilities were still strong. The figures come across as relaxed patricians standing in gorgeous architectural settings, and the decorations of leaves, fruits, birds, stars, and blue and gold skies are very elegant.

Nikolaos Orphanos

Location: Between Apostolou Pavlou and Irodotou
Opening hours: Tues.–Sun. 8:30 am–3:00 pm. Closed Mondays.
Admission: Free

This church is part of a monastery, and the capitals and columns include material recycled from early Christian churches. The shape of the interior has been altered from the original three-aisle basilica. However, the wall paintings are among the best preserved in Thessaloniki.

Unknown artists
Wall paintings, 1310–1320 CE

Following tradition, these paintings are a mix of standing figures and narrative scenes. Typically, saints are on lower levels, with scenes of

The funeral of the Virgin, c.1310–20, Byzantine fresco. (Church of Nikolaos Orphanos, Thessaloniki)

the Passion of Christ and Mary's Dormition on the next level. The highest level shows the Resurrection and events that followed. In the apse Mary stands commandingly, acknowledged by angels and accompanied by scenes of the Annunciation and Nativity.

These are late Byzantine works, comparable to those in Ayoi Apostoli. With the exception of the distinctly Greek face, they are comparable to art in the Western churches of the late Middle Ages. The figures are modeled in the round and in a variety of postures, albeit with a preference for frontal poses with weight being taken more on one leg. Drapery has a key role in defining the body beneath. The treatment of narrative scenes varies from the traditional practice of putting events from different times into the one composition to the more modern convention of focusing on a central dramatic action.

Hossios David

Location: Off Timotheou.
Opening hours: Mon.–Sat.: Except for the usual period after lunch, a caretaker is available to open the church and explain the frescoes.
Admission: Donation.

Unknown artist(s)
Mosaic, late 5th century

If possible, don't miss this treasure. The mosaic in the apse is among the oldest in Thessaloniki. The building, formerly part of a monastery, survived use as a mosque and was reconsecrated in 1921. Twelfth–century wall paintings of the life of Mary are outside the apse.

The large mosaic takes us back to the style and subject matter of early Christianity in a world that was still Greco-Roman in culture. The subject is called the Theophany—Christ showing himself in glory to the world. He appears as a young man declaring his role as the central figure of the universe and the future judge who will be enthroned at the world's end. The universe is symbolized by swarming rivers in prosperous landscapes and by the prophets and evangelists who foretold its nature and its end. The evangelists are at the four corners of the rainbowed throne: Mark the lion, Luke the ox, John the eagle and Matthew the angel. The crouching figure at the (viewer's) left is said to be the prophet Ezekiel. Both the freedom of composition and the clarity of color are striking.

Basilica of Saint Dimitrios

Location: Ayiou Dimitriou.
Opening hours: As for churches.
Admission: Free.

There have been many churches on this site. The one you see now is the largest church in Greece, built on the site where Saint Demetrios, patron of the city, was martyred in the 4th century CE. A native of the city and son of an eminent family, he had been made a subconsul of Greece by the Roman emperor Erculius Maximus. When he converted to Christianity, he set about converting others, thereby earning the wrath of Galerius who questioned, humiliated, imprisoned and tortured him. From prison, he worked notable miracles before Roman soldiers speared him.

In accordance with tradition, the church's front door faces west and the sanctuary is at the eastern end. Once you are through the porch or narthex inside the entrance, you are in a basilica church, a form adapted from Roman building. The body of the church is the nave with two rows of columns on each side creating four aisles. At the eastern end, the colonnades turn to the right and left respectively to create cross aisles or transepts. Above, where the nave crosses with the transepts, is the dome. The apse is a quarter of a sphere, filled with a gigantic modern mosaic. Large piers help to support the dome.

Of the twenty columns flanking the nave, eight are green and the others white. The columns and their capitals are a mix of new and reused materials. The four piers are square and faced with marble except where mosaics have been uncovered. The ceilings are timber, which allows the building to be quite spacious because it does not have to support huge weights at the top. Above the side aisles are galleries, originally for women, who could look down into the church. The outer walls have numerous windows whose circular apertures let in disciplined rays of light that penetrate the space unobtrusively.

As you enter, your eye is drawn to the various points of light around the space. The altar is fenced off from the areas set aside for the congregation and a further area behind the altar is reserved for the priests who conduct parts of the liturgy from there.

Unknown artists
Mosaics, 5th–9th centuries CE

Nine mosaics remain from the many undoubtedly beautiful ones that adorned the basilica before a fire in 1917. Although they span several centuries of Byzantine craftsmanship they are consistent examples of the early style. Seven of the nine concern Saint Dimitrios. We see him as a consul summoned by an angel with a trumpet from a cloud-filled sky. Children bring him gifts. He stands with four priests, with the bearded builders of the church and with his arm around a deacon. We see him also standing protectively over a small boy and a girl. In all of these, light, clear colors, serene faces and idealized landscapes transmit a feeling of purity and innocence, at odds with the violence he and other Christians endured from their Roman overlords.

Crypt

The entrance to the crypt is easy to find from inside the basilica on the right of the altar.

Opening hours: Tues to Sat. 8:00 am–8:00 pm, Sun., 10:30 am–8.00 pm, Mon.12:30 pm–7:00 pm

Underneath the crossing is a crypt—part of the former Roman baths containing a lot of pillars and arches that support the sanctuary above.

Within is a marble basin that once contained holy water and subsequently the miraculous oil of myrrh associated with Saint Dimitrios. The oil was also kept in pots, some of which can still be seen. The space now houses a well organized and annotated display of the site's history.

Hagia Sofia

Location: Plateia Ayias Sofias

Like the Basilica of Saint Dimitrios, Hagia Sofia is built over Roman structures and has colonnades and first-floor galleries. The difference is the large dome that sits on a Greek cross formed by the nave and side aisles. It has similarities to the great church of Hagia Sofia in Istanbul, dedicated to divine wisdom.

Unknown artists
Sculpture, 5th century CE and later

The only remains of original 5th-century work in stone is on the capitals at ground level on the north side (the left side from the main entrance). Some of these playfully adapt the acanthus leaf motif of Corinthian columns to a swirling motion. Another treats the capital as a set of four surfaces tapering from a square top—an arrangement that will later accommodate symbolic and narrative figures.

Unknown artist(s)
Mosaic, 9th century CE

There are early mosaics remaining on a vault near the sanctuary, but the great piece is a majestic scene of the Ascension in the dome. Its use of space alone is masterful, especially given the theological requirements for portraying the event. The twelve apostles, Mary, and two angels are set around the circle of the dome, each framed by trees in a rocky landscape. Two more angels carry an already transfigured Christ into the celestial spheres. Christ, Mary, and the angels take the event in their stride but the apostles are clearly flummoxed or confounded by what has happened. The blues, white, and some browns on a gold field seem the natural colors of such an event.

The huge *Mary and the Child* on a gold ground in the apse is of uncertain date, possibly about the 12th century.

Ayoi Apostoli

Location: Ayiou Dimitriou

Unknown artists
Mosaics and wall paintings, from 1310 CE

Although substantial changes in style have occurred over the centuries since early Christian artists adapted Greco/Roman styles, typical arrangements of figures and stories persist. In Ayoi Apostoli (the Holy Apostles) the image of Christ Pantocrator dominates the center of the space and presides over the mosaic scenes from his life. On the lower levels, wall paintings tell more stories from the Christian texts and offer images of saints and scholars.

These are similar to the last of the Byzantine mosaics, and they are mannered in style. We see in them a return to Hellenistic tastes for elaborately draped and posed figures, an attraction to emotional and dramatic moments and gestures and a search for realism that can only be at odds with much of the subject matter. This tension, manifest in a work such as the transfiguration (in the upper west arch), takes the works into the realm of surrealism.

There is more of Byzantium to be seen in Thessaloniki. The guide *Wandering in Byzantine Thessaloniki* (E. Kourkoutidou-Nikolaidou and A. Tourta. Kapon Editions) is comprehensive and learned.

Archeological Site and Museum of Vergina

Location: 50 miles (80 kilometers) west of Thessaloniki (from where you can catch a bus), and about 8 miles (12 kilometers) from Veria.
Contact details: Tel. +30 331 92347; www.culture.gr
Opening hours: 8:30 am–3:00 pm Tues.–Sun., Closed Mondays.
Admission: Mid-range (Euro 5–8), discount Euro 4.

Vergina was built on what was the first capital (Aigai) of ancient Macedonia. It is now best known as the site of the tomb of Philip II, uncovered in 1977 when it was still stocked with a treasure of fine gold-work. The treasure was moved to the Archeological Museum of Thessaloniki but has now returned to be part of a brilliantly conceived exhibition of the tombs. There are splendid wall paintings and other treasures. The tomb and many other wealthy finds made in 1977–8 are still almost intact, with their treasure undisturbed—since 336 BCE when Phillip was assassinated at his daughter's wedding—and the finds are considered to be some of the most important of the last century. Although a detailed look at the site is beyond the scope of this book, it is easy to guide yourself around this site.

Windmills in the mountains of Crete

Trail 8:
The Minoan Trail—Crete
and Santorini

Thera

SANTORINI **Akrotiri**

Heraklion

CRETE

Agios Nikolaos

Kritsa

Phaistos

(Trail 8 | **The Minoan Trail**

Crete

Crete is a significant site in Greek mythology. Zeus was born there, in a cave on Mount Ida (14 miles, 22 kilometers) from Anogia. In the form of a white bull, Zeus coupled with Europa to produce Minos, legendary king of Knossos and founder of Minoan civilization. Beneath his palace the Minotaur roved the Labyrinth, which Daidalos, father of Icarus, had designed. (The word labyrinth descends from *labrys* or double ax with which Knossos is associated.) Minos forced Athens to send regular batches of young women and men to be devoured by the Minotaur, until the monster was slain by Athenian Athenian hero Theseus.

The colorful and vital art of Crete had a strong influence beyond the island and its near neighbor, Santorini. Although Mycenaeans seem to have taken over Crete around 1400 BCE, Mycenaean art was virtually a branch of Minoan art. Minoan art uses both stylized and realistic forms with ease and vigor. It also survives in more varied media than the art of other periods. Painting, for example, was highly prized in many periods, but only Minoan painting has survived to any extent. Painting, small-scale sculpture and pottery are the prize pieces. The palaces, as re-imagined, are impressive. Craft objects such as gold jewelry, seals and boxes are beautifully made.

The marvelous art suggests a society that was dynamic, creative, and ordered. Long before Greek culture spread across Greece, Minoan culture shone in the Aegean and had a strong influence on its successors. The Minoans were a sea-loving people and traded with their neighbors in the islands and on the African coast. Their art celebrates their love of nature as well as their social and religious life.

The main city in Crete is Iraklio. The traditional English spelling is Heraklion. Crete and Santorini are both reachable by ferry or plane.

Heraklion Archeological Museum

Location: The museum is to one side of Elefetherias Square in the center of Heraklion. Follow signs to Kentpo or Museio.

Contact details: Tel. +30 281 022 6092; www.culture.gr

Opening hours: Daily from 8:00 am–5:00 pm, Mondays 12:00 noon–5:00 pm.

Admission: Mid-range (Euro 5–8). A combined ticket for Heraklion Museum and the archeological site of Knossos is Euro 10 or Euro 5 discount.

The museum gives an overview of the Minoan world and is truly a unique opportunity to explore a wonderfully lively and varied art. Most of the exhibits are from Minoan palaces, settlements, and tombs in Crete. After the earthquake of 1700 BCE palaces were rebuilt at Knossos, Malia, and Phaistos and a new palace was built at Zakros. Photographs of the sites from which the exhibits come hang around the walls—usually appearing as low lines of stone, except for colored drawings of reconstructed palaces at Knossos.

The collection is displayed chronologically. Rooms are numbered, and the glass cases are numbered seriatim. Sometimes, you may have to hunt

The Bull in Minoan Art

The bull has long been a symbol of majestic strength and almost uncontrollable violence. Minoan art refers frequently to bulls in apparently sacred contexts, and often depicts bull-leaping, which had the extreme danger of bull-fighting without the blood. Both men and women participated in the sport, the women in male dress. The idea was to seize the horns of the charging bull and vault over its back.

Apart from its obvious thrills as a sport, bull-leaping is thought to have had a religious meaning in itself or at least some significance in religious celebrations. Experts are satisfied that the sport was practiced and might be the source of the myth of the Minotaur.

Greek legend has it that Zeus, in the form of a white bull, coupled with Europa and produced Minos, the founder of Cretan civilization. Whether this later myth drew on Minoan mythology, presumably via the Mycenaeans, is impossible to assess. The correspondences are strong and the cultural transitions from one civilization to the next would have been gradual despite the abruptness of natural disasters, invasions and political realignments.

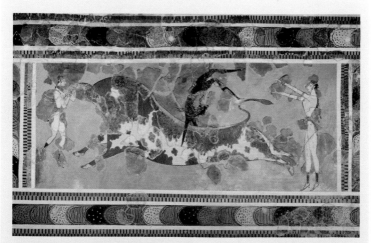

Bull leaping. Fresco from Knossos. 1600–1400 BCE.
(Archeological Museum of Heraklion)

around to find the numbers on the cases. We give exhibit numbers when possible, but not the names of artists, as no one knows who they were.

Adjoining the foyer is a special exhibition on bull leaping, which you may wish to look at first.

Unknown artists
Bull with leapers, libation vessel, Exhibit 4126

In this depiction of the bull-leaping theme on a ritual vessel, the figures are small enough to be children, and the bull exceptionally large. The crafting of the jug is neat: its handle would make pouring easy and its three legs would make it more stable than a realistic four-legged piece.

Ivory figure of an acrobat, Exhibit 3, 1700–1450 BCE

Other works in the museum confirm that this slender figure in mid-flight is a bull-leaper. The figure celebrates youth, daring and the human capacity to harness if not control the bull's power. There are indications that the figure is wearing clothes of gold. There were several leapers, male and female, all wearing very little. Because this figure is about a foot (30 centimeters) long, if there were a bull in the original sculpture the whole piece would have been about a yard (a meter) long and about half as high.

Room I

Room I is a treasure trove, almost worth a visit on its own. It starts about 7000 BCE and spans five millennia. Objects from Neolithic times—7000–3500 BCE—are in Cases 1–2. Cases 3–18 contain human and animal figurines and vases from the Bronze Age before the Minoans built their palaces (3500–2000 BCE).

The case numbering goes around the walls and ends in the rows in the middle of the room. Especially notable are Cases 1, 2, 7, 8, 12, 13, and 18a.

Pottery and figurines from Knossos and elsewhere, Case 1, Neolithic period

The pottery shows the longevity of geometric patterning as decoration. The female figurines (e.g. no 2716) testify to sculptors' efforts to create a lasting shape from lasting materials such as baked clay. The figures may represent a deity or, like the animal figures, be intended as votives. For the animal, painting has served to define features. The markings on the female figure are harder to interpret.

Male torso from Knossos, Case 2, Exhibit 2623, 7000–3500 BCE

In the middle of the case is a small (4 inch/10 centimeter) but compelling marble male torso. One of the legs is broken. The body is well observed and its strength contained in broad shoulders and a muscled thigh. Like many other figures, the arms fold in and are somewhat stunted compared to the rest of the anatomy. The translucent marble simulates the warmth of skin, and marks the early stages of a love affair with the material that will preoccupy Mediterranean art and its descendants for millennia.

Stone jug from the island of Mochlos, Case 7, Exhibit 1201
Jewelry boxes in stone, Exhibits 2719 and 1282, Pre-palace period 3500–2000 BCE

The jug is particularly handsome because of the way in which color variations and the veining in the rock have been exposed and decorate the body of the vessel. The shape is timeless.

Sprawling dogs form the handles on the lids of two jewelry cases; both are thought to be the work of the same craftsman and carved from a greenish colored stone. The dogs are stretched out to fit the geometry of the hatching on the lids, back leg at right angles, the tail in a carefully contrived curve, paws marked.

Libation vessel from Mochlos, Case 8, Exhibit No 5499, Pre-palace period

Libations were a part of rituals—including burial rituals—so their shapes had symbolic value. This one will pour from the breasts of a woman with her arms typically folded across her body. The function and symbolism combine to indicate that this is probably the figure of a deity connected directly to maternity and to maintaining human life and bringing fertility to the world.

Figurines, Neolithic and Pre-palace periods including Cycladic figures, Case 13, 3500–2000 BCE

The many Bronze Age figurines here offer a synopsis of figure styles that will be explored over and over in Western art. Although more elegantly abstracted and in a more attractive material than Neolithic work, they do not necessarily suggest greater skill. They do, however, appeal to modern taste for abstraction.

The more abstract among them are Cycladic, some almost dagger-shaped. Most are naked with arms folded across the belly. On the face, the nose usually protrudes. Sometimes lips and eyes are recessed. Breasts are those of young women or girls, indeed no bigger than those on some male figures.

There is a variety of ideas. One figure is wrapped, another dressed. Some have rounded arms; on others the arms are indicated by line. There are rounded lips, tilted heads, separated or joined legs, rounded or flat bellies, big ears and pin heads. Twins stand up from a common base. Only one (Exhibit 287) is seated and conceived in three dimensions.

Turn now to Case 18a, the pyramidal case in the middle of the room.

Ivory figurine found at Archanes, Case 181a, Exhibit 440, Pre-palace period 3500–2000 BCE

This lustrous ivory figure, about 4 inches (10 centimeters) in height, mimics the usual marble Cycladic types. The sculptor has carved out the shape of the head and neck; the arms cross at the midway point on the body. The dotted area may represent clothing; the legs have been made with a line and then with an incision separating them; the toes are turned up.

Room II

Room II contains objects from the first Minoan palaces, which were destroyed by earthquake. This so-called old palace period covers 2000–1700 BCE. The pieces come from the palaces of Knossos and Malia and from peak sanctuaries on mountaintops.

Kamares style pottery, 2000–1700 BCE

About half the cases in Room 2 are devoted to inventive and colorful pottery in the Kamares style (named after the sanctuary of Kamares on Mt Ida above Phaistos, where the first of these samples were found.) The delicacy, variety and in some cases fragility of the pieces suggest that they were destined for the palace elite. They were also renowned enough to be exported to the mainland, other islands, the Middle East and Egypt. The Kamares exhibits continue in Room III with finds from Phaistos.

The skill of the potters is clear in both the range of items, from very fine tableware to solid vessels for storage, and in the range of shapes. The white decoration on a black ground is enlivened by reds and yellows, and motifs vary from geometric, with a preference for curves and whorls, to naturalistic—floral, vegetal, and animal. People and narratives, however, do not appear. Textures are also exploited, often with baroque effect.

As well as the pottery there is a host of miniature sculptures in the room. Case 21a includes a display of the double-headed axes—a major symbol of the palace at Knossos. Case 24 offers an interesting selection of human figures.

Figurines, 2000–1700 BCE, Cases 24 and 29

The top shelf of this case has some models of buildings using features seen in reconstructions at Knossos. The columns are tapered at the base and apparently freestanding supports for (probably cult) objects. Sets of rooms are double-storied and the bull's-horn symbol appears in miniature.

The bulls and human figures on the shelf below are probably votaries—offerings taken up to a peak sanctuary. Both males and females have their arms raised in a common gesture, presumably of worship. The woman's gown is closely belted at the waist, falling in gathers to her feet and she wears a headdress.

The male figure on the shelf below, Exhibit 405, wears a loincloth, a belt, and a prominent knife. The raised arms are breast beating.

The detail of the figures in this and in surrounding cases shows interest in style and individuality. Dress is clearly an important aspect of a leisured palace life. Even the sketchy details of faces reflect individual moods and a taste for comic or theatrical effects. Animals and figures could well be participating in games or staged processions. The long, protruding nose with large eyes can still be seen today on the streets of Heraklion.

The votary collection continues in Case 29 (and others) where the object is a limb. These probably represent injured parts that bearers or well-wishers seek to have cured. Overall the votaries and sanctuaries point to a polytheistic religion identified with sacred sites—basically like the religion that sustained historic Greece. We cannot be sure, however, that the Greek practice of depicting gods as human figures, so central to Greek art, was used by the Minoans.

Town Mosaic, Case 25

These faience tiles found at Knossos depict buildings from various aspects, plants, animals, and people. They almost certainly fitted together to make a composite picture of a real or ideal town, and may have decorated a household box or chest. They show important detail of Minoan architecture: the houses are two- and three-storyd with light wells inside; flat roofs, double doors and windows and stone work on the façade. The details correspond to houses excavated on Santorini and to parts of dwellings, such as windows, that appear in Minoan painting.

Room III

Room III has more Kamares ware from Phaistos, as well as the famous Phaistos disc.

Pottery from Phaistos, Cases 32–3, 2000–1700 BCE

The bravura of the pottery from Phaistos suggests the palace was a leading center of the time. The decoration uses geometric, vegetal, animal and marine motifs, but these themes are also carried into the overall shapes of the vessels.

The Phaistos Disc, Case 41, 2000–1700 BCE

The Phaistos disc is a rare example of Minoan writing. It consists of two sides of hieroglyphs in sequence spiralling into the center, but there is not enough here to decipher. Signs are repeated, indicating that they are seals pressed into wet clay. In each circle, a human figure walks in the same direction. The signs may be syllables or may represent ideas. The vertical lines within the spirals may be markers of words—in which case, the signs are syllables—or they may indicate lines, as in a poem. Meanings can be guessed at for many of the signs but the connections elude interpretation.

Dancing figures, Case 42, Exhibit 10583, 2000–1700 BCE

The dish in red, white and brown and the base of the bowl nearby are decorated with free-flowing dancers, symmetrically placed. Similarly sketched figures are in different postures on the top of the bowl. The simplicity and distortion make the bowl look modern. Greeks still have dances reminiscent of this. Some of the figures on the bowl are gathering and apparently offering flowers, which suggests that they and the dancers are part of a ceremony, perhaps involving a mixture of god-figures and priestesses.

Finally, in Case 42 you will see a display of a tableware set, whose rococo detailing testifies to the wealth and sophistication of the palace culture at Phaistos.

Writing in Greece

The earliest writing in Greece has been unearthed in Crete, from the Minoan era. From the old palace period, the Phaistos Disc (in Case 41) uses seal impressions in clay that are either ideograms, where a sign represents an object or an idea, or syllables, or more likely, a mixture of both. Other cultures in the Middle East and Egypt used such systems, but the meaning of the Minoan language signs has not been unlocked.

From the New Palace period there are examples of a script that used sets of lines. The first of these is called Linear A (Case 44). Linear A is scratched into clay or written with ink, presumed to be in the Minoan language and hence undeciphered.

From late in Minoan civilization, after the spread of Mycenaean civilization, is Linear B. This combines syllable signs, ideograms and lines and circles to represent numerals (see Case 69) Linear B inscriptions from Knossos and Pylos were deciphered by an English architect and Classical scholar Michael Ventris, who died in 1956, aged 34. For a time, he followed false trails trying to relate the script to Etruscan, and believing it to be Minoan, which was not a Greek language. Finally, in 1952, in a broadcast on the BBC, he was able to announce that Linear B tablets were in "a difficult and Archaic Greek ... five hundred years older than Homer and written in a rather abbreviated form." (See The Decipherment of Linear B by John Chadwick, his collaborator, first published in 1967.)

The Greek alphabet was adapted from the Phoenician alphabet, which—according to Herodotus—was brought to Thebes by Cadmus around 1400 BCE. The Phoenicians had an alphabet about that time, but linguists date its appearance in Greece about 500 years later. The Greeks borrowed consonant signs that suited their sounds and added vowels. Eventually they wrote from right to left.

The English alphabet descends from the Greek via Etruscan and Roman adaptations.

Room IV

After the earthquake of 1700 BCE new palaces were built in Knossos, Phaistos, Malia and Zakros. This brilliant New Palace period produced art of great sophistication. Further disasters ended the New Palace period about 1450 BCE. After that, only Knossos was rebuilt and the Mycenaeans dominated Crete.

Cup with writing, Case 44, Exhibit 2630, 1700–1450 BCE

The writing inside the little vessel, reproduced on paper beside it, is a script in Linear A; the ink used was cuttlefish ink, which could be used on other surfaces such as papyrus—a plant which, known for its use in Egypt, also appears in Minoan paintings.

Pottery and writing fragments Case 49, 1700–1450 BCE

Jars with Linear A markings are also on display in Case 49. The black dribbles on fragments of pithoi used for storage are thought to show which fluid was in the vase.

This case also contains several superb vases with floral and marine motifs. Especially attractive is one covered with a woven grass pattern in browns (unnumbered). In this instance, nature has provided a geometric patterning, but overall there is a trend away from geometric decoration towards naturalism.

Snake goddesses, Case 50, Exhibits 65 and 63, 1700–1450 BCE

These fascinating and forbidding figures, among the largest pieces of sculpture found in Minoan sites, are among the plum pieces of the museum. Both are proudly bare-breasted, wasp-waisted and clothed in heavy skirts and bold helmets. One with a tiered skirt brandishes snakes; the other has them slithering around her arms, head and waist. Experts see these as goddess or priestess figures in a snake cult. (Several vessels in Case 46 have been identified as breeding dishes for snakes.) Snakes were later associated with the underworld and the formidable expressions on the statues suggest they were here as well. The Minoans' mastery of various media and the spaces they created in their palaces tempts speculation that there may have been other larger sculptures that have now perished.

Bull's head rhyton (ritual vessel). 1700–1450 BCE. (Archeological Museum of Heraklion, Lauros/Giraidon/Bridgeman Art Library)

Bull's head rhyton, Exhibit 1368. Case 51, 1700–1450 BCE

This rhyton celebrates the beauty and purity of animal strength. The hard materials are precious—finely veined and incised black stone for the head, rock crystal and a pink stone for the eyes, shell for the nose. The left side of the head is original, but the horns, of gilded wood, are restorations. For libations, the bull's head was filled from the back and poured from the mouth.

Another depiction of a bull leaping, Exhibit 57 in Case 52, is a rare example of painting on a glass-like pane of rock crystal. Other animals are depicted in faience (glazed pottery work).

Dress, Exhibit 58, *Cow*, Exhibit 68, *Goat*, Exhibits 69, all in Case 55 ; *Gaming board*, Case 57, 1700–1450 BCE

Minoan potters were exceptionally skilled in miniature work in most media. Their faience works are among the best pieces in the collection. Exhibit 58 models an elaborately crafted skirt like those worn by the snake goddesses. Why pieces such as this were made is unknown. However, the plaques of a *Cow* and *Goat* suckling their young demonstrate the vivid naturalism of which Minoan artists were capable.

The famous gaming board in Case 57 and made from ivory, rock crystal and glass paste is a hint that fragments of faience such as the animals above formed part of larger pictures.

Room V

Room V moves towards the final phase of Minoan palace civilization at Knossos in the century following 1450 BCE. There are several items of historical interest in the room. The biggest vase on the back wall, with the palms, is a reminder of trade and cultural exchange with Egypt.

Case 69 contains tablets and other inscriptions in Linear B, while Case 70a has a model of a Minoan house found at Archanes, a settlement near Knossos. The space is intricate and well lit, with enclosed rooms for winter and an open upper storey.

Room VI

Exhibits in Room VI come from the end of the New Palace era and from the Post-Palace period, i.e. 1450–1300 BCE. They are mainly items from cemeteries.

The pottery has become rather harsh, perhaps made in imitation of metal vessels. The seals and rings, however, retain the inventiveness of earlier Minoan work and demonstrate again their great skill with miniatures and jewelry.

The helmet made of boars' tusks (Case 82, Exhibit 175) and another of bronze, are the most striking of a large number of weapons displayed here. The Old and New Palace periods seem to have been peaceful and prosperous. The appearance of much weaponry in the Post-Palace period is taken as evidence of the occupation of Crete by the martial Mycenaeans, i.e. the Greeks. The tusks are sewn into a leather cap.

Room VII

Here, and also in Room VIII, are some remarkable works in stone from the New Palace period (1700–1450 BCE). Inside the entrance is a display of large double-axes, a ubiquitous symbol of construction and destruction, hence, perhaps, of life and death.

> *The Harvesters' Vase*, Case 94, Exhibit 184;
> *The Chieftain's Cup*, Case 95, Exhibit 341;
> *Rhyton with various scenes*, Case 96, Exhibit 498

All three pieces are from Ayia Triada, near Phaistos. The stone is a soft soapstone or steatite (meaning "like dough" in Greek).

The Harvesters' Vase (Exhibit 184) is a complex scene conceived as a lively and jolly procession. The men are in pairs, probably returning from winnowing in the fields outside the settlement. The scene may depict a special occasion, such as the end of the harvest. There is a musician in the group and several singers. The leader is in ceremonial dress—his jacket imitating fish scales or waves. The sculptors have taken care to show the group as a mix of individuals in varied and somewhat disorderly action and showing various emotions.

The Chieftain's Cup (Exhibit 341) is also known as *The Report* because the smaller figure shouldering a staff appears to be making an announcement to the larger figure with the long tresses and the out-thrust scepter. Each figure has been given an individual character that fits the role being played. The man with the scepter opens his shoulders and stands high; the other slumps slightly in a posture of subservience.

The conical *Rhyton* (Exhibit 498) has four bands of sporting scenes. The second band from the top shows the familiar sport of bull-leaping. The other three feature boxing and wrestling. Some of the contestants wear only a loincloth, others are in armor.

All three of these are scenes of action. Key moments have been selected to show character and illuminate the emotions of the participants.

The bronze figurines in several cases nearby are by and large in ritual postures. Those labeled adorants offer a closed-fist salute to the forehead. Others raise the open palm in a form of salute. Their proportions are elongated, with a marked sway-back posture. Most are male. The modeling—as of the leapers—suggests young males extending themselves to the full.

Potters' wheels, Case 100

The potting wheel, the impetus for huge advances in pottery, was developed somewhere in the islands before the first Palace Period. Here we have two discs of clay that would have spun on a wooden machine. One of the discs has the double-ax symbol, which suggests that the craft enjoyed considerable status among rulers, gods or both.

Room VIII

Items in this room are from the palace at Zakros in the New Palace period. The first case we look at is 109, a wall case.

Crystal libation vase, Exhibit 2721, Case 109

This exquisite vase is expertly fashioned from a piece of rock crystal. Its translucence, as well as the decoration with gold and precious stone, fits its use as a vessel for taking libations. Since libations are ritualistic drinks, the vessels are necessarily precious, in effect the crockery of the gods. The elegance and delicacy of the work on the crystal justifies the preciousness of the metal collar and jade-colored bead handle. The vase suggests great wealth both in its materials and workmanship.

Rhyton with reliefs of wild goats, Exhibit 2764, Case 111

Made of green stone, this rhyton was discolored by fire in the Minoan palace at Zakros. Its finely crafted low relief depicts the peak sanctuaries that Minoans placed high in the Cretan mountains—there are chapels in similar positions today. The carving shows a rocky landscape with a building. Goats climb the rocks and squat heraldically around the building. The sanctuary building is walled and surmounted by a bull's-horn symbol. A central door has spiral decorations; beneath a staircase within the sanctuary are three altars. The observation of goats seated on their haunches and looking about—their heads twisted in different positions—and of goats climbing, is masterful and gives life to an essentially static subject.

Stone vessels, Case 118

Finds from the palace at Zakros, not unearthed until the 1960s, come from the richest period of Minoan art. Of particular note among the ritual stone vessels from a shrine is a bold limestone jug (2720) with a double neck and question mark shaped handles.

The same case contains another pieced-together bull's head, said in the museum guide to have been found outside the Temple area and probably in use to stave off disaster at the time of the destruction of the palace.

Other items to note in Room 8 are copper ingots and elephant tusks used as currency (Case 113) and an important collection of pottery vessels with marine motifs (Cases 106, 110, 113 and 114).

Room IX

Room IX contains finds from the New Palace period in Eastern Crete.

Seals, Cases 124 and 128

The displays in this room of seals and impressions from seals repay close examination. Seals in Case 124 are of clay and from various sites. Seals in Case 128, of hard, semi-precious stones, are from the 300-year period after the earthquake of 1700 BCE. They are, of course, of great historical interest and wonderful examples of miniature sculpture. The range of subjects is large, from human heads and figures to hieroglyphs, fantasy animals, dance scenes, insects and grotesques. The amount of detail that can be packed into a tiny space is often astonishing.

Rooms X and XI

Rooms X and XI contain works from the end of Minoan civilization (1400–1100 BCE) and the beginnings of Hellenic Geometric periods (1100–800 BCE). Cult figures, such as the females in Cases 133,

140 and 148 are more ungainly than their earlier equivalents and beginning to be more abstracted.

Room XII

Room XII shows more developed examples of the Geometric-period style period that takes us into the early archaic movement across the Greek world.

Vase of bull with Geometric decoration, Geometric period 900–600 BCE

On the corridor wall, between two giant vases decorated with sphinxes, is a terracotta vase decorated with a bull grazing. This image is at eye level, near the top. It illustrates what might be seen many times around the room—the tension between persisting with natural forms and symbols, such as the bull, and the urge to abstraction in decoration. The strength of the haunch is emphasized by a darkening sweep of color; the saddle becomes triangular and below its point, a symmetrically placed penis. A circular shape represents the rippling of the front joint and the length and angle at which the head is held are emphasized by lines. The style is somewhere between natural realism and decoration, with the artist tending to the formal decorative side of the craft. The skill is in the resolution of these two directions.

Vases and objects in the rest of the room show recognizable human, animal and vegetal shapes coexisting with Geometric decoration, albeit from different places and still over a period of more than two centuries. Nearby sphinxes and other depictions of birds and figures in the same room show marked influences from Egypt and the Middle East.

Room XIII

Minoan carpenters and potters were also coffin makers. This room is full of sarcophagi from 1500–1200 BCE, all but two of them empty of bones. Bodies would have been doubled up to fit into the half-size burial boxes. Some are squarish in shape, others more like tubs. The tub shapes are decorated with scenes and symbols both inside and out.

Burying the dead in wood or clay coffins goes back to the 3rd millennium and continues for most of the Minoan period. The sarcophagi here are from its final centuries. It is claimed that burial in a coffin was, as now, the common fate of the dead and not a privilege of the wealthy. We can assume that much of the decoration drew on the pottery of the time and some represented the paradise to which the dead were being sent. The doubled-up position of the bodies—like the fetal position—is said to symbolize birth, or in this case rebirth in another world.

Go upstairs from Room XIII to see the Minoan paintings.

Upper floor: Rooms XIV, XV, and XVI

The most prominent object in Room XIV, in a case in the center of the room, is a sarcophagus that differs from the rest in that it is painted with a number of scenes.

Painted sarcophagus from Ayia Triada, Case 171, 1400–1300 BCE

This treasure of Minoan art has surfaces of painted plaster, and the scale of the painting suggests it was used for a highly important or royal burial. Most of the scenes deal with worship and death but the light background gives it a lively look. The side that you face when you come in shows a bull being sacrificed while flutes are played. The bull's blood is collected in a bucket by a procession of women—presumably priestesses. The first in line has her hands on the bull's head. On the right of the sacrificed bull, a priestess wearing a sheepskin offers another sacrifice in front of a sanctuary. A black bird—probably a symbol of death—sits on top of a double ax. The scene is set out like a strip or frieze and is framed by spiral patterns with flowers set into the centers of the spirals and by a series of rosettes and vertical patterns. The colors are fresh, bright and cheerful. The faces are consistently long-nosed and large-eyed.

Go around to your left. This (north) end shows a red-haired couple drawn by goats. The compacting of the image to fit the end space adds to the impression of motion.

On the east side, a priestess is emptying a container, probably the blood of the sacrificed bull on the first side. She is beside another two double axes with dark plumed birds perched on them. Another priestess follows her with buckets balanced on her shoulder and a musician playing an instrument with seven strings. Behind him, three men in sheepskins are offering animals and a model of a ship to a man who is standing between a tree and a building. This could be the dead person and the ship a symbol of passing into another world, perhaps where there are animals to hunt.

On the south side, a chariot drawn by winged griffins carries a pair of women—no doubt goddesses. Above, a large bird—an eagle or a bird of prey—flies towards them, perhaps bringing them news from the future.

Priestess at an altar, detail from a sarcophagus from a tomb at Ayia Triada, Crete. Painted plaster on limestone, Late Minoan Period, c.1390 BC. (Archeological Museum of Heraklion, Crete, Greece/Bridgeman Art Library)

On the walls around these rooms are recreations of wall paintings and two low reliefs from the palace of Knossos, numbered 1–15; from Amnisos, numbered 16–17, and from Ayia Triada, numbered 18–24. (These may be in other rooms, depending on the demands of temporary exhibitions.)

That any fragments of paint on plaster (usually painted on to dry plaster) survived is extraordinary given that it was from a period 1800–1300 BCE. What you see now as apparently complete paintings are largely recreations based on small fragments. Extensive reworking amounts to guesswork and is disputed. Some critics dismiss them as misleading, as they do the recreations of the palace at Knossos.

Whatever the case, the images are striking. Some fragments such as the lilies (Exhibits 14 and 16), Room XIV and *The Wildcat* (Exhibit 20, Room XIV) and *La Parisienne* (Exhibit 27, Room XV) seem to be mostly in a good state of preservation. The fact that you see the head of *La Parisienne* is important to the impression of the whole piece.

Minoan painting is probably religious in theme and hence may represent not the real world of people but the realms of gods. Animals are symbolic and landscapes and interiors might represent the next world. Women are white-skinned (from living indoors?) and the men brown.

Fresco Painting

The Minoan frescoes are famous for the fluidity and vitality in their depictions of figures, animals and nature. To paint these glorious works, the process was as follows: first a layer of mortar on the wall was covered with lime stucco; next it was divided into three zones with lines of string lightly pressed into the wet plaster as a guide for the artists; then a general design was laid down in a light color and large areas painted in while the plaster was still wet. This process is known by the Italian name of "buon fresco." Final details were painted in after the plaster had dried—this second technique is "fresco secco." The artists used red and yellow earth pigments. Their black was carbon, and their blue a synthetic pigment obtained in Egypt. Colors were made lighter by mixing the pigments with limewater. Some of the frescoes found in the Akrotiri excavations on Santorini had been painted over, as is common with such works in later European art.

Dolphins and bull leapers

Two blue dolphins are arched against a white sea, with traces of blue suggesting clear water. This is probably the most striking image in the room but may not be faithful to the original. Models used for recreating the bull-leapers can be found in sculptures in the museum, but also call for a leap of faith.

Relief head of bull, c. 1600 BCE

The making of this piece as a painted relief helps give a stronger idea of the original. Only the head has survived and some indication of horns, most of which appear in restoration. It is said to have come from a scene of the capture of a bull, painted around 1600 BCE. The observation of the powerful animal trapped in an agonizing situation is acutely recorded.

La Parisienne

This figure of a lavishly made-up woman has been dubbed *La Parisienne*. Boubelina from the movie version of Kazantzakis's *Zorba the Greek* would fit just as well. Boldly painted and coiffed, her face is like many other faces in Minoan art—long nose and large eyes, their appearance enlarged by cosmetics. The painter has taken a little liberty with the curl falling over the forehead, a flirtatious detail which probably earned her the nickname. She is one of a set of figures being offered libations.

The Palaces

The art of the Heraklion Archeological Museum comes from many Minoan sites around Crete. A visit to at least one such site is necessary to round out your feel for the period and its art. The four largest Minoan settlements were (in order of size) Knossos, Phaistos, Malia and Zakros. Of these, Knossos is not only the largest but also the most easily reached from Heraklion. Malia is also close to Heraklion. Phaistos is in the south and Zakros at the extreme east of the island.

Each of these sites consisted of a palace surrounded by a town. The sites themselves date back to Neolithic times. Each has the ruins of an old palace built around 1900 BCE and destroyed, possibly by an earthquake, about 1700 BCE. The destroyed palaces were replaced by new palaces that lasted till about 1450 BCE when they, too, were destroyed or badly damaged. What event destroyed them so abruptly is not known. Knossos was then inhabited by Greek-speaking Mycenaeans whose language was that of the famous Linear B tablets. The preceding languages of the non-Greek Minoans—written in Linear A and in hieroglyphics—have not been deciphered.

The palaces were in prime locations and not fortified, which suggests a peaceful, prosperous civilization lasting about half a millennium. Externally, the island was protected by its sea power, as Herodotus notes, incidentally adding that Minoans were not Greeks. Internally, political arrangements among the various cities of Crete probably acknowledged Knossos as the main power.

The palace walls were built of a mixture of cut stone and rubble, plastered over and painted. The tapering columns were inverted tree trunks. Surrounding dwellings were sometimes of stone but mostly of mud brick. Excavators, most notably at Knossos, have attempted partial reconstructions of parts of the palaces.

The Cretan palaces followed a fairly common design, with affinities to designs in nearby kingdoms of the Middle East. The centerpiece was a large courtyard from which two- or three-story sets of rooms radiated to lesser courtyards and monumental entrance staircases. Life revolved around the central court with access to fairly modest royal apartments, cult rooms and extensive storage rooms for giant *pithoi* (terracotta urns) containing oil, wine and grain. To the outsider, however, the design was less coherent. After the entrance are sets of rather small rooms with devious passageways. Legend says that the founding king Minos of Knossos kept the Minotaur in a labyrinth beneath his palace. The palace's labyrinthine design might have contributed to the legend.

Part of the design is a theatrical area, an open-air space on the edge of the palace. It is terraced on one side, presumably for spectators at ceremonies of the kind depicted in paintings.

Knossos

Location: About 3 miles (5 kilometers) southeast of Heraklion. Buses leave from the bus station at the port.

Contact details: Tel. +30 281 023 1940; www.culture.gr

Opening hours: The site is open daily from 5:30 am–3:00 pm.

Admission: Entrance fees are Euro 6 or Euro 3 discount. A combined ticket with Heraklion Museum is Euro 10 or Euro 5 discount.

THE MINOAN TRAIL — CRETE AND SANTORINI

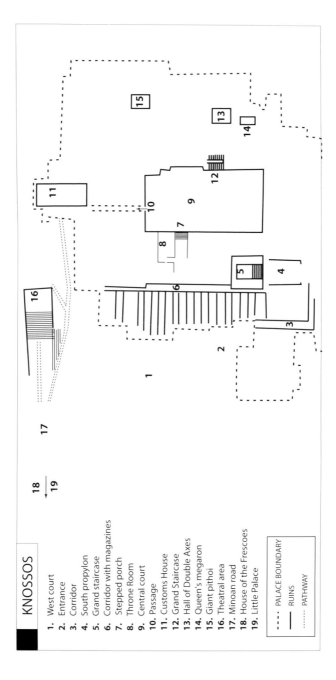

KNOSSOS

1. West court
2. Entrance
3. Corridor
4. South propylon
5. Grand staircase
6. Corridor with magazines
7. Stepped porch
8. Throne Room
9. Central court
10. Passage
11. Customs House
12. Grand Staircase
13. Hall of Double Axes
14. Queen's megaron
15. Giant pithoi
16. Theatral area
17. Minoan road
18. House of the Frescoes
19. Little Palace

- - - PALACE BOUNDARY
——— RUINS
.... PATHWAY

Knossos was undoubtedly the grandest of the Minoan palaces, and the only one to be rebuilt a second time after the New Palace phase. Its name is probably the Minoan name for the city: it is mentioned in Linear-B tablets as ko-no-so. Though known from ancient times, the site was not excavated until early in the 20th century. Its chief excavator, Sir Arthur Evans, undertook restoration work that would not be done today, but it does help us to visualize aspects of the original. Columns have been reinstated, copies of the heavily restored wall frescoes in the Heraklion museum appear in various rooms, and the functions of rooms have been deduced or imagined. As for the frescoes, remember that the reconstructions were put together from small fragments, so there was a lot of guesswork involved. The diagram shows the layout of the site.

The central palace can be entered from several sides. The usual and most impressive entrance is via the large paved area of the **west court** **(1)**. To your left is the **theatrical area (16)**. In front are magazines or storage rooms and on your right, an **entrance (2)** that takes you to a **corridor (3)**, called the corridor of the procession. After a left turn you reach the **south propylon (4)**, part of the south entrance. Up to this point the copies of reconstructed frescoes on the wall are of a religious, or at least ceremonial, procession. Youths (identified as males by their brown skin) carry drinking vessels. They are sufficiently alike to suggest they are typical of their culture: slim, strong with long noses, full lips, almond eyes, and ornamental hairdos featuring blue scalps and black plaits.

Beyond the south propylon is a **grand staircase (5)**. From the left corner at the top of the staircase there is a long **corridor (6)** with many magazines off it. A right turn from the corridor takes you towards a **stepped porch (7)** and into the **central court (9)**. Left and down some steps is the **throne room (8)**. The throne (dubbed the "throne of Minos") is as it was found on the site. Some archeologists suggest that there was a ceremony occurring in the throne room when the palace was abruptly destroyed. The throne is backed by reconstructions of painted griffins in a stylized landscape. Both the monsters and the landscape offer clues to Minoan culture. Griffins have lions' bodies and eagles' heads. Lions are universal symbols of strength across Africa, Europe, and the Middle East. Eagles, the strongest of the birds, are still plentiful in Crete. Griffins were symbols in both Minoan and Greek cultures. During the period of these paintings, the two cultures probably mixed. We cannot say for sure what griffins symbolized to the Minoans, but their heraldic grouping around the throne suggests power and prestige. To the Greeks, the monsters certainly signified strength. Apollo rode a griffin and griffins guarded the treasure of the Hyperboreans, the inhabitants of the ideal land beyond the north (boreas is Greek for north). Griffins went on to be Christian symbols, representing the union of earth and heaven.

The landscape is probably also symbolic—a collection of signs rather than observations of nature. The plants are hard to identify, perhaps because their subject is derived from painting elsewhere (e.g. of Egyptian papyrus). Wavy lines in the background are likely to be mountains (plentiful in Crete) enclosing a valley with a river along which the plants grow. The placing of this landscape with monsters behind a "throne" suggests that the room was used for ceremonies and the throne for a presiding priest or priestess (other frescoes suggest the latter). This in turn suggests that the Minoans shared with Egyptians the symbolism of youth, fertility and prosperity embodied in plants growing beside water.

Minoan snake goddess from the palace of Knossos. c. 1700–1450 BCE.
(Archeological Museum of Heraklion/Lauros/Giraudon/Bridgeman Art Library)

On the north side of the central court (left of where you entered the court) **a passage (10)** leads to the **customs house (11)**. On the east side of the central court is the east wing that contained royal apartments. This had four storeys connected by another **grand staircase (12)** that emerged fairly intact from excavation. It is naturally lit by a well and the use of colonnades instead of solid walls. A passage after the colonnades leads to the **Hall of the Double Axes (13)**. The double axes are a common emblem in Minoan imagery—as we have seen from the huge examples in the Heraklion museum. The ax has symbolic power in many cultures, perhaps because it is both creative tool and brutal weapon.. The interesting aspect of the Minoan ax is its double blade, suggesting the ambiguities of destruction and creation. To the right of the hall is the **queen's megaron (14)** with a copy of the famous dolphin fresco. Some distance to the north side of the east wing are the magazines or storage rooms of the **giant pithoi (18)**. From there you go through the north entrance, with the fresco of the charging bull and the creatively named "customs house" area (because it faced the sea) to the **theatrical area (16)** similar to an earlier "theater" at Phaistos. It has seats for about 500 on two sides and a raised platform in the corner, which might have been for the quality to watch whatever games or ceremonies were staged there. From the theatrical area a **Minoan road (17)** runs past the **House of the Frescoes (18)** to the **Little Palace (19)**. Important discoveries of sculpture and painting were made here and are now in the Heraklion Museum.

Phaistos

Location: 38 miles (62 kilometers) from Heraklion. Buses go from the long-distance terminal in Heraklion.
Opening hours: Daily 8:30 am–3:00 pm except Monday (12.00 pm–17.00 pm).
Admission: Euro 4, Euro 2 discount. Combined ticket for Phaistos and Agia Triada Euro 6, Euro 3 discount

Phaistos is on the southern side of Mt Ida with a wonderful view of the fertile plain of Messara—Crete's largest plain. Legends have the city founded either by Phaistus, son of Herakles (whence the name) or by the Cretan lawmaker Rhadamanthys, brother of Minos. It is probably best known now for the much discussed Phaistos Disk, an undeciphered set of hieroglyphics found in Phaistos and displayed in the Heraklion museum.

Phaistos has not been restored in the manner of Knossos so the visitor sees what the archeologists found, more or less untouched. Its overall layout of palace with staircases, apartments around courtyards and an impressive "theatral area" is comparable to Knossos and well worth the visit, especially on a fine day when both the site and view can be enjoyed. Two miles (3 kilometers) west of the site is the Minoan villa of Agia Triada, the ruins of a Mycenaean village and the graveyard where the superb sarcophagus in the Heraklion museum was found.

Malia and Zakros

Two more archeological sites well worth visiting are Malia, a huge site by the sea only about 20 miles (35 kilometers) from Heraklion (open Tuesday-Sunday from 8:30 am–3:00 pm, entrance fee Euro 4, Euro 2 discount) and Zakros in the far east of the island on a beautiful site (open daily 10:00 am–3pm, Euro 3, Euro 2 discount). The ancient names for these sites are not known. Malia is a half-day trip out of Heraklion. Zakros could be added to trip to Agios Nikolaos, (below).

Other Visits in Heraklion

The church of Ayia Aicaterini (Saint Catherine of Sinai), behind the main church of Heraklion and the old church of Ayios Minas, is a pleasant gallery of church painting from the 14th to 16th centuries. Overall they illustrate the persistence of Byzantine painting. The prime pieces however are by the 16th-century painter Damaskinos, who combines Byzantine with Venetian influences. El Greco, a Cretan, might have worked here.

Agios Nikolaos Archeological Museum

Opening hours: 8:30 am–3:00 pm, Closed Mondays.
Contact details: Tel. +30 284 102 4943; www.culture.gr
Location: The museum is on the road from Heraklion before you reach the port.
Admission: Low range (Euro 1–4).

In ancient times Agios Nicolaos was the harbor of Lato. It is now a resort center with a museum that opened in 1970 and houses attractive displays of material excavated in nearby parts of eastern Crete.

The museum is pleasant to look around—smallish, its rooms laid out chronologically around a central courtyard. In addition to the works we have identified below, there are a few other items to seek out: in the early sections there are very interesting Neolithic works; in Room 6, the photographic display of Cretan hieroglyphics show a quite wonderful delicacy and precision; and, near the exit, a skull still wears a delicate wreath of olive leaves. When found, he still held in his mouth the fare to pay the ferryman for his ride to the next world.

Fresco of a prince with lilies. Minoan painting. c. 1500 BCE. (Archeological Museum of Heraklion)

Room 1

Unknown artist

Bird-shaped vase, Early Minoan, Found at Hagia Photia,
2600–2300 BCE

There is an air of the alert little mother hen about this piece. Three
legs ensure that it will be a stable vase, but it is the figure itself that
attracts the eye. The pertly angled head and neck, incised eye, and
protruding tail establish a lively little figure. Quite heavy incisions
show the lie of the feathers and emphasize the swell of the body.
Whether for ceremonial or domestic purposes, the potter has
observed his subject well.

Other pieces nearby also use decorative incision that draws attention to
shape and line.

Room 4

Unknown sculptor

Goddess of Myrtos, Case 16, Early Minoan, c. 2300–2200 BCE

The figure is a libation vessel presented as a female with distinct
facial features. She has the air of a ceremonial figure, but that
could mean that she was a guardian or priestess rather than a
goddess. Her small head sits at the top of a very long neck. Her
skinny arms hold a peaked jug. Her body is bell shaped with two
small but conspicuous stuck-on breasts. The pubic area appears
below as a triangle of red painted lines. A painted rectangular
pattern, covering parts of her back and sides but leaving the
front of her figure exposed, may be clothing or a ceremonial
cloak.

A jug that is an exact replica of the one she holds is nearby (Case 14). It
is generously curved with bold lines running from shoulder to base. It
has all the air and grace of a classic piece of design, as can be expected
among objects that stand the test of use.

Various pieces of gold jewelry found in graves and displayed nearby
are appealing, especially for the delicacy of the work and the play of
light across their juxtaposed surfaces. In comparison with our own
times, gold seems to have been used imaginatively.

Room 5

Unknown artists
Various sarcophagi, including Exhibit 262

Terracotta sarcophagi are small. It is often said that the corpses therefore had to be folded into them, which would have been done while they were still warm, but it might be equally true that the size of the sarcophagus was limited by the size of the potters' kilns.

This one (Exhibit 262) is shaped like a bathtub and decorated with a sea theme. Dominating the exterior are the eyes and tentacles of an octopus linked to a continuous line, which may represent moving water or seaweed. There is a row of waves around the rim. At each end on the interior, land and wave designs establish the environment for a corpse, while a fish with a huge frontal eye arches down towards wave patterns on the floor. It is tempting to look for meanings: the decoration may be symbolic of a journey over the sea to a new life, or simply associated with the life of the person to be buried.

Among others in this collection is one with a side divided into three panels, a bird at each end, and what are possibly mountain peaks in the panel between. The bird on the left grips a wriggling worm. Both birds have a fierce frontal eye. With claws holding the earth and powerful wings trailing behind, they seem poised and ready for action. In the interior, a line like a river or road runs around the walls, suggesting a landscape rather than abstract decoration. If it is a landscape, spots on the floor—which is marked off around the base—may represent what is seen from the air.

Room 7

Unknown artists
Stand for a vessel, AE 12684, late Minoan, c. 1300–1350 BCE

The tower-shaped stand, alone in its case, was made to hold a vessel like the one it is displayed with, which was found in the same area but not actually with it. The dark and red painted decoration stands out dramatically against the original pale-colored clay. Double arches in the base lighten its overall appearance. At the top, alternately painted and unpainted double horns suggest a ceremonial use but other decorations—chevrons, hatching, bars, enclosed diamonds—may be abstract.

Nearby in Case 57, another stand—also featuring the double horn decoration—is made to hold the slim base of a vase, which would have been a libation vase.

Room 8

Unknown sculptor
Head, Exhibit 8440, c. 700–600 BCE

The smile recalls the Archaic smiles of the kore. Originally, the face was painted. There are still traces of blue on the eyebrows. The wide open eyes have pin pricks at the center of the pupil, suggesting that they were constructed with the use of a compass but their effect is to suggest a kind of innocence. The hair and headdress, although stylized, are simple.

Byzantine Chapel of Panayia Kera

Location: In Kritsá, which is a short trip out of Agios Nikolaos. The chapel is on the roadside a mile (1.6 kilometers) before you reach the village.

Contact details: Tel. + 30 284 105 1525; www.culture.gr

Opening hours: 8:30–3:00 daily except Monday.

Admission: Low range (Euro 3).

The beautifully set chapel of Panayia Kera contains absorbing Byzantine frescoes from the 13th and 14th centuries. The frescoes are well preserved, and, at least on a bright day, well lit. The central aisle, with the earliest works, follows the common pattern for storytelling, with the Ascension in the vault at the altar end, scenes from the life of Christ along the walls and scenes of the end of the world at the entrance end. Saints and doctors of the church (with black crosses on their vestments) fill the lowest level. The painting, within its conventions, is exceptionally vigorous.

The side aisles date from the next century, the 14th, and demonstrate changes that came in a period of renaissance in Byzantium. The aisle nearest the entrance traces the life of Mary's mother Ann (largely via apochryphal stories). By contrast with the multi-event compositions of the central aisle, the scenes from the life of St Ann feature a dramatic moment in a story. In the far aisle, opposite the entrance on the lower part of the wall, is a unique portrait painting of a local couple of the time.

The work from both centuries reveals an interest in naturalistic detail—in, for example, animals and buildings—alongside great skill in making essentially stylized faces and figures look individual through posture and expression.

Santorini

Modern Santorini, the Thera of prehistoric times, is the most southern of the Cycladic islands and close to Crete. In the eras that preceded the catastrophic volcanic eruption that blew the island apart in about 1500 BCE, it was home to both Cycladic and Minoan cultures, and lives on in

Wall paintings from Akrotiri, Santorini. C.1500 BCE. Prehistoric Museum of Thera.

legend as the possible lost island of Atlantis. Today the main town of Fira, with its blue and white houses scaling the steep sides of the old volcano and overlooking the Aegean, is an masterpiece of art in itself.

There are two museums, both worth visiting. The new museum, devoted to prehistoric art from ancient Thera, is rich in art from the archeological site of Akrotiri, which was preserved under volcanic ash and lava. The Archeological Museum houses material from the Geometric period onwards.

Planes and ferries go to Santorini from Athens; however, a ferry trip to or from Heraklion is shorter. Buses from Fira, the main town, go to the ferry. Taxis go from the airport.

The Museum of Prehistoric Thera is in the center of town and well marked. To get to the Archeological Museum, follow signs to the cable car, going upwards towards the clock tower. Large stones outside the entrance mark the spot.

Museum of Prehistoric Thera

Location: Fira, in the center of town
Contact details: +30228 602 3217; www.culture.gr
Opening hours: 8:30 am–3:00 pm Tues.–Sun. Closed Mondays and public holidays.
Admission: Low-range (Euro 1–4). One ticket admits to both museums in Fira. A mid-range ticket (Euro 8, concessions Euro 4) is available for both museums and the Archeological sites of Akrotiri and Ancient Thera.

As you enter this big, open gallery, there is a display of early Cycladic figures from 2700–2300 BCE. Many appear as simple, schematic shapes, smoothed as though they had been held in the hand for generations. Others, with large heads and arms folded across the belly, are more realistic in their depiction of details of the human body though, as the proportions show, they conform to non-realistic styles.

Unknown artist
Marble basin, Exhibit 4210, Early Cycladic, 2700–2300 BCE

The marble basin is a little under a yard (90 centimeters) in diameter. Its generous size invites the eye to dwell on the curve and the colors revealed in the marble, and is a reminder of seemingly universal qualities in the art of different places and times. To shape the bowl, the artist would have used very simple tools.

Unknown artists
Cycladic jugs, especially Exhibits 135, 101, 102, and 138, 2000–1500 BCE

In the first alcove on the right is a display of middle Cycladic jugs. Some seem to have derived their shape from birds with their heads tipped back as though drinking. The simple markings on the neck and body are worn like an adornment.

Exhibit 135 is at the end of the display on your left as you face into the alcove. Note what look like decorated nipples on the throat. It is hard to know what these mean. Alongside is a smaller jug decorated in a style that calls to mind the dot paintings of Australian Aborigines.

Further along are Exhibits 101, 102, and at the end of the case Exhibit 138—all recognizable as examples of the same style with bands of color at the neck and base and decorated with pairs of nipples (or eyes). Swallows—caught in mid-flight and pictured in a few confident brush strokes—dart across their surfaces. Swallows were frequently used as a motif, possibly because they were common.

Unknown artists
Three pithoi, Exhibits 225, 226, and 227, Early Bronze Age

A pithos is a large pottery jar, typically used in ancient times for storing oil or grain. Painted signs show what they were used for— Exhibit 225 on the right for reeds, Exhibit 226 in the middle (probably) for grape-vine roots and Exhibit 227 for liquid.

Unknown artists
Painted offering table, Exhibit 253, 1600s BCE

The offering table is made of stone and clay and was reportedly found in the excavations of Akrotiri in the same room as the much admired fresco of *The Fisherman* (which you will see soon). Archeologists are convinced that tables like this served some ceremonial purpose but do not know what exactly what that purpose was. If the painted surface were laid out in a line, it would present an underwater frolic about 4 feet (30 centimeters) long. Dolphins with grumpy eyes or searching looks, some with profiles a little like a platypus, cruise among the weeds of the underwater world. Later, dolphins were to become powerful symbols for the Greeks, sometimes associated with Apollo himself and sometimes identified as the beings who conducted souls to the next life. Whatever the state of their beliefs, the association of island people with the sea would have made it and its life forms an obvious subject for their art.

Unknown artist
Fragment of a wall with rosettes, Fresco Exhibit 252, c. 1600 BCE

It is interesting how many frescoes have been found on Santorini. The fact that a large number of the buildings had frescoed walls suggests a stable and prosperous town life.

Rosettes are a commonly used Minoan motif, here and in Crete, and presented in the colors commonly used in their frescoes. Blue rosettes with sixteen points are grouped in fours, surrounded by a raised relief in white. The rosettes look ready to spin like cogs in their ordained space. Notice how the dark outlines strengthen each separate shape but still draw the whole image together.

Unknown artist
Fragments of frescoes from The House of the Ladies, Akrotiri,
including major areas of a room, Exhibit 264, Exhibits 261–3,
c. 1600 BCE

The first fragment shows a female who inclines forward as she moves to our right. There is not enough of the original fresco left for us to establish what the story is, even though the image is clear. She is a deep-bosomed woman of mature build and, as was the Minoan custom, shown at about two-thirds of her real size. She boasts a carefully constructed hair-do and large earrings, a standard Minoan profile and the white skin used to depict women. Her dress is low cut and her nipple, like those on many jugs, is decorated. She is looking up and seems to be reaching out towards a figure in front. There are many possible rituals associated with women's business—puberty, preparation for marriage, conception, giving birth. Perhaps this is one and she is in a robing ceremony, looking upwards towards a goddess or priestess figure.

Behind her is a painted canopy of stars that may be a painted-wall-within-a-painted-wall. Whichever, the starry pattern is a device that gives light and depth to the scene and keeps the frescoed area bright. Above her is a line of frieze.

Fresco Exhibits 261–3, 1600s BCE

Next is a room where the fresco could be confidently reconstructed. A strongly colored border establishes the height of the walls and the area originally decorated. The subject repeats images of papyrus (a sedge native to southern Europe and Egypt) each with three flower heads and growing out of stylized rocks. They stand against a pale background with no features and no horizon, which design gives an impression of infinite depth and makes a smallish room appear to be a bright, large space.

The next fragment shows a younger woman moving against the same starry background as we saw before and with the same frieze above—they are part of the same composition. Unlike the older woman, she is upright and alone. She wears little jewelry—a large round earring and an unpretentious necklace. Her role may be ceremonial.

The two women were on opposite walls outside the papyrus room in Akrotiri. Nanno Marinatos, author of *Art and Religion in Thera* (Mathioulakis, Athens), theorizes that they may depict those who attended ceremonies in the papyrus room. The idea is plausible and provokes speculation about the significance of the papyrus motif. In Egypt, papyrus was associated with fecundity and fruitfulness. We don't know if that was the case here.

Beyond are displays of pottery with lilies, bulls, goats, diving dolphins and birds—all well observed and portrayed with finesse. Exhibits 417 and 418 are boar rhytons with curiously innocent expressions, handsome tusks and perky ears. Exhibits 413 and 414 are Cretan vases with complex and varied patterning that covers their bodies—evidence of the abundant trade between the islands. Exhibit 413 has darker colored bands, dots, spirals and rosettes that stand out against the paler colored clay and make for a visually rich surface. Exhibit 414 carries the double-headed ax on a broad area of decoration immediately below the handles.

Continue across to the other side of the gallery to view a number of charming frescoes. The first one you approach shows four-legged animals—perhaps goats or sheep—alert to the life around them, heads up, caught listening and watching, their feet lightly on the ground.

Next are extensive fragments from a panorama. The lower part of the walls features monkeys that climb about with easy grace. Scholarly artists have filled any gaps in the scene. Wherever they appear in

Minoan frescoes, the convention seems to be to show monkeys as blue. These appear as graceful, lively animals and many of them sport an elegantly curled tail.

A frieze that is deeper and more ornate than that in the House of the Ladies takes up the upper part of the walls. Perhaps the room itself had some special significance and was therefore more decorated. In this upper zone, multiple straight lines establish a band for continuous interlocking spirals. The repetition is striking. One of the effects is to contrast with the pale background of the monkey fresco below, again providing a lightness and depth to the pictorial work.

The following frescoes, formerly in the National Museum in Athens, are to be displayed in this museum in the future. This is part of the national plan to return works to their home in storage. There is no firm date for their unveiling here, but you may be lucky enough to view them.

Unknown Minoan painter(s)
Very large fresco showing mainly naval activity with scenes of life on shore, c. 1550—1500 BCE

Here are 23 feet (7 meters) of fresco, much of it original, with some clear-cut Minoan elements—such as diving dolphins—but in many respects the work has its own attractive style. There are many missing elements, but everywhere you look, there are more vignettes of activities associated with life in a seafaring economy. On land, we see a lion chasing antelopes; on the shore, a city; in the water, boats seemingly involved in some sort of regatta with dolphins arching over them; a line-up of soldiers with shields, apparently about to repel some intruders; and, immediately behind them, sketches of rustic activity. In the water, very Minoan-looking youths frolic. In a palace, a number of the aristocracy are on towers, watching people jumping into small craft on the opposite shore and heading towards them. Shepherds on the hillside and a crowd of people on the shore are also watching the arrival.

We need not assume in a work of this sort that the various scenes are synchronous. As in the Bayeux tapestry, scenes in different parts may portray events of different times. However it is interpreted, the fresco shows an outstanding narrative skill that enables a lot of absorbing detail to be gathered together with great liveliness and a sense of patterning. One of its strengths is that coherent compositions are created with a comparatively limited range of colors.

Unknown Minoan painter(s)
The Fisherman, c. 1500–1500 BCE

An almost entirely preserved fresco, found at Akrotiri, shows a dark-skinned fisherman, in profile except for the chest and shoulders, which are nearly front-on to the viewer. He is naked except for a necklet and his hair is in the same fashion as the boxers—black curls arranged on a crown dyed or colored blue. The fish are drawn to suggest an abundant catch, which he holds with pride. He stands easily in his world and has the air of living in a sort of paradise. The predominant colors of the Minoan palette are here: the brown figure on a light ochre background with touches of green and blue. Colors are also grouped in the bands of color at the top. Above all, the image gains in strength because it stands out as a sinuous silhouette.

Unknown Minoan painter(s)
Fresco of a priestess, c. 1550–1500 BCE

The trademark range of ochres along with blue and some red make up this appealing figure. The drawing mixes profile and frontal views. The overall effect is of the person advancing towards the viewer's right, yet the head and arm are shown in profile against a frontal upper body. The shape of the garment contributes to the overall realism of the figure. When modern painters, in particular Picasso, show different views—side and frontal—within the one figure, the deliberate effect is to lose realism in favor of a multi-faceted abstraction. Here, similar multiple views of a body retain an air of great realism. The nose, the eye and the hairstyle are typical of Minoan drawing in this period.

The Archeological Museum

Walking up to the Archeological Museum you see wonderful views of this blue and white island.

Location: The Archeological Museum is a short walk uphill from the Prehistoric Museum.

Opening times: 8.30 am–3.00 pm Closed Mondays.

Admission: The ticket from the Prehistoric Museum also admits to the Archeological Museum. There is also a combined ticket for both museums and the archeological sites of Akrotiri and Ancient Thera.

Contact details: Tel: +30 228 602 2217.

Amphoras from Cycladic workshops, 1700s BCE

In the first room, amphoras from Cycladic workshops show such mastery of the art of decoration that it is hard to imagine it was ever bettered.

Bands of abstract shapes, lines, squiggles and bars divide the surfaces into discretely decorated areas and yet the effect is of a single coherent design. On an amphora in Case 1, a bird looks back over its wing and tail, thus fitting neatly into a space between uprights that may be abstract decoration or tree trunks or blades of grass. If the various decorations represent the real world, what are they? After all, the bird is clearly real.

In an unnumbered case at the end of the room, on another amphora, another strong-legged bird—this one with a mighty wing—steps over and among triangular shapes that may be stones or mountains, its frontal eye and curved beak recalling Hitchcock's *The Birds*. In the same case, a more simply and boldly decorated amphora shows a pair of horses drinking or eating side by side to form a symmetrical image where bands of horizontal lines and areas of vertical lines or small abstract shapes make a pleasing picture that could be of this world or the next. There is both grace and simplicity in the drawing.

Another amphora, also unnumbered, shows a bird whose body and tail are built up of continuous lines that draw attention to the neat space it stands inside. A worm or perhaps a snake dangles wriggling from its beak.

A Daidalic statue of a mourning woman, Exhibit 392, c. 650 BCE

Dressed in a plain brown dress belted at the waist and falling to her feet, the woman is shown apparently tearing her hair which is banded at the forehead and then falls free. Her eyes are wide and her look intense. The figure is memorable, mostly because of its simplicity but also because, as a mourner, she was made to communicate intense emotion.

Attic black-figure cup, c. 575–550 BCE

This piece looks like a big cake dish. It is displayed standing on a mirror so that you can see the decoration on the under side. All of the decoration is warlike. Around the rim are stylized waves and ships, probably on their way to war. In the center, Poseidon, the god of the sea, battles with the giant Polybotis. Below is a massive conflict with chariots and hoplites leaving for battle or engaged in the fight.

The archeological sites associated with these museums both make interesting visits. The site of Ancient Thera (the post-earthquake city) is a steep climb from the town, with a fabulous view. It is open from 8.30 am–3.00 pm every day except Monday, when it is closed. The pre-earthquake settlement of Akrotiri is at the southern end of the island, accessible by bus or taxi. There, you can see the remains of houses from which the collection in the Prehistoric Museum comes. The site is open from 8.30 am–3.00 pm but closes on Mondays.

If you feel like something quite different, a boat trip leaves from Fira for a tour around the spectacular crater of the volcano: details can be had from tourist agencies in the main square. Take your swimsuit and wear solid shoes.

The Minoans have provided the last—some would say the best—of our Trails through the art of Greece. No matter which Trails you were able to follow and what order you took them in, we are sure that you have found a range and depth of art that few travelers anticipate when they first visit Greece. Time has sorely depleted their world, but the gods are not dead.

Paros Village, Paros, Cyclades

Other Notable Figures in Greek Art

The most important figures in Greek art are in the introduction. This appendix lists more minor figures and includes artists as well as writers.

Aeschylus, 525–456 BCE: An Athenian writer of tragedies whose trilogy *The Orestia* includes *Agamemnon*, the best known of his plays. He held public office and fought at Marathon and Salamis. Pausanias records that Aeschylus had his war record "as witnessed by the trees at Marathon and the Persians who landed there" inscribed on his tombstone; he made no reference to his poetry.

Agorakritos, 5th century BCE: A sculptor of the Classical period, Agorakritos was a member of Phidias's group that worked on the Athenian acropolis. Despite his prominence in his day, little reliable information has survived, even in ancient writers, about his life or his works.

Apollodoros, circa 1st century BCE: *The Library of Greek Mythology* (translated by Robin Hard, Oxford World's Classics) from the 1st or 2nd century CE, is an invaluable mixture of the learned and the popular. The work is attributed to this Greek author, but details about his life and achievements are uncertain.

Aristophanes, circa 448–380 BCE: An Athenian comic dramatist. Among his works are *The Acharnians*, *The Birds*, *The Clouds,* and *The Wasps* which are chiefly satires of Athenian social and political life.

Euphranor, mid 4th century BCE: Sculptor and painter from Corinth. Like his contemporary, Lysippos, he wrote about proportions in sculpture.

Euripides, 485–406 BCE: Athenian tragic dramatist. Major works are *Alcestis*, *Iphigenia* in *Tauris and Medea.*

Herodotus, 480–420 BCE: Greek historian from Helicarnassus, hailed as father of history and author of *The Histories*, which recounted and reflected on the events of the Persian war against Greece. He was the first writer to attempt an objective account of the past and to see history as a way of understanding human nature. See *The Histories* (translated by Aubrey de Selincourt, Penguin Classics).

Herodus Atticus, 2nd century BCE: Of Roman origin, Herodus Atticus was an administrator and a wealthy patron of the arts in Greece.

Hesiod: A poet from central Greece thought to have lived about 700 BCE. He is the author of *Works and Days,* a book of advice about how to live, and probably of the Theogony, which describes the origins of the gods and the world.

Kalamis, 5th century BCE: Sculptor, perhaps of the charioteer at Delphi. His work was well thought of by ancient writers, but no originals survive (unless the attribution of the charioteer is correct).

Kritios, 5th century BCE: Sculptor, perhaps of the charioteer at Delphi, perhaps of the kouros that bears his name in the museum of the Acropolis in Athens.

Libon of Elis, 5th century BCE: Architect of the Temple of Zeus at Olympia. Elis is the name of the region in which Olympia is situated.

Lysippos, 4th century BCE: A sculptor who developed a canon based on eight rather than seven that served to elongate the human figure. Ancient authors praise his huge output. His wealthy patrons included Alexander. See also Polykleitos the Elder.

Pindar, circa 518–438 BCE: A lyric poet, author of *The Odes* dedicated to athletes at the Pan Hellenic games. (Olympian games at Olympia, the Pythian Games at Delphi, the Nemean Games at Nemea, and Isthmian Games at Corinth.) Born near Thebes of a notable family, he was apparently a prolific writer, but only his odes to victories at the games survive as complete poems. Nonetheless, he is esteemed as Greece's greatest lyric poet. See Pindar, *The Odes,* translated by C. M. Bowra, Penguin Classics.

Plato, 427–347 BCE: An Athenian and one of the most influential philosophers in Western culture. Author of *The Republic* and a number of Dialogues in which Socrates is the chief protagonist. He began his career as a student of Socrates.

Plutarch, circa 45–120 CE: Greek historian and, in later life, a priest in Delphi. He wrote a number of biographies including one on the life of Pericles. See *The Rise and Fall of Athens,* translated by Ian Scott-Kilvert, Penguin Classics.

Polykleitos the Elder, 5th century BCE: Sculptor. He wrote a canon setting out proportions for the human body in which the head was 1/7th total height. See Lysippos.

Polykleitos the Younger, 4th century BCE: Responsible for the Temple of Asklepios at Epidauros.

Pythagoras, 5th century BC: A Greek sculptor who lived and worked in Rhegium, Italy. There are no works attributed to him with certainty. Ancient writers admired him for his sculpting of the body, especially of athletes.

Socrates, 469–399 BCE: An Athenian philosopher who set an example of critical enquiry, especially into morality, that is still revered. He left no writings of his own and is known through the writings of others, especially the *Dialogues* of his student Plato. He fell foul of Athenian authority, was charged with denying the gods and corrupting youth, and was obliged to kill himself by drinking poison. Plato describes his death in *The Last Days of Socrates*.

Sophocles, 496–406 BCE: Athenian author of tragedies. Among his Theban Plays are *King Oedipus* and *Antigone*.

Timanthes, 4th century BCE: None of Timanthes's paintings have survived, but a version by a Roman painter of one of his paintings of Iphigenia was found in the House of the Tragic Poet in Pompeii. Ancient Roman orators and writers (Pliny, Cicero, Quinilian) praised his work for its emotional power, especially his portrayal of the men participating in the sacrifice of Iphigenia.

Vitruvius, late 1st century BCE–early 1st century CE: Roman author of a treatise *De Architectura*, which set out to systematize Greek architecture.

The Ancient World

This appendix lists places and people of the ancient world. The persons are sometimes real, but more often they are from myth, as much of Greek art uses myth as its subject matter. These are stories of gods and goddesses, heroes, and lesser beings that symbolize human motivation and behavior. Some are intended to explain the nature of the world, some are stories told for dramatic effect, and some give accounts of events that probably occurred. Sometimes, established historical events and daily life provide a subject or a motive for art work.

Achilles: The son of King Peleus and the sea goddess Thetis. When he was an infant, his mother tried to protect him by dangling him in the waters of immortality but held him by the heel, which therefore remained dry and vulnerable. In *The Iliad*, Achilles, now the strongest and swiftest of the Greeks, kills Hector, a prince of Troy, but then dies when Paris wounds him in the heel.

Aegisthus: Clytemnestra's lover, who took advantage of her husband, Agamemnon's absence during the battle for Troy.

Agamemnon: descendant of Atreus of Mycenae and leader of the Greek forces in the Trojan War. Agamemnon eventually returned home only to be slaughtered by his wife's lover, Aegusthus. His son Orestes later avenged his death.

Alexander the Great, 356–323 BCE: A great military leader and conqueror of as much of the world as he could reach before dying at the age of 33. Tales of his exploits and their cultural influence color European and Asian history.

Amazons: A race of warrior women. The battle against them is called the Amazonomachy.

Amymone: One of the 50 daughters of Danaus, Amymone was in a dry country with her father who sent her to look for water. Tired out, she fell asleep. A satyr tried to rape her and she cried out to Poseidon for help. He chased the satyr off with his trident. She then agreed to make love to him, after which water flowed from the spot that his trident had hit.

Antony, 83–30 BCE and Cleopatra, 69–30 BCE: Among the world's most famous lovers. He was a Roman general. She was the pharaoh of Egypt. After the defeat of their navy, they each committed suicide.

Aphrodite: A daughter of Zeus and goddess of love and beauty. Particularly associated with Corinth, she was born from the sea and her symbol is a shell. She was the mother of Eros, also known as Cupid.

Apollo: The son of Zeus and Leda the swan, and god of poetry, music, healing and prophecy. In ancient times, the oracle at his shrine at Delphi made pronouncements about future events. As god of music, he appears with a lyre. He often carries a bow.

Ares: The son of Zeus and Hera, and the god of war, Ares usually appears in armor carrying shield, spear and sword. He supported Troy in the Trojan war.

Ariadne: A daughter of the Cretan King Minos. Ariadne fell in love with the Athenian Theseus and led him through the maze so that he could kill the Minotaur. At first Theseus promised to marry her, but when he left she died broken-hearted.

Artemis: Apollo's sister, who remained a virgin. As a huntress and the protector of the Amazons, she is usually shown carrying her bow and was especially honored in the mountainous parts of Greece. She took part in the war between the gods and the giants.

Asklepios: A pupil of the centaur Chiron and god of healing. Asklepios was associated with serpents, which are still the symbol used by pharmacists. One of his descendants, Hippocrates, gave his name to the oath still taken by graduate members of the medical profession where they swear to seek to preserve life.

Athene: A powerful goddess who was born out of the head of Zeus already clothed in armor. She made mankind a gift of the olive tree. As the goddess of wisdom, she was associated with the owl. She was also goddess of warfare and patron of Athens and in this guise, often wears a helmet and carries a shield known as an aegis. She is known under several names: Athene Nike (victory); Athene Parthenos (virgin); Athene Polias (god of the city); Athene Promachos (champion).

Atlantis: A legendary island sometimes identified as the ancient island of Thera, today known as Santorini.

Atreus: Rival with his brother for the kingdom of Mycenae, which he won with the help of Zeus. When his wife and brother became adulterers, Atreus took revenge by having his brother's children killed and served up to him at dinner as a stew. A tomb known as the Treasury of Atreus is at the archeological site at Mycenae. Agamemnon was a descendant of the family.

Attica (Attic): Athens and its region.

Aulis: A port near Thebes.

Cadmus: Legendary founder of Thebes was a king's son who traveled to Greece in search of his sister Europa. His wedding to Harmony was a major event attended by all the gods.

centaur: A mythical creature where the torso of a man is seemingly grafted to the body of a horse, The mix of man and animal is similar to the minotaur and the satyr. Centaurs feature on the metopes of the Acropolis. Except for Chiron, who was a teacher, they were brutal.

Centauromachy: A war against the centaurs.

Chiron: The most important of the centaurs. Unlike his generally violent race, he was friendly and learned and taught medicine and various arts to Achilles and Jason. When he was wounded by Herakles, his immortality became a great burden and he agreed to die instead of Prometheus.

Cyclades: A group of some 200 islands in the Aegean Sea. Cycladic art takes its name from the islands

Danaus: A man with the ferocity of a wolf who was chosen to be king of Argos, Danaus was the father of 50 daughters.

Daphne: A nymph who turned herself into a laurel tree to escape the amorous attentions of Apollo.

Delphi: In ancient times, the site of Apollo's shrine and the home of the oracle. It remains a place of wonder where the remains of temples and shrines are poised above a deep valley, overlooking the olive groves of Amphissa and the sea.

Delphic oracle: A prestigious source of advice for over a thousand years. People sought Apollo's advice by consulting the oracle at Delphi who spoke for him. His priests gave ambiguous and sometimes meddlesome answers and the whole procedure gathered notoriety.

Demeter: A daughter of the Titan couple Cronus and Rhea and protector of agriculture. Her daughter Persephone was captured by Hades, the king of the dead, and taken to live with him in the underworld. Demeter went there to rescue her but was only partially successful, and Persephone had to live half the year in the underworld. The world of nature endures winter in memory of Demeter's grief and celebrates with her in spring, when Persephone returned to the world of the living. Associated with agriculture, Demeter is shown with ears of corn and especially associated with Eleusis.

Dionysos: The god of wine and frenzy. He was a favorite in Crete and often shown accompanied by satyrs.

Electra: Daughter of Agamemnon and Clytemnestra. Following Agamemnon's murder, Electra and her brother Orestes avenged their father's death.

Erechtheus: A mythical king of Athens whose body was part snake. According to Homer, Erechtheus's parents were Earth and Hephaestus. Reared by Athene, he installed Athene Polias as goddess of the city. He shares the Erechthion with both Athene and Poseidon and is hailed as founder of the Pan Athenaic festival. During a war with Eleusis, an oracle promised victory if he sacrificed one of his three daughters. He chose one, but all three chose death. He was subsequently killed by Poseidon.

Eros: A personification of love, often shown as a winged boy who fires arrows at humans and causes them to fall in love.

Europa: A young girl who was playing on the beach at Sidon when Zeus saw her and immediately fell in love. He made himself into a white bull and swam off with her. Their coupling resulted in Minos, the mythical king of Crete after whom, in recent times, Minoan art was named.

Giants: The earth, Gaia, gave birth to the giants in anger after Zeus punished her children the Titans. The battle between the gods and the giants was a popular subject for temple and altar friezes, such as on the Acropolis. They could assume terrifying shapes. In Delphi, they appear as creatures part snake, part dragon, and part human.

Gigantomachy: The revolt of the giants against the gods. The giants could only be killed by an alliance of god and human. Thus the super-hero Herakles became the god's ally.

Glauke: A wife of the hero Jason who endured pain and suffering at the hands of Medea, his previous partner.

Gods: Immortal beings who lived on Mount Olympus. They did not grow old or die. The myths told how, from time to time, they visited earthly shrines and met people. Some gods had a strong association with a bird or animal and may originally have been thought of as animals. They often seem to provide an explanation for otherwise inexplicable events.

griffins: Birds with the bodies of lions and terrible beaks. Sacred to Apollo, they occur again in Byzantine imagery.

Hebe: A daughter of Zeus who personified eternal youth and became Herakles's wife after he achieved immortality.

Helen: The daughter of Zeus and Leda the swan, said to have been the most beautiful woman in the world. Though she was married to the Greek King Menelaus, she was "given" to the Trojan prince Paris by the goddess Aphrodite. The Greeks fought Troy to get her back. During the years of battle that followed, goddesses variously supported Greeks or Trojans.

Hephaistos, Haphaestes: The husband of the goddess Aphrodite, associated with working fire and metal.

Hera: The wife and sister of Zeus and associated with the peacock, symbol of long life.

Herakles: A child of Zeus and a mortal mother who lived as a hero, distinguished from humans because of his astonishing strength. He undertook the 12 labors shown on the metopes at Olympia. Despite his super-human strength, his pursuit of the 12 tasks demonstrates how persistence is necessary for anyone to achieve their potential. At the end of his human life, he went to live among the immortals and married Hebe, the goddess of youth. He is often shown wearing the skin of the lion of Nemea and carrying a club.

Herakles's 12 labors: In the order displayed in Olympia Museum the twelve are:
- To kill the lion of Nemea, which was terrifying the valley.
- To kill the Lernaean hydra, a fire-breathing snake with nine heads.
- To kill the Stymphalian flesh-eating birds.
- To tame the Cretan bull, which was ravaging Knossos.
- To capture the Keryneian deer, which had gold horns.
- To take the belt of Hippolyta, queen of the Amazons.
- To capture the Erymanthine boar, a terror to all who encountered it.
- To tame the horses of Diomedes, who were reared on human flesh.
- To capture the oxen of Geryon, a three-bodied giant.

- To bring back the golden apples of the Hesperides, which Atlas gave him in return for relieving him of holding the earth.
- To drag the monster Cerberus from the underworld.
- To clean the Augean stables, which were clogged with dung.

Hermes: A son of Zeus and a nymph named Maia. As the gods' messenger, he sports winged sandals, a broad-brimmed hat and a courier's staff. He made the first lyre out of tortoise shell and cattle intestines. He invented the pan pipes, sold them to Apollo and in return was allowed to be a soothsayer. His principal task was travelling with the spirits of the dead to the underworld. As bearer of news between heaven and earth, he resembles the archangels of Christianity.

Herodes Atticus, second century CE: A wealthy Greek with great standing among the Romans who financed many public buildings including the Odeon in Athens (which still bears his name) and the stadium at Delphi. He became an archon, a consul, and a senator.

Heroes: In the Greek world, great men of some past time who often had a god for a parent. Renowned for their bravery and honor, heroes knew they were not gods, recognised the power of fate and accepted death and mortality as their lot. Gods might intervene in their lives but they depended on human qualities like strength and cunning and only occasionally called on supernatural aid.

Hector: A Trojan warrior slain by Achilles as revenge for the killing of Achilles's lover Patroclus.

Hestia: The goddess of the family hearth,

Hoplite: In ancient Greece, a foot soldier who was heavily armed and owned his weapons and armour.

Jason: A hero who gathered many of the best of the Greek heroes to voyage in the Argonaut to capture the Golden Fleece. He succeeded with the help of Medea, whom he married and according to some versions abandoned.

Keramos: An Attic hero said to have invented the art of pottery—hence the word "ceramic."

Marathon: Marathon was the site of a victory in 490 BCE of the Athenians over the Persians. Marathon foot races commemorate the story that the messenger Phidippides ran to Athens with the good news and then dropped dead.

Maenads: The female followers of Dionysos, the god of revelry, who are often shown playing a double flute or joining a hectic dance.

Medea: The woman who helped the hero Jason to get the Golden Fleece after he promised to marry her. When he abandoned her, she killed their children and dipped his new wife's wedding dress in poison.

Memnon: Son of Eos the dawn, who fought in the Trojan War against the victorious hero Achilles. His mother's tears are the morning dew.

Menelaus: King of Sparta whose wife Helen was taken to Troy by her lover Paris. To regain their honor, the Greeks besieged Troy for ten years.

Minos: A legendary king of Crete and one of the three children of Europa and

Zeus (who wooed Europa in the form of a white bull). Minos had a
labyrinth built under his palace to contain the Minotaur, a man with a
bull's head who ate human flesh. The Athenian hero Theseus, helped by
Minos's daughter Ariadne, found the way through the labyrinth and slew
the Minotaur.

Nessos: A centaur who was defeated by the hero Herakles and subsequently
operated a ferry to take people across the River Evenus.

Nestor: King of Pylos who called on the Greeks to make war on Troy and
avenge Menelaus whose wife Helen had left him for Paris, a prince of
Troy.

Nymphs: Mythical beings who are not human or gods but spirits pictured
as beautiful young women. Some live in trees, some in watery places
or on mountains. Occasionally one falls in love with a man, invariably
a hero.

Odysseus: A hero of the siege of Troy noted for his courage and cunning.
Homer's *Odyssey* tells of his ten year journey home and of how, to resume
his place, he had to kill the suitors who had gathered around his wife.

Oedipus: A king of Thebes who unwittingly killed his father and married his
mother.

Olympus: In reality, a mountain in the northeast of Greece; in ancient times,
believed to be the permanent home of the gods, inhabited by Zeus, his
divine family and immortal associates.

Orestes: The son of Agamemnon and Clytemnestra, When his mother and her
lover murdered his father upon his return from the Trojan Wars, Orestes
strove to avenge his father. Many stories tell of these deeds.

Paris: A prince of Troy to whom Aphrodite promised the most beautiful woman
in the world, who turned out to be Helen, wife of the Greek king
Menelaus. When Paris went off with her—whether she went willingly was
not an issue—the Greeks waged a ten-year war against Troy. Homer tells
stories about the war and the heroes who fought in it.

Pelops: The founder of the Olympic Games. Pelops was killed in battle and
served to the gods as a sort of stir-fry that they would not eat. Instead they
reassembled his body and he went on to be the father of Atreus.

Pericles, 495–429 BCE: The Athenian leader at the time of the city's greatest
glory, he was personally wealthy, well educated and an eloquent speaker.
He persuaded Athens to rebuild the city that had been destroyed during
wars with Persia, and employed Phidias to supervise Athens's new
acropolis.

Perseus: The hero who killed the gorgon Medusa and became king of the
Mycenean city of Tiryns. Because it was predicted that her son would kill
her father, Perseus's mother Danae had been kept locked up by her own
father. However, Zeus found and seduced her, and years later the adult
Perseus did accidentally kill his mortal grandfather. Perseus's greatest
heroic exploit was to kill Medusa the gorgon. One look from the gorgon
turned you to stone but he had winged sandals, a shoulder bag and a

helmet. He could fly with the sandals, he could see the gorgon's reflection in the shiny helmet and cut off her head without looking and he had the shoulder bag to carry the head away. On the way home, he rescued his future wife Andromeda.

Persephone: The daughter of Zeus and Demeter, she was taken by her uncle Hades to live in the underworld. Because she ate six pomegranate seeds, she was fated to live six months of the year with him, during which time her mother grieved and the world endured winters.

Parthenon: The Athenian Parthenon was built on a rocky hilltop in Athens in the fifth century BCE. Dedicated to Athene Parthenos, the city's guardian goddess, it stands poised above the city, with the remains of other shrines and temples, floodlit at night and taking on the varied colors of the sunlight during the day.

Peisistratos, 602–527 BCE: A ruler of Athens described as a tyrant.

Pirene, Peirene: A weeping woman after whom a spring in Corinth is named. Her child was accidentally killed and, as a spring, she wept forever.

Piraeus: The port adjoining Athens, built in the 5th century BCE.

Paris: A prince of Troy who stole Helen from her husband King Menelaus, thus leading to the siege of Troy by princes and warriors from all over Greece.

Philomela: The sister of Prokne who was transformed into a nightingale.

Polyphemus: A cyclops and son of Poseidon, he captured Odysseus on his long way home from Troy. Odysseus got the giant drunk and told him that his name was "Nobody." Odysseus and a companion then put out the giant's eye with a sharpened pole. When the giant cried out that "Nobody" was attacking him, his fellow giants took no notice and Odysseus escaped.

Poseidon: A brother of Zeus and god of the sea and watery places including rivers, he usually carries a three-pronged spear called a trident. He had innumerable affairs with both immortal and mortal women. He was also associated with earthquakes, when the earth seems to behave like the sea.

Prokne: A sister of the mythical King Erechtheus of Athens, married to the King of Thrace. The king raped her sister, Philomela, and cut out her tongue to silence her. In revenge, Prokne killed their son Itis and had him cooked and served to his father.

Prometheus: A Titan who stole fire and gave it and its power to mankind. As punishment, he was chained to a rock where an eagle attacked his immortal liver.

Pythagoras, 569–475 BCE: A philosopher and mathematician born on Samos, who believed that mathematics was deeply embedded in reality and that some symbols had mystical significance. His famous theorem states that in a right-angled triangle, the sum of squares of the sides that make up the right angle is equal to the square of the third side.

Satyrs: Demon spirits of nature, shown as half-men, half-beasts. They accompany Dionysos, are associated with male sexuality, and prey on nymphs.

Selene: The moon goddess who rode across the sky in a silver chariot.

Sirens: Sea monsters, half-bird half-woman, whose birth is sometimes associated with stories of Herakles. They lived on a Mediterranean island and lured sailors—except for the wily Odysseus—to their death with sweet singing and music.

Solon: A thinker who gave Athens the laws and values that opened the way for the growth of democracy. He died in 559 BC.

Sphinx: A winged monster, part woman, part lioness, sometimes a symbol of depravity, known for asking riddles.

Theseus: An Athenian hero who conquered the Minotaur, a half-man monster with a bull's head. In this task, he had the help of Ariadne, the king's daughter, but he abandoned her and joined in the Argonauts' search of the Golden Fleece. He features on the Acropolis.

Titans: In Greek mythology, a race older than the gods; the children of the sky, Uranus, and the earth, Gaia.

Triton: The three-pronged trident carried by the god Poseidon.

Virtues: The four virtues of the world of Ancient Greece were courage, temperance, justice and wisdom. They do not mean what we mean by these terms today.

Zeus: Chief among the gods of Ancient Greece. His birthplace was Crete and he lived on Mount Olympus. His shrine was at Olympia. He is sometimes shown hurling a bolt of thunder and assumed many shapes in pursuit of beautiful women and at least one boy.

Glossary

acanthus: The leaf of a plant represented in Corinthian capitals. See diagram, page 22.

acropolis: The high point of a town, containing its sacred and public buildings.

acroteria: Small sculptures, or stands for them at the peak and the ends of a pediment.

aegis: a protective cloak of metal or goatskin, often associated with Athene and sometimes used as a shield. In some sculptures of her it is fringed with snakes with Medusa's head in the center.

agora: The marketplace and a principal gathering place of towns in ancient Greece.

amphora: A double-handled jar with a narrow neck, typically used in ancient Greece to store wine and oil.

arcade: A series of arches supported by columns.

Archaic: See Introduction to Greek art, page 20.

architrave: Part of the entablature. The entablature is between the columns and the roof. The architrave is the section in contact with the columns. See diagram, page 22.

aryballos: A scent-bottle.

askos (plural askoi): a jug with a spout and a handle on the top, sometimes in the shape of an animal.

basilica: Originally a Roman building with a row of columns creating an aisle on either side. Some early Christian churches were adaptations of these buildings. Later churches, down to quite modern times, have used the same design.

bead-and-reel: Pattern used in molding, made up of rounded, outward-curving sections.

bouleuterion: In a Roman city, the meeting place of the boule or city council.

capital: The molded top section of a column, different in style in each of the three Greek orders: Doric, Ionian, and Corinthian. See diagram, page 22.

caryatid: A column sculpted in the form of a woman, a caryatid supports the porch (as in the Erechthion) or frieze of a temple.

cella: The inner room of a Greek temple where the statue of the god or goddess was installed.

centaurs: half-man, half-beast creatures of mythology.

chiton: A garment worn by females, and also, though rarely in art, by men. It is the Ionic equivalent of the Doric peplos but has buttons on the shoulders.

See diagram, page 54. It consists of a piece of cloth about 9 feet by 4.5 feet. (3 meters by 1.5 meters) folded to form a square, then fastened at the shoulders leaving gaps for head and arms, and worn with a belt. See diagram, page 54.

chryselephantine: Works in gold and ivory.

Classical: See Introduction to Greek Art, page 23.

columns: In Greek building, the upright supports which, with their related features, are divided into three separate orders: Doric, Ionic and Corinthian. See diagram, page 22.

corbel: A stone that juts out from the wall and can support the weight of building above.

Corinthian capital: Designed by Kallimachos (q.v.) with smaller volutes than the Ionic ones that often seem more two dimensional. Its acanthus leaves and flowers create a rounded capital. See diagram, page 22.

cornice: The upper and projecting part of the entablature in a Greek building. See diagram, page 22.

dipylon: An oval shape with two half circles cut from each side so that it looks like an hourglass.

Doric order: Developed in the architecture of mainland Greece somewhere about the 7th century BCE. It has columns with twenty flutes, plain capitals and makes use of metope. See diagram, page 22.

egg and dart: A pattern used in Ionic architecture and derived from an Egyptian pattern of alternating lotus flowers and buds. The buds became egg shapes. The dart shapes were originally the stamen of open flowers with petals curving back to buds on either side.

entablature: The parts of a building supported by the columns, consisting of architrave, frieze, and cornice. See diagram, page 22.

ex voto: An offering made to the gods in thanksgiving; in Christian times, offerings made especially to saints.

frieze: In an ancient Greek building, part of the entablature, often carrying sculpted ornaments and scenes.

fresco: Painting done directly on to wet plaster on a wall.

fluting: Vertical grooves carved into columns. See diagram, page 22.

Geometric: See Introduction to Greek art, page 22.

golden section, the: The idea that the most pleasing proportions are achieved through geometry, attributed to the mathematicians of ancient Greece and probably also understood by the Egyptians. It is achieved by dividing a line in three such that the smallest length has the same proportion to the middle-sized length as the middle length has to the whole. The theory is that preserving these proportions gives the eye the greatest satisfaction.

Hellenistic: See Introduction to Greek art, page 24.

himation: A loose-fitting outer garment worn by both men and women in ancient Greece, consisting of a large rectangular piece of cloth draped over one shoulder and under the opposite arm. See diagram, page 54.

hoplite: Foot soldiers in ancient Greece who wore armor from head to toe and carried circular shields. They formed disciplined phalanxes that presented a wall of shields and spears on all four sides. They owned their own finely decorated armor and their weapons.

Ionic order: One of the basic styles of Greek architecture, along with Doric and Corinthian.. The Ionic order developed in the Greek culture of Asia Minor in about the fifth century BCE. The Ionic column has twenty-four flutes and instead of the plainer Doric capital, has a double scroll. The egg-and-dart molding is common in Ionic building as is the leaf-and-dart. See diagram, page 22.

kore (plural korai): A young girl sculpted in the Archaic style.

kouros (plural kouroi): A young man sculpted in the Archaic style.

kouratrophos: A statue of a mother and child.

krater: A large bowl with two handles used in ancient Greece to mix wine and water.

kylix: A shallow cup with two handles and a stem, used in ancient Greece.

larnax (plural larnakes): A coffin or ossuary found inside tombs.

libation: A ritual where pouring out wine or oil becomes a religious act or sacrifice.

lozenge: A diamond shape, often used as a vulva shape to symbolize women, hence the womb, and by extension, the underworld.

maenads: Women who take part in the orgies of Dionysos.

meander: A decorative line used extensively in Greek art. It is continuous and forms oblong shapes by doubling back on itself.

metope: In a frieze, sunken panels with relief carving placed between slabs decorated only with vertical grooves.

Minyan: The first wheel-made pottery, which was of a uniformly gray color. Schliemann named it after Minyas, a legendary king.

mosaic: Pictures or designs of colored pieces stuck on to a surface. From very early times, Greeks developed mosaics especially for pavements. Most surviving mosaics date from Roman times. Byzantium raised mosaic to a high art.

nike: The personification of victory as a winged female moving at high speed. Sculpted nike appear on many buildings. Athene sometimes takes the form of Athene Nike.

Odeon: A building similar to a theater but roofed and used for musical performances, commonly found in ancient Greek and Roman cities.

order: A style with distinctive elements—in Greek architecture one of three: Doric, Ionian, and Corinthian. See diagram, page 22.

palmette: A stylized palm leaf adapted from the Mesopotamian tree of life and often found in the decoration of ancient Greek buildings.

Parian marble: Marble from Paros, one of the Cycladic islands.

pediment: The triangular end of a roof that often carried sculpture in ancient Greek temples.

Pentelic marble: Marble from Mt Pentelos near Athens.

peplos: A Doric garment worn by girls and women. It is a single piece of woven
    cloth 4 feet by 6 feet (about 1.20 by 2 meters) without sleeves and held in
    place with pins and a belt. It may be worn alone or with a himation or
    tunic over it. See diagram, page 54.

periptero: A street kiosk.

peristasis: A colonnade of columns around the cella or inner part of an ancient
    Greek temple.

pithos (plural pithoi): A storage jar.

propylaia: Ceremonial entrance to a sanctuary.

proskenion: The front of a stage (proscenium).

repousse: Metal work where the pattern is raised by hammering thin material
    from the back.

rhyton: A drinking cup with ritual uses in ancient Greece. It could take different
    forms, many of them referring to animals.

skene: A stage building from which actors entered and exited.

spolia: Material from ruins that is re-used in another building.

stoa: In a Greek town or city, a covered arcade, usually running alongside a line
    of shops and buildings.

swastika: A sign with four arms around a central point. It is an ancient symbol
    and its use—representing activity and regeneration—is widespread. The
    four 'arms' are bent at the elbow and point to the direction in which it
    revolves. For the ancient Greeks who liked to represent the qualities of the
    universe through geometry, it must have been an evocative image.

theater: A common building at any religious site in ancient Greece, and used in
    early times for Dionysiac festivals. By the 4th century BCE, theaters were
    used for tragedies, especially identified with the Athenian playwrights
    Aeschylus, Sophocles, Euripides, and Aristophanes.

tholos: A circular domed building.

tiropitta: A cheese pie.

triglyph: A decorative panel in a Doric frieze consisting of four vertical lines
    sunk into a panel. See diagram, page 22.

volute: The spiral shape carved on an Ionian capital and incorporated in
    Corinthian capitals. See diagram, page 22.

votive: An object offered to a god and representing a vow.

Index